30 DAYS
TO UNDERSTANDING

HOW
TO LIVE AS A
CHRISTIAN

30 DAYS
TO UNDERSTANDING

HOW
TO LIVE AS A
CHRISTIAN

MAX ANDERS

WORD PUBLISHING
Dallas • London • Vancouver • Melbourne

30 Days to Understanding How to Live as a Christian

If you are interested in having Max Anders speak to your church, organization or special event, please contact:

interAct Speaker's Bureau
330 Franklin Road
Suite 120, Box 897
Brentwood, TN 37024-0897
Telephone: 800-370-9932
Facsimile: 615-370-9939

Library of Congress Cataloging-in-Publication Data

Anders, Max E., 1947–
    30 days to understanding how to live as a Christian / Max Anders.—
1st ed.
        p.   cm.
    Includes bibliographical references.
    ISBN 0-8499-3577-6
    1. Theology, Doctrinal—Popular works.   I. Title.   II. Title: Thirty days to understanding how to live as a Christian.
BT77.A45   1990
248.4—dc20   90–39731
                                                                          CIP

Printed in the United States of America

4 5 6 7 8 9   LB   9 8 7 6 5 4 3 2 1

Other books in the "30 Days" series

CONTENTS

Acknowledgments / *ix*

Introduction / *1*

Section One: The Human Condition and the Ways of God

1. What Gives Me Meaning in Life? / *5*
2. How Does God See Me? / *19*
3. How Do I Fit into God's Plan? / *29*

Section Two: Just What Does God Expect From Me?

4. Love God / *43*
5. Love Others / *55*
6. Esteem Yourself / *65*
7. Be a Steward / *79*
8. Be a Servant / *87*

Section Three: What Has to Happen for Me to Be Holy?

9. The Work of God / *97*
10. The Word of God / *107*
11. Personal Commitment / *117*
12. Other Believers / *127*
13. Time and Trials / *137*

Section Four: Spiritual Snares

14. Intellectual Intimidation / *151*

15. Materialism / *165*

16. Spiritual Discouragement / *175*

17. Carelessness / *189*

18. Toying with Sin / *199*

19. Spiritual Exhaustion / *213*

Section Five: Spiritual Warfare

20. Spiritual Warfare / *227*

21. Spiritual Armor / *239*

22. The Battle for the Mind / *255*

Section Six: Spiritual Disciplines

23. Prayer / *267*

24. Worship / *279*

25. Balancing Life's Competing Priorities / *289*

26. Using Your Spiritual Gifts / *299*

27. Sharing the Good News / *307*

28. Knowing God's Will / *319*

29. Spiritual Vigilance / *329*

30. Living a Life of Love / *341*

Notes / *353*

Suggested Reading / *359*

About the Author / *365*

ACKNOWLEDGMENTS

I would like to thank the people who helped in one way or another with this book. Thanks to my friends Doug Sherman and Walter Crutchfield who reviewed the manuscript and gave many helpful suggestions. Thanks to Anita Harris who proofread the manuscript. Thanks to Holly Dunham and Nora Duckett who helped with the editing of the manuscript. Thanks to Howard Morrison who read the manuscript and made many helpful suggestions, and who also wrote the "Response" sections at the end of each chapter. Thanks to Keith Aycock who first exposed me to some of the thinking presented in the first section. Finally, thanks to Dr. Bill and Pattie Walker for the use of Turtle Cove.

INTRODUCTION

A fter a ministry engagement in St. Louis some time ago, I had several hours before I had to be back to the airport. I had never seen the downtown area of St. Louis with its historic baseball diamond and old buildings, nor had I seen the Great Arch. I hopped in my rental car and began driving down the interstate which I knew would take me near the area. When I got close, the Great Arch stood so high above everything else that I had little difficulty using it to guide me to its base.

I had never been there before. I drove down obscure streets, the names of which I had never heard. I went past buildings I had never seen and navigated intersections I had never been through. I turned right when I should have and left when I should have, even though no one had told me how to get there. It took some tricky maneuvering, but I finally arrrived at the base of the Great Arch on the banks of the Great River, the Mississippi.

I made it to my destination without directions from anyone, because I could see clearly where I wanted to go. The goal stood high above everything else, and I was able to make all the right decisions along the way simply by keeping the goal in sight.

This is a parable of what I think is missing with many of us in our Christian walk. We do not see clearly where God is taking us. Therefore, we get confused along the way. "Now let's see," we ponder, "did that preacher say we were to hang on, or let go? Should I turn left or right here at the intersection of Faith and Doubt? Am I going in the right direction at all?"

The goal of this book is to raise a Great Arch for the Christian life, so that we can gain a better understainding of God's goal and general strategy for our lives. When that is clearly seen, making the daily decisions along the way becomes much easier.

1

Certainly, you will not understand *everything* about the Christian life as a result of reading this book. No one understands everything about the Christian life, and there will still be many questions on the thirty-first day. However, you will have an overview understanding which will provide a good foundation for your continued learning.

Other writers may have omitted some information from a book like this and included other information. I respect that. But this information seemed to me to be foundational, and while someone might wish that we could include more, few would think we should include less.

There is another point I think is important to make. There are many specific and deeply personal aspects to living the Christian life about which there is much room for responsible disagreement in the Christian community, such as the filling of the Holy Spirit, the sovereignty of God, and the free will of man, the eternal security of the believer, etc. I have deliberately avoided most of those. Instead, I have chosen to focus on the more general areas about which there is historic agreement among Christians, and to hold up the goals of the Christian life for us to see more clearly. If we understand generally where God wants us to go and how He is going to get us there, we will be less apt to make major detours, and will more easily recover from any minor detours.

Bon Voyage, and may God be with you.

THE HUMAN CONDITION AND THE WAYS OF GOD

*God's purpose in creating you is
that He wants to demonstrate
to the universe through you
that He is who He says He is and,
in the process, wants to fulfill
all your deepest longings.*

O N E

WHAT GIVES ME
MEANING IN LIFE?

*When you are Irish, one of the first things
you learn is that sooner or later this world
will break your heart.*

Senator Patrick Moynihan
(after hearing about the assassination
of President John F. Kennedy)

I n his book *When All You've Ever Wanted Isn't Enough,* Rabbi Harold Kushner writes:

> I was sitting on a beach one summer day, watching two children, a boy and a girl, playing in the sand. They were hard at work building an elaborate sand castle by the water's edge, with gates and towers and moats and internal passages. Just when they had nearly finished their project, a big wave came along and knocked it down, reducing it to a heap of wet sand. I expected the children to burst into tears, devastated by what had happened to all their hard work. But they surprised me. Instead, they ran up the shore away from the water, laughing and holding hands, and sat down to build another castle. I realized that they had taught me an important lesson. All the things in our lives, all the complicated structures we spend so much time and energy creating, are built on sand. Only our relationships to other people endure. Sooner or later, the wave will come along and knock down what

5

we have worked so hard to build up. When that happens, only the person who has somebody's hand to hold will be able to laugh.[1]

I remember how surprised I was when, as a young adult, I finally came to the conclusion that life was not going to unfold like a Walt Disney movie. I remember watching "Pollyanna" on television and thinking how wonderful it was—nice people living in a nice town, with just a touch of interpersonal conflict, which was resolved so that everyone lived happily ever after. I thought that if you just worked hard and were sincere and didn't do anything foolish, everything would work out the way you wanted it to.

Finally, when my eyes were opened to reality, it was a shock. Many things do not work out the way we want them to, regardless of how hard-working, sincere, and wise we are. For many people, this causes a crisis.

Give Me Meaning

Gimme! Gimme! Gimme! Most of us have stood, toe to toe, eyes popping, neck veins bulging, saliva flying, screaming at life. Most of us have grabbed life by the throat, slammed it up against the wall, sunk our thumbs into its jugular, and shrieked, "Give me meaning! Give me purpose! Give me peace! Give me happiness! Give me something worth living for! I demand it! I cannot go on without something worth living for!"

And for many of us, life stares back like a zombie, with unblinking eyes, emotionless, silent, unruffled, and untouched by our outburst. Nose to nose with us, it breathes its foul, uncaring breath into our nostrils as its unfocused eyes look past us, unconcerned and even unaware of our presence. It was as though it never heard us.

With rage, fueled by alarm, we wail, "But you promised! You promised me meaning, purpose, and love. You led me to believe that I could succeed, that I could matter, and that someone would care! You lied. . . you lied. . . you lied!"

Mixed with panic and despair, we slump to the floor, eyes unfocused, head drooped to our chest, wondering where we go from here. We cannot give up. Yet we cannot go on. Meanwhile, life turns its back and shuffles away from us, leaving us alone. We think our heart will break, we think our mind will split, we think our soul will shrivel like week-old roses.

As we lie in a heap on the floor of life, thinking we are looking at the *end,* we actually may be looking at the beginning. What a wonderful and marvelous place this is. What a privilege and opportunity it is to utterly come to the end of one's hope—not only to run out of answers, but to run out of questions. To be beyond fighting, to come to that suspended animation where we are so confused and so weak that we can neither fight nor run.

The End of Yourself

When you face this critical juncture, when despair seems most certain and hope seems least likely, you are on the verge of triumph. You must seize the day! You must grasp the moment! For you see, when you come to the end of yourself, you find the beginning of God. And there, and nowhere else, you find the answers you seek. You find fulfillment for the longings of your soul.

Like rats in a maze, we shuffle panic-stricken down every blind alley, looking for our way out, choosing every tunnel except the one that leads to God. That is the only tunnel that isn't a dead-end. But often, we will not take that tunnel until we become completely convinced that it is the only one left. Then and then only can our deepest longings be fulfilled. Then and then only will our thirst be slaked. It is as Blaise Pascal once wrote:

> All men seek happiness. This is without exception. Whatever different means they employ, they all tend to this end. The cause of some going to war, and of others avoiding it, is the same desire in both, attending with different views. The will never takes the least step but to this objective. This is the motive of every man, even of those who hang themselves.[2]

And he went on to say:

> There once was in man a true happiness of which now remain to him only the dark and empty trace, which he in vain tries to fill from all his surroundings, seeking from things absent the help he does not find in things present. But these are all inadequate, because the infinite abyss can only be filled by an infinite and immutable object, that is to say, only by God Himself.[3]

That is the answer! And that is the reason it is such a glorious and hope-filled thing to come to the end of one's self. Until we have done so, we will be tempted to try still another option other than God, and to do so is to delay further the fulfillment of the deepest longings of our soul. We were meant for God. We were created *by* Him, and *for* Him, and until we find ourselves *in* Him, we are still short of our journey.

Do we still think we can find our deepest longings fulfilled elsewhere? Is it not enough that Solomon wrote 3,000 years ago that he had tried everything, and it had not satisfied? He was surrounded by pleasure, wealth, accomplishment, relationships, fame—everything. He succeeded to a far greater degree than any of us have time, money, or talent to succeed, and he said it was like bottling wind or eating gravel. In the end, it is God and God alone who satisfies.

From Anthony and Cleopatra, to Henry VIII to Howard Hughes, is it not enough that wealthy and talented people throughout the ages have been among the most miserable and pitiable people ever to stalk the abandoned halls of earth? Is it not enough that the wealthy, talented, and beautiful Hollywood types of today often become the most haunted and tormented of souls? Is it not enough to observe that poor and simple people are often happy?

We find ourselves unhappy, unsatisfied, unfulfilled, and we instinctively long for "things absent," as Pascal said, rather than to seize that which is "present," namely, God Himself.

Meaning is to be found in God and God alone. That is the only message of this book. There is no other answer. If we accept that premise, great discoveries await us. We can sail on like Columbus, for just over the curve of the earth are our greatest discoveries, and the very thing we were looking for when we set sail.

It Is Okay to Want to Be Happy

There is a nagging suspicion that it is not all right to want to be happy. That if we were truly unselfish, we would not worry about being happy. C. S. Lewis has written to that question:

If there lurks in most modern minds the notion that to desire our own good and earnestly to hope for the enjoyment of it is a bad thing, I submit that this notion has crept in from Kant and the Stoics and is no part of the Christian faith. Indeed, if we consider the unblushing promises of reward and the staggering nature of the rewards promised us in the Gospels, it would seem that Our Lord finds our desires not too strong, but too weak. We are half-hearted creatures fooling about with drink and sex and ambition when infinite joy is offered us, like an ignorant child who wants to go on making mud pies in a slum because he cannot imagine what is meant by the offer of a holiday at the sea. We are far too easily pleased.[4]

Even something as staid as the *Westminster Confession* agrees that the chief end of man is to glorify God and enjoy Him forever. John Piper, in his book *Desiring God,* goes one step further. He asserts that the chief end of man is to glorify God *by* enjoying Him forever.

Many Scripture passages indicate that deep, "bone crushing" longing isn't unspiritual, but rather, it is a sign of God drawing us to Himself. He intends to be the one to fulfill those deep longings.

> As the deer pants for the water brooks,
> So my soul pants for Thee, O God.
> My soul thirsts for God, for the living God.
> (Psalm 42:1–2)

> O God, Thou art my God;
>   I shall seek Thee earnestly.
> My soul thirsts for Thee,
>   my flesh yearns for Thee,
> In a dry and weary land where there is no water.
> (Psalm 63:1–2)

Our longings have been given to us by God. It is not wrong for us to long for meaning and purpose and significance and love. He has given us such longings, because He wants to be the One to fulfill these longings. And, He has created us so that only He *can* fill these longings. It is not wrong to long. It is wrong and self-destructive, however, to look outside of God for the fulfillment of them.

If we pursue God as the fulfillment of our longings, then our longings cannot be too strong and our pursuit too ambitious.

The price, of course, in our pursuit of God is absolute. Everything good we long for is found in Him, so if we move away from God, we move away from the fulfillment of our longings. If we follow God completely, we move toward the fulfillment of our longings. God knows that. He knows that sin maims and destroys. That is why, in His love, He calls us to total obedience.

You may have heard the following story as a sermon illustration:

"I want this pearl. How much is it?"

"Well, " the seller says, "it is expensive."

"But how much?" we ask.

"Well, a very large amount."

"Do you think I could buy it?"

"Oh, of course, everyone can buy it."

"But, didn't you say it was very expensive?"

"Yes."

"Well, how much is it?"

"Everything you have."

We make up our minds. "All right, I'll buy it," we say.

"Well, what do you have?" he wants to know.

"Let's write it down."

"Well, I have ten thousand dollars in the bank."

"Good. Ten thousand dollars. What else."

"That's all. That's all I have."

"Nothing more?"

"Well, I have a few dollars here in my pocket."

"How much?"

We start digging. "Well, let's see—thirty, forty, sixty, eighty, a hundred, a hundred twenty dollars."

"That's fine. What else do you have?"

"Well, nothing. That's all."

"Where do you live?" He's still probing.

"In my house. Yes, I have a house."

"The house, too, then." He writes that down.

"You mean I have to live in my camper?"

"You have a camper? That, too. What else?"

"I'll have to sleep in my car!"

"You have a car?"

"Two of them."

"Both of them become mine. Both cars. What else?"

"Well, you already have my money, my house, my camper, my cars. What more do you want?"

"Are you alone in this world?"

"No, I have a wife and two children. . ."

"Oh, yes, your wife and children, too. What else?"

"I have nothing left! I am left alone now."

Suddenly the seller exclaims, "Oh, I almost forgot! You yourself, too! Everything becomes mine—wife, children, house, money, cars,—and you, too."

Then he goes on. "Now listen. I will allow you to use all these things for the time being. But don't forget that they are mine, just as you are. And whenever I need any of them, you must give them up, because now I am the owner."[5]

It does not only cost all that we *have*. The price is all that we *are*. In return, God promises to fulfill the deepest longings of our soul. He promises to satisfy us with Himself.

God's Desires

Through You

This is God's intention: God is good, and He wants to demonstrate to the universe *through you* that He is who He says He is! This is a blockbuster idea! God is good, and He wants to demonstrate it to the universe through you!

In addition to being good, He is a number of others things. God is also:

- omnipotent—all powerful

- omniscient—all knowing

- omnipresent—everywhere present

- holy—untouched by sin

- just—consistent to His word

- merciful—desires to spare us from judgment

- loving—cares about our welfare

And He wants to prove and demonstrate all these things to the universe through you!

Let's mull this over a moment. Getting this idea into our mind is like trying to get a mattress into the back seat of a small car. It usually takes more than one attempt.

God is omnipotent, and He wants to demonstrate to the universe *through you* that He is omnipotent. God is merciful, and He wants to demonstrate to the universe *through you* that He is merciful. God is good, and He wants to demonstrate to the universe *through you* that He is good. God is love, and He wants to demonstrate to the universe *through you* that He is love. And so on. He exercises all His attributes to our benefit.

Everything must flow out of this belief. If we are off at this point, we will be way off in the end. They say that on a moon shot from the Kennedy Space Center, if the launch were off by just one degree leaving the earth, it would miss the moon by hundreds of miles. The same is true with our Christian experience. We must begin with a proper understanding of the character of God. If we have a deep faith in His character, then it will keep us from "doubting" when the going gets tough.

And, if we believe deeply in His purpose—to demonstrate to the universe through us that He is who He says He is—then it will help us hang in there when life comes down on us like a thunderstorm in July, wind raging, lightening flashing, thunder clapping, and hail pounding.

Love Is Giving

I remember as a young boy the first Christmas present I ever gave a girl. It was a bottle of cheap apple blossom perfume and a frail necklace. I put them in a small brown paper sack and then pondered how to wrap them. A commercial for aluminum foil on television had shown some Christmas boxes wrapped in aluminum foil and graced with brightly colored bows. It presented a crisp, clean image. I liked it.

I didn't have a suitably sized box, so I just wrapped the brown paper bag in aluminum foil. I couldn't find a bow, but at the time that didn't seem important. I carried the present around with me through two recess times at school trying to work up the courage to give it to her. Finally, at the last recess of the day, I pulled the present out of my back pocket and thrust it at her.

"What is this?" she eyed it suspiciously. I hadn't realized how crumpled the "present" had become in my back pocket. Crumpled and without a bow, it looked all the world like an old sandwich. The vision of the bright, clean presents on TV was somehow missing, but I was in love (albeit, puppy love), and nothing could stop me from "giving" something to demonstrate it. As I think back on it, my ears flame with embarrassment. But it is an example of the fact that "love" is deeply motivated to "give."

The Bible teaches that the central characteristic of love is that it "gives." In John 3:16 we read, "For God so loved the world that *He gave. . . .*" and in Ephesians 5:25 we read, "Husbands, love your wives just as Christ also *loved* the church and *gave . . .*" Throughout the Scripture, we see love "giving," (emphasis mine).

God loves us. That means He wants to *give* to us, and in return, to receive from us our worship, our praise, and our fellowship.

As we search the New Testament, we see God Himself desiring for three things:

1. A community of beings to whom He could reveal Himself, from whom He could receive glory, praise, worship, and with whom He could give and receive love.

2. A community of beings of whom He could be the Head, and with whom and through whom He could rule all creation.

3. A community of beings into whom He could build His likeness, to form a living reflection of Himself, an eternal dwelling place of God, to glorify Him forever.

Angels could not satisfy these desires. Robots could not satisfy these desires. No beings could satisfy these desires unless they were created in His image. That was where "Man" came in. He was created in God's image and held the potential of having the relationship with God that He envisioned.

When Adam and Eve sinned, they rejected God's original plan. There were only two solutions: destroy creation or restore creation.

Restoration

God chose to offer restoration to man. He offered to forgive man's sin and restore him to the fullness of God's image and the life and relationship He originally envisioned. This offer comes through Jesus. By believing in Him and receiving Him as our personal Savior, God restores us to a relationship with Him. Then, God develops a community of beings who believe in Him.

To fulfill His three-fold desire to have a community of beings to whom He could reveal Himself, of whom He could be the Head, and in whom He could build His likeness, God set about a three-fold plan:

1. God's plan was to create a spiritual family whom He can love and accept in eternal fellowship. In Jesus, *we are that family.*

2. Jesus' plan was to create a spiritual body to function as an extension of the incarnation of Christ; to share in the significance of ruling with Him forever, and to find our identity in Him. In Jesus, *we are that body.*

3. The Holy Spirit's plan was to create a spiritual temple of living stones into whom He can invest His likeness and power, competent to serve and glorify Him in eternal fulfillment. In Jesus, *we are that temple.*

By bringing us into His Family, by bringing us into His Body, by making us part of His living Temple, He gives to us the things which satisfy the deepest longings of our souls. Being part of the family satisfies our longing to be loved and secure. Being part of the Body satisfies our longing to do something significant with our lives. Being part of the living Temple satisfies our longing to be competent to do that which is pleasing to God.

His motivation to love is an expression of His character. Out of His love, He gives us that which is exactly what our souls long for: security, significance, and competence.

Out of His love, God gives us His forgiveness, His love and fellowship, a share in His universe, His character, His glory, His wealth, and His power. Out of His love, He gives us membership in His Family, membership in His Body, and membership in His Temple. Accomplishing this takes all God's attributes. It takes His love, His mercy, His grace, His knowledge, His power, His presence. By doing all this through a once-fallen race, God demonstrates to the universe through us that He is who He says He is.

Earthly Visitors and Relationships

C. S. Lewis once said, "Pride is the mother hen under which all other sins are hatched." The original sin of man is pride—putting himself at the center of his own life, raising himself above God. God wants man to willingly step down from the throne of his life, and put God on the throne. God wants a family, a body, and a temple, but with Christ at the center.

This life is not the *end* for us. It is the *means*. It is not the destination; it is a journey. Our task is to live in this world, in light of the next world. It is to live in time with the value system of eternity. It is to move through the world doing the things that are important to heaven. It is to see ourselves as visitors on this planet. We sojourn here, all the while preparing ourselves and others for heaven.

Any other perspective will bring frustration and disillusionment at God's refusal to "bless us." If we put our hopes only in this world, they will be treated worse than a Yankee manager in a Dodger dugout. Certainly, we are free, within the will of God, to make things as good for ourselves as we can. In addition, we are responsible to improve the world and make it as good a place to live as we can. But the moment we cease living with a sense of detachment for the pleasures of this world, we start borrowing trouble. We put ourselves on a collision course with the brick wall of reality. It will steal from us our joy in life, make us ineffective in the world, and rob God of His glory.

Our earthly fathers picture the relationship our Heavenly Father wants to have with us. The feelings of hope and joy and promise that an earthly father feels when he holds his newborn son for the first time, God feels for us when we become reborn in Christ. The joy that brings tears to a young father's eyes, the dreams for the future, the longing for the relationship—these are the emotions God must have toward His reborn children. Luke 15:10 says, "there is joy in the presence of the angels of God over one sinner who repents." If the angels, how much more the Father!

God loves us more than any of us have the capacity to realize. We are like a two-year old who has little capacity to realize the depth of his earthly parents' love. The question is: Will we let Him pour His love out on us by giving ourselves to Him completely?

> I urge you, therefore, brethren, by the mercies of God, to present your bodies a living and holy sacrifice, acceptable to God, which is your spiritual service of worship. And do not be conformed to this world, but be transformed by the renewing of your mind, that you may prove what the will of God is, that which is good and acceptable and perfect. (Romans 12:1–2)

Heavenly Father, please help me to take the step of total commitment to you. I believe that fulfillment is found only in you . . . but help my unbelief. Give me the courage. Give me the strength. Give me the vision. Help me believe and help me respond. I now give myself totally to you. Help me to understand all that it means, and help me to be faithful. I pray in the name of Jesus, my Savior. Amen.

REVIEW

1. Give Me Meaning

When we reach the end of *ourselves,* then we find the beginning of *God.*

2. It Is Okay to Want to Be Happy

Yes, meaning in life is to be found only in *Christ.* Our deepest longings were given to us by God, and He wants to be the One to meet them. In fact, He is the only one who *can* meet them. The price is *total commitment* to Him.

3. God's Desires

God is *good,* and He wants to demonstrate to the universe through us that He is who He says He is. He will prove it by making us His *Family,* His *Body,* and His *Temple.* All this is done through Christ.

4. Earthly Visitors and Relationships

We must let Him pour His *love* out on us by *giving* our lives to Christ.

As a memory exercise, write in the missing words in the paragraphs below. Notice that they are the same words as the italicized words in the paragraph above.

1. Give Me Meaning

When we reach the end of _____, then we find the beginning of _____ .

2. It Is Okay To Want To Be Happy

Yes, meaning in life is to be found only in _____. Our deepest longings were given to us by God, and He wants to be the One to meet them. In fact, He is the only one who *can* meet them. The price is _____ _____ to Him.

3. God's Desires

God is _____, and He wants to demonstrate to the universe through us that He is who He says He is. He will prove it by making us His _____, His _____, and His _____. All this is done through Christ.

4. Earthly Visitors and Relationships

We must let Him pour His _____ out on us by _____ our lives to Christ.

RESPONSE

Questions for Group Discussion or Personal Exercises

1. Where or to whom is the world turning today to fulfill its deepest longings?

2. Use some resources (concordance, basic doctrine book, Biblical encyclopedia) to do a brief character study of God. What words do you find to describe Him?

3. As you look back at your life, can you identify other purposes that you might have pursued other than knowing God? Are there some that you are pursuing right now?

4. Is it hard (due to your personality or family background) for you to *receive* from God? How do you think you could begin to overcome that?

5. When have you *felt* most loved? By whom? Why? How did you know? What would God have to do to demonstrate His love to you? List from Scripture as many things as you can where God has already done things for you because He loves you. (See Ephesians chapter 1 for starters.)

T W O

HOW DOES GOD SEE ME?

> *The doctrines of grace humble a man with-*
> *out degrading him, and exalt a man with-*
> *out inflating him.*
>
> Charles Hodge

T he development of an eternal perspective, that is, seeing this world as God sees it, is one of the most crucial mental transformations a Christian must experience. We are creatures of this world, but we need to think and act as creatures of the next world.

Have you heard the story of Little Lord Fauntleroy? It is a very heartwarming story, and is a good illustration of this.

> The son of an English earl marries an American woman, and is consequently disinherited. Some years later, he dies at sea, and his widow and son live humbly in New York City. The disinherited man's father, the Earl of Darringcourt, becomes aged and is concerned for the succession to his fortune and family line. His ten-year-old American grandson is his only legal heir, so he sends a representative to America to offer to have his grandson come to live on the fabulous estate as Lord Fauntleroy, and eventually succeed him as Earl of Darringcourt. There is one catch. Little Lord Fauntleroy's American mother who was the cause of the original disinheritance, an exemplary woman with whom Lord Fauntleroy is very close, cannot live on the estate. The story of the initial conflict and misunderstanding, and the subsequent

healing and restoration of relationships is a touching one in which everyone eventually lives happily ever after.

When the Earl of Darringcourt's representative first comes to America with the proposal, a circumstance arose which is analogous to the life of a Christian. He describes what life will be like as Lord Fauntleroy. Wealth, power, honor, glory are his. He is a royal heir. Yet, he will have to wait until he gets to England to experience it. For now, he will have some limited benefits, but for the most part, until he crosses the Atlantic, the life of Lord Fauntleroy has to wait.

Nevertheless, the representative stresses, it is important to begin thinking and acting like Lord Fauntleroy now for three reasons. First, because there are decisions and actions right now that require his attention. Second, because he needs to begin practicing now for the expanded role that will come to him when he gets to England. And third, because he *is* Lord Fauntleroy, and that fact is momentous enough in itself. Lord Fauntleroy ought to act like Lord Fauntleroy. Period.[1]

I mention this story in *30 Days to Understanding the Bible*, but it is also helpful here. The situation for the Christian is similar. The Bible presents a picture of a future which is difficult to imagine. Power, glory, wealth, and honor are ours. But in large measure, we must wait until we get to heaven to experience it. Nevertheless, we are children of God now, and we ought to act like it.

God Sees Me as Righteous in Christ

If we want to understand how to live, we have to understand who we are. We all live consistently with how we see ourselves. Therefore, we must see ourselves as God sees us—no more and no less.

Many of us observe our own inconsistency in the Christian life and fear that our name brings a stench to the nostrils of God in heaven. "Will He let us into heaven when we die?" we wonder. Probably so, because of Jesus, but we can imagine God standing at the pearly gates with His arms folded across His chest, tapping His foot impatiently, heaving a sigh, and saying, "Well, I probably shouldn't, but, come on in. I'm letting you in because of Jesus, but I sure hope you shape up now that you're here!" It is hard to imagine how God could see us as righteous when we know full well we aren't. Is God blind? Or is He pretending He doesn't see the things that we do in the dark?

The reason we think we aren't righteous is because there is a new reality we haven't embraced. We don't understand exactly what happened to us when we became a Christian. Ephesians 2:1 says, "And you were dead in your trespasses and sins . . ." In what sense were we dead? Physically? We were dead spiritually, separated from God.

In John 3, Jesus says to Nicodemus, "You've been born once, Nicodemus, and that makes you a member of this physical kingdom. But my kingdom is spiritual, and if you want to be a member of my spiritual kingdom, you must be born again, spiritually." Being born again, He explains, happens when we believe in Him, and receive Him as our personal savior (John 1:12). This new spiritual self which is born again is holy and righteous. It does not sin. For example, Ephesians 4:24, where this new spiritual self is described says, "put on the new self, which in the likeness of God has been created in righteousness and holiness of the truth."

Note also several verses in Romans 7 which describe the new spiritual self as the "inner man." This inner man "does not wish to sin" (v. 16), "wishes to do good" (v. 18), "joyfully concurs with the law of God" (v. 22), and "serves the law of God" (v. 25). Paul then goes on to say, "So now, no longer am I the one doing [evil], but sin which indwells me" (v. 17). He repeats it: "If I am doing the very thing I do not wish, I am no longer the one doing it, but sin which dwells in me (v. 20)."

We rarely hear this taught as clearly as it is stated in Scripture, I think, because we fear it will give rise to a "the devil made me do it" approach to the Christian life where we do not take responsibility for our sin. This could hardly be farther from the truth, however. In Romans 6:12–13, Paul states equally unambiguously, "do not let sin reign in your mortal body that you should obey its lusts, and do not go on presenting the members of your body to sin as instruments of unrighteousness; but present yourselves to God as those alive from the dead, and your members as instruments of righteousness to God."

In 1 Corinthians 11, we see some Christians who were taken to the spiritual woodshed by God because of their sin. Paul says that because of flagrant and prolonged sin, some Corinthian believers suffered, were sick, and even died. Nowhere does God take sin in the life of a believer lightly. And nowhere does Paul suggest that God does not hold us accountable in this life for our actions. But the Scripture does differentiate between this "sin" on the one hand, and the true spiritual self which has been born again on the other hand. This true self does not sin, according to Romans 7.

In his commentary on Ephesians, John MacArthur states clearly that the redeemed Christian is not two natures but one. Then he goes on to say of the new self:

> So righteous and holy is this new self that Paul refuses to admit that any sin comes from that new creation in God's image. Thus his language in Romans 6–7 is explicit in placing the reality of sin other than in the new self. He says, "Do not let sin reign in your *mortal body* (6:12), and do not go on presenting the *members of your body* to sin" (6:13, emphasis added).
>
> In those passages Paul places sin in the believer's life in the body. In chapter 7 he sees it in the flesh. He says, "No longer am I the one doing it, but sin which indwells me" (v. 17), "nothing good dwells in me, that is in my flesh" (v. 18), "I am no longer the one doing it, but sin which dwells in me" (v. 20), and ". . . the law of sin which is in my members" (v. 23).
>
> In those texts Paul acknowledges that being a new self in the image of God does not eliminate sin. It is still present in the flesh, the body, the unredeemed humanness that includes the whole human person's thinking and behavior. But he will not allow that new inner man to be given responsibility for sin. The new "I" loves and longs for the holiness and righteousness for which it was created.[2]

Somehow, this "new self" doesn't always come out on top in our actions. It is impeded by the force of sin in our bodies. However, the bodies we are in now will never make it to heaven. We will die and be given new bodies when we go to heaven. If the Lord returns, we will be given new bodies on the spot. With new bodies which will also be holy and righteous, we will finally serve the Lord in complete righteousness.

So is God blind? Does He pretend He doesn't see the things we do in the dark? No! How can He see us as righteous? He is looking at this inner man which has been redeemed and does not sin. He understands that sin is in the flesh, and that this body of flesh will never make it to heaven. It will be discarded, and our redeemed inner selves will stand before God housed in redeemed bodies, and we will finally serve and love Him unimpeded by any influence of sin whatsoever.

This in no way solves all the problems we have understanding everything. But it is true to Scripture. We are a new self which does not sin. Paul calls this the "inner man" in Romans 7. It is this new righteous self that we must identify as the true person we are. In the same chapter he says that in our "outer man," if you will, the flesh, dwells sin. We are essentially spirit beings, housed in a body of flesh. In the relationship between the two, the new righteous self is not always expressed consistently.

Nevertheless, and this is the importance of embracing the new reality, our inner righteousness will be expressed *more* consistently if we see ourselves accurately—as holy and righteous beings housed in bodies which pull us toward sin.

When temptation to sin comes our way, we can say, "That is not the new *me* wanting to sin. That is the power of the flesh in my body (Romans 7:23). It is a fraud, an impostor. It has not come from inside the true spiritual *me*. I do not have to yield to its lure. I can resist it, and I choose to do so!"

We must embrace this new reality and begin living as who we have become. Instead of trying to go our own way and do our own thing, we must accept who we are in Christ and live accordingly. As we do, we receive the happiness and meaning we long for. Happiness and meaning are not gotten by pursuing them. They are gotten by pursuing God who then grants us happiness and meaning as a by-product of our relationship with Him.

We Must Define What We Are Living For

One night a mother fixed a special meal for her family: turkey with mashed potatoes and gravy, corn, green beans, cranberry sauce, and apple pie for dessert. It was everyone's favorite meal, especially when it came at a time other than Thanksgiving. The aroma filled the house, and as the children came in from playing, they could hardly wait for dinner to begin. The last child appeared only a few minutes before dinner time and sat through the meal without eating, even though he especially loved those foods. Why? Because he had filled up on peanut butter at a friend's house. In settling for something good, he had lost his appetite for the best.

The same applies to our spiritual appetites. Some people don't have much of an appetite for spiritual truths because they have satisfied themselves with lesser things.

We have two fundamental longings: (1) the desire to love and be loved, and (2) the desire to live a life of meaning and purpose. God alone can meet these longings completely and unendingly. No doubt, some things can fulfill them temporarily, but only God can meet them completely and unendingly.

Problems come when we either do not know or do not believe that God alone can meet these fundamental desires, or we begin to try to get them met outside of God, usually through people, possessions, and circumstances. The problem is, of course, that people, possessions, and circumstances don't always cooperate with us. When they go haywire, it frustrates our longings for love and meaning in life.

There are two things wrong with getting trapped into thinking that these "things" will satisfy you. First, by themselves, they don't. Not for long, anyway. They are a mirage. Once you have what you thought would bring you happiness, your horizons expand, your desires increase, and you want more. Like the donkey chasing the carrot, you never catch it.

The second thing is that it keeps you from the greatest commandment to love others. We tend to think of sin as doing or thinking something immoral or unethical or dishonest. And, these are sin. But there is a much more common pattern of sin, and that is *not loving others*.

If our primary goals in life are to hit a financial home run, or climb the ladder of corporate success, or "land" a beauty queen as our wife, then people are mere commodities. They either help us or get in our way. If they help us, the illusion of friendship exists. But if they get in our way, they are to be gone around, run over, or thrown away. They aren't any good to us.

If we love people based merely on whether or not they help us reach our goals, we are living in terrible sin. We are failing at our greatest commandment toward our fellow men. We are failing to love them as ourselves. So what if we don't use drugs, beat our kids, kick the dog, or rob banks? The Bible says we are to love people and use things. We get it backwards. We love things and use people. We are flagrant sinners if we fail to love others.

So our task is to love others and not view them as commodities. But how do we cope with the pain when people, possessions, and circumstances leave us with unfulfilled dreams? First, we must hold our dreams lightly. It is not wrong to dream, nor is it wrong to try to move people, possessions, and circumstances toward noble goals. But if the will of God does not bring us what we long for, we must let go of those dreams. We must not demand them for happiness. The Bible does not promise the fulfillment of our desires here on earth.

Second, we must look to God for the fulfillment of our deepest longings. When we find ourselves falling on hard times in a relationship, or in finances, or with our health, or other circumstances, we must understand that God may not change those circumstances. Instead, He will meet us at our point of need with His grace. He will grant to us the joy of having our deepest spiritual longings fulfilled in Him, in spite of circumstances.

Happiness is rooted in two things:

1. Hope for the future. When we put our hope in heaven, we can tolerate disappointment in temporal things.

2. Spiritual goals. When we live for spiritual goals, we cannot be thwarted.

Our task, then, is to redefine what we are living for.

God, and God alone, loves us perfectly and forever. No one else is able to love us so totally. He, and He alone, can give us purpose and meaning in life completely and forever. Nothing else can do so. When we feel the longings and dissatisfactions rising up in our soul, we must recognize that it is God that we long for. It is heaven that we seek.

Our Great Task Is to Begin Living Like Whom We Have Become

We have seen, then, that we are new creations—that we have been created in holiness and righteousness. True, we are housed in a body which still pulls us toward sin. Nevertheless, our spiritual selves have been crucified with Christ. We have died from the power of sin. We are not slaves to sin any longer. We can choose not to sin. We can present our bodies to the Lord as instruments of righteousness, rather than being instruments of unrighteousness. (See Romans chapter 6.)

Our great task is to have our outer life conform to our inner life. As we said, our inner man is holy and righteous. Therefore, our outer lifestyle should be holy and righteous. Our inner man loves God and others as Christ does. Therefore, our outer lifestyle must be one of loving God and others.

If our great task is to have the lifestyle of the outer man conform to the righteousness of the inner man, this requires a radical transformation of our mind, emotions, and will. We have old programming, old habits, old values, and old attitudes which do not die immediately or easily. Just as it took a long time to put them in place, it may take a long time for some of them to be changed, replaced by Christ's attitudes. Nevertheless, that is our great task—to cooperate with God in the process of transforming us into the character image of Christ. Remaining chapters in the book are intended to spell out more clearly how this can happen.

I have been crucified with Christ; and it is no longer I who live, but Christ lives in me; and the life which I now live in the flesh I live by faith in the Son of God, who loved me, and delivered Himself up for me. (Galatians 2:20)

Heavenly Father, help me understand who I have become in Christ. Help me see myself as You see me. And then, Heavenly Father, change me into the character image of Your Son, so that my outer life will conform to my inner character in Christ. I pray in His name. Amen.

REVIEW

1. God Sees Me as Righteous in Christ

In Christ, we are *forgiven* of all our sins, born again, and spiritually ready for *heaven*. In Him, we are *righteous*, serving the law of Christ.

2. We Must Define What We Are Living For

Though our spirit has been *born again* in Christ, we are still housed in a fallen body, in which the power of sin dwells. Therefore, our outer actions *fail* to reflect our inner character.

3. Our Great Task Is to Begin Living Like Whom We Have Become

We must *cooperate* with God in transforming us, from the inside out, so that our outer *actions* will conform to the inner *reality* of our new birth.

As a memory exercise, write in the missing words in the paragraphs below. Notice that they are the same words as the italicized words in the paragraph above.

1. God Sees Me as Righteous in Christ

In Christ, we are _____ of all our sins, born again, and spiritually ready for _____. In Him, we are _____, serving the law of Christ.

2. **We Must Define What We Are Living For**

Though our spirit has been _____ in Christ, we are still housed in a fallen body, in which the power of sin dwells. Therefore, our outer actions _____ to reflect our inner character.

3. **Our Great Task Is to Begin Living Like Whom We Have Become**

We must _____ with God in transforming us, from the inside out, so that our outer _____ will conform to the inner _____ of our new birth.

RESPONSE

Questions for Group Discussion or Personal Exercises

1. Has the first stage of transformation (salvation) happened in *your* life? If not, read the Gospel of John, chapters 2 and 3. Notice Jesus' emphasis on each character's personal need to be born again in his spirit.

2. Memorize Galatians 2:20. Discuss where you can see evidence of Christ living in you. You might start by looking at the character issues of Galatians 5:22–23. Which of these are more evident in your life now than they were before you became a Christian? Which of these still need more work?

3. What area of your life is Christ wanting to see the great change or transformation? If it is a particular character trait, study that trait as it appeared in the life of Jesus.

THREE

HOW DO I FIT INTO GOD'S PLAN?

*A man can no more diminish God's glory
by refusing to worship Him than a lunatic
can put out the sun by scribbling the word
"darkness" on the wall.*

C. S. Lewis

In ancient Persia, if you came into the presence of the king
unbidden, it cost you your life. The chasm between monarch
and mortal has always been difficult and dangerous to cross. If this
is true with kings, how much more so with God? How does one
approach God? On what basis might we be accepted into His presence and establish a relationship with Him? How can we be properly related to God?

God is, in a sense, a monarch, and there are certain rules
which apply in our ability to approach Him. Yet, unlike most mon-
archs, God earnestly desires our fellowship. He encourages us to
come to Him. Billy Graham, in his book *How to Be Born Again*, tells
an interesting story which captures this fact so well.

> Picture a courtroom. God the Judge is seated in the judge's seat,
> robed in splendor. You are arraigned before Him. He looks at
> you in terms of His own righteous nature as it is expressed in the
> moral law. He speaks to you:

29

God: "John (or) Mary, have you loved Me with all your
heart?"

John/Mary: "No, Your Honor."

God: "Have you loved others as you have loved yourself?"

John/Mary: "No, Your Honor."

God: "Do you believe you are a sinner and that Jesus Christ
died for your sins?"

John/Mary: "Yes, Your Honor."

God: "Then your penalty has been paid by Jesus Christ on
the cross and you are pardoned. Because Christ is righteous, and
you believe in Christ, I now declare you legally righteous." [Can
you imagine what a newspaperman would do with this event?]

Sinner Pardoned
Goes to Live with Judge

It was a tense scene when John and Mary stood before the Judge
and had the list of charges against them read. However, the
Judge transferred all of the guilt to Jesus Christ, who died on a
cross for John and Mary.

After John and Mary were pardoned, the Judge invited them
to come to live with Him forever.[1]

Pardon and Christ's righteousness come to us only when we
totally trust ourselves to Jesus as our Lord and Savior. When we do
this, God welcomes us into His intimate favor. Clothed in Christ's
righteousness, we can now enjoy God's fellowship.

Faith is the key to a relationship with God. If we believe in
Him, He adopts us as His spiritual child, and the relationship we
might imagine existing between a model earthly father and child is
a picture of the spiritual relationship we then have with God.

God's strategy in developing his relationship with man has
been consistent throughout the ages. There are four main elements in the program of God: revelation, faith, blessing, and reproduction.

1. Revelation: God reveals truth to man.

    In the earliest days, He did this directly, through direct
    contact, or dreams and visions, or angels, and so on. Now,
    His primary way is through the Bible.

2. Faith: God asks man to live by faith.

Many of the things which God asks of man in the revelation take man in the opposite direction of his natural inclinations. Therefore, man will only respond if he believes God! Such is the nature of faith. You believe something you can't see! You act on something that is unnatural! You subordinate your own instincts to someone whom you believe has greater wisdom.

3. Blessing: God blesses the faithful.

   As man lives for God by faith, trusting God and obeying him as best he knows how, God blesses that man and gives him a quality of life that makes his life of faith deeply satisfying.

4. Reproduction: Others desire to know God.

   Finally, when others look at the "child of God" and see the blessing that comes to him through his relationship with God, a thirst is created in some lives to want to know God also.

How these principles worked themselves out is quite different in the Old Testament than it is in the New Testament. We are now going to look at each of these principles and see how they are revealed in the Old and New Testaments.

The Old Testament: The Fruit of the Vine

Revelation: God Reveals Truth to Man

God revealed Himself to the people in the Old Testament in many different ways. In the earlier days, it was entirely through miraculous means, since none of the Bible was written. After the Old Testament was being recorded, they had the benefit of that Scripture.

This revelation asked the Old Testament people to act in ways that departed from the normal behavior. For example, they were not to amass horses to themselves as military resources. God would fight for them and protect them from all enemies as long as Israel remained righteous.

They were to refrain from labor or commerce every seventh day. Every seventh year, they were to let their land lie fallow for the entire year. God promised to bless their business and agricultural pursuits to such an extent that they would have plenty.

They were to give almost 30 percent of their income in tithes and offerings for national taxes and for the functioning of the sacrificial and priestly system. God promised to prosper them economically if they would obey these commands, so that, not only would they not be poor, they would be fabulously wealthy.

Faith: God Asks Man to Believe and Obey the Revelation

If you believed that an invisible God would protect you from enemies, you would be willing to forego the development of a cavalry and chariot warfare. If you did not trust God to protect you, you would disobey and raise all the horses you could to protect yourself.

If you believed that an invisible God would prosper your farming to such an extent that you could actually not plant one year out of seven and spend that year in praise to the Lord, you would obey and forego planting the seventh year. If you did not trust God to prosper you, you would disobey and raise all the crops you could, to supply yourself.

If you believed that an invisible God would prosper you financially, so that you could afford to give 30 percent of your money for national and religious purposes, you would obey and tithe your income. If you didn't trust God to prosper you, you would disobey and keep the money for yourself.

These are just three examples of how God's revelation took man in the opposite direction from his natural inclinations. His natural inclination is to protect himself, supply himself, and fund himself. Faith requires that you believe God and do things His way.

Blessing: God Blesses "Living by Faith"

If the Israelites would trust God to meet their needs and obey His commandments, God promised to give them, not just subsistence, but abundance beyond comprehension in every area of their national life.

Now it shall be, if you will diligently obey the Lord your God, being careful to do all His commandments which I command you today, the Lord your God will set you high above all the nations of the earth. And all these blessings shall come upon you and overtake you, if you will obey the Lord your God. Blessed shall you be in the city, and blessed shall you be in the country. Blessed shall be the offspring of your body and the produce of your ground and your herd and the young of your flock. Blessed shall be your basket and your kneading bowl. Blessed shall you be when you come in and blessed shall you be when you go out.

The Lord will cause your enemies who rise up against you to be defeated before you; they shall come out against you one way, and shall flee before you seven ways. The Lord will command the blessing upon you in your barns and in all that you put your hand to, and He will bless you in the land which the Lord your God gives you. The Lord will establish you as a holy people to Himself, as He swore to you, if you will keep the commandments of the Lord your God, and walk in His ways. So all the peoples of the earth shall see that you are called by the name of the Lord, and they shall be afraid of you. (Deuteronomy 28:1–10)

God put His word on the line in unambiguous terms. Marvelous blessing was theirs if they were obedient from the heart to His commandments.

Reproduction: Others Want to Have Faith

God did not choose the nation of Israel to the exclusion of all the other people in the world. He chose Israel in order to reach all the other people in the world. God's idea was to so bless Israel that the other nations of the world would see the "thumbprint" of God on their national life and desire to know their God, because of the quality of life He had given Israel.

This is stated in Psalm 67 as succinctly as anywhere in the Bible:

> God be Gracious to us and bless us,
> And cause His face to shine upon us
> That Thy way may be known on the earth,
> Thy salvation among all nations.
> Let the peoples praise Thee, O God;
> Let nations be glad and sing for joy.

> For Thou wilt judge the peoples
>   with uprightness,
> And guide the nations on the earth.
> Let the peoples praise Thee, O God;
> Let all the peoples praise Thee.
> The earth has yielded its produce;
> God, our God, blesses us.
> God blesses us,
> That all the ends of the earth may fear Him.
>   (Psalm 67:1–7)

There it is in black and white. God blesses Israel, that all the ends of the earth may fear Him. Fear here does not mean "fright or terror," rather it means respect or reverence.

But God's blessing is always tied to the obedience of His commandments. Israel, however, was never very successful at living righteously for very long. The longest sustained period of righteousness for the nation overlapped David's reign and the first part of Solomon's reign. There was a period of perhaps as long as sixty years of sustained righteous national living. As a result, this was the period of greatest blessing on them as a nation. It was stupendous, and its effect on the surrounding nations was observable.

We read in 1 Kings 10 that word of the splendor of Israel was spreading. Even the queen of Sheba heard of the glory of Jerusalem and the wisdom of Solomon. So fascinated was she by the reports of Israel's grandeur that she came for a closer look. Solomon displayed to her his palace, the city of Jerusalem, and the temple, one of the most glorious buildings ever built.

After the queen had seen everything, the Bible says in verse 5, that "there was no more spirit in her." She swooned! Then she began to babble. "It was a true report which I heard in my own land about your words and your wisdom. Nevertheless, I did not believe the reports until I came and my eyes had seen it. And behold, the half was not told me. You exceed in wisdom and prosperity the report which I heard" (1 Kings 10:6–8).

Then she broke out in spontaneous eulogy to God. "Blessed be the Lord your God. . ."

This was the way it was supposed to work. The people of the world see the splendor of Israel, and their attention is drawn to God.

The New Testament: The Fruit of the Spirit

God's dealings with the nation of Israel were very much physical and were designed to picture or foreshadow the spiritual truths which would be presented in the New Testament. The Old Testament sacrificial system was intended to picture, in literal terms, the spiritual work which would be done by Christ on the cross in the New Testament. The beauty of the temple was designed to picture the glory of God. The physical blessing of protection and food was designed to picture the spiritual protection and nourishment which is ours in Christ.

The blessings in the Old Testament were conspicuously material and physical—the fruit of the vine. The blessings in the New Testament are conspicuously spiritual—the fruit of the spirit.

Revelation: God Reveals Truth to Man

The revelation from God in the New Testament is quite different from the Old Testament. Christ said that He came to fulfill the law. Now that He has come and died for our sins, and has risen again from the dead, there is now no longer any need for the sacrificial system. There is no need to observe the Mosaic Law. We no longer have to worry about not planting the seventh year, and so on, because, whereas Israel was a physical kingdom designed to picture the coming spiritual kingdom, now the spiritual kingdom is here. If Jesus' kingdom were of this world, we would have to be concerned about some of those things. But it isn't, so we don't.

Nevertheless, the nature of the revelation remains the same. It asks us to function in a way contrary to our natural inclinations. If we would keep our life, we must lose it; if we want to be great, we must become a servant. If we are to be strong, we must be gentle. It is better to give than to receive. Pursue the kingdom of God first, and all our material needs will be met. Reality in the New

Testament is that which is *not* seen, while that which is seen is a counterfeit. We must live for the next world instead of this one.

Faith: God Asks Man to Believe and Obey the Revelation

All of this, going against our natural inclinations, is most unnatural—just as unnatural as the commands in the Old Testament. And faith is required just as much in the New Testament as in the Old. It all boils down to the same thing. If we believe God, we obey the commands. If we don't, we don't. The opposite of obedience is not disobedience. It is unbelief. Our disobedience is linked to lack of faith.

Blessing: God Blesses "Living by Faith"

In the Old Testament, God blessed the Israelites with material abundance. In the New Testament, the material blessings are no longer operative. God blesses the Church with spiritual abundance. If we live in faith, trusting and obeying God, He gives us, rather than the fruit of the vine, the fruit of the spirit: love, joy, peace, patience, kindness, goodness, faithfulness, gentleness, self-control (Galatians 5:22–23). If you ask someone what he wants out of life, he will say, "I just want to be happy." If a person is happy, life has meaning. The blessing which is promised to the faithful child of God in the New Testament is greater—peace, love, joy.

Reproduction: Others Want to Have Faith

In the Old Testament, God promised to raise Israel higher than the other nations of the world by bestowing material abundance. In the New Testament, He promised to raise individual Christians higher than the world by bestowing spiritual abundance. "Let your light so shine before men in such a way that they may see your good works, and glorify your Father who is in heaven" (Matthew 5:16). "Do all things without grumbling or disputing; that you may prove yourselves to be blameless and innocent, children of God above reproach in the midst of a crooked and perverse generation, among whom you appear as lights in the world" (Philippians 2:14–15). It is our inner spiritual abundance, not our outer material abundance, that shows God to the world.

When we live as we ought, it calls attention to the Lord and encourages others to become Christians. "A new commandment I give to you, that you love one another, even as I have loved you, that you also love one another. By this all men will know that you are My disciples, if you have love for one another" (John 13:34–35). And, as Christ is accurately portrayed and proclaimed to the world, people will be drawn to Him to become Christians.

The Consequences

We see, then, that to be properly related to God, faith is the central issue. Faith is critical, because it is the only thing we can do and still not do anything. It is the one response we can make and still not be responsible for saving ourselves.

By faith, we become His spiritual children, and by faith, we read His revelation, believe it, and respond accordingly. In doing so, we are eligible for His spiritual blessing which has three primary consequences:

1. God is glorified. As we live in trust and obedience to God, striving to live according to the Scriptures, our lives gradually begin to take on the character of God Himself. When this happens, the world begins to get an accurate picture of who God really is, because they begin to see Him in us. The value and worth of God begins to be known publicly, and in this way, God is glorified.

2. Man is satisfied. We who are His spiritual children experience the pleasure of the life which God grants to us. Peace, love, and joy become ours in increasing measure.

3. Others are evangelized. As others see the quality of life available to the children of God, some will desire to know God because of what they see of Him in our lives.

God be gracious to us and bless us, and cause His face to shine upon us—that Thy way may be known on the earth, Thy salvation among all the nations. . . . God blesses us, that all the ends of the earth may fear Him. (Psalm 67:1–2,7)

> *Heavenly Father, help me to be obedient to You from the heart. May my life of willing obedience bring glory to You, rich satisfaction to me, and may Your blessing in my life cause others to want to know You because of what they see of You in me. Amen.*

REVIEW

1. The Old Testament: The Fruit of the Vine

When Israel believed God and *obeyed* Him from the heart, God *blessed* Israel with great *material* wealth which reflected God to the world.

2. The New Testament: The Fruit of the Spirit

When the Church believes God and *obeys* Him from the heart, God *blesses* the Church with great *spiritual* wealth which reflects God to the world.

3. The Consequences

When the world sees the blessing of God resting on His children, three things happen: God is *glorified,* Christians are *satisfied,* and others are *evangelized.*

As a memory exercise, write in the missing words in the paragraphs below. Notice that they are the same words as the italicized words in the paragraph above.

1. The Old Testament: The Fruit of the Vine

When Israel believed God and _____ Him from the heart, God _____ Israel with great _____ wealth which reflected God to the world.

2. **The New Testament: The Fruit of the Spirit**

When the Church believes God and _____ from the heart, God _____ the Church with great _____ wealth which reflects God to the world.

3. **The Consequences**

When the world sees the blessing of God resting on His children, three things happen: God is _____, Christians are _____, and others are _____.

RESPONSE

Questions for Group Discussion or Personal Exercises

1. What is the most important thing you are doing to learn the Bible?

2. What are three things you could do to be more effective in learning it?

3. When did you first discover that the Bible was written to reveal God to you personally?

4. Create a list of things for which you are believing God. What are you trusting Him for that only He can do?

5. Relate an experience from the past where someone wanted to know more about you because of what they saw in your life (an associate, classmate, relative, neighbor, or acquaintance).

JUST WHAT DOES GOD EXPECT FROM ME?

There are five things and only five things that God asks of each individual. All the teaching sections of the Bible and all the commands can be fitted into one of these five areas.

F O U R

LOVE GOD

*To be free to sail the seven seas, you must
make yourself a slave to the compass.*

Anonymous

E very freedom has a corresponding bondage, and every bondage has a corresponding freedom. You can be free from the
toothbrush and a slave to cavities, or you can be a slave to the
toothbrush and free from cavities.

You cannot be free from the toothbrush *and* free from cavities.
That kind of freedom does not exist. By nature that is what we
want. Absolute freedom. But we can't have it. It simply doesn't
exist. The athlete can be a slave to training and excel, or he can
be free from rigorous training and fail. The salesman can be a
slave to good marketing techniques and succeed, or he can have
sloppy technique and starve to death. There is no such thing as
total freedom. Always, there is one bondage, and one freedom.
You choose.

One of the keys to life, then, is to *choose well* your freedoms and
your bondages. This is true for the Christian and his relationship
with God. Everyone who is a Christian wants a significant, meaningful relationship with God. The question is, how is he going to
get it?

43

Is he going to make himself a slave to God and be free from sin, or is he going to be free from God and a slave to sin? Those are the only two choices. It makes sense to make ourselves a slave to God, because everything that God asks *of* us, He does so in order to give something *to* us.

There are five things God asks of us. When you take all the commands and responsibilities in the New Testament and put them into "like" categories, you can find five things God wants from us. He wants us to *love Him, love others, esteem ourselves, be a steward,* and *be a servant.*

All the commands and all the instruction in the Bible are directed toward these five goals. All of them will fit into one of these five categories.

In order to gain these five things, God asks us to:

1. Love and worship Him.

   In Matthew 22:37, we read that the greatest commandment is that we love the Lord our God with all our heart, and with all our soul, and with all our mind.

2. Love our neighbor.

   Further, in Matthew 22:39 we read that the second great commandment is to love your neighbor as yourself.

3. Love ourselves.

   Again, in Matthew 22:39, we see that we are to also love ourselves. To fail to esteem ourselves is to deny the value that God has attributed to us and to fail to see ourselves as God sees us.

4. Be a steward of our resources.

   We are to consider ourselves to be stewards, not owners, and ambassadors, not sovereigns. We are to allocate our resources according to God's value system, and serve Him in all we own. In Matthew 6:25–34 we read, "seek first His kingdom and His righteousness, and all [*your true needs*] will be added to you" (emphasis added).

5. Give our lives away.

Rather than to direct our lives for the accumulation of people, possessions, and the control of circumstances, God asks us to live a life of servanthood toward others. In Mark 10:45, we read, ". . . the Son of Man did not come to be served, but to serve, and to give His life as a ransom for many."

These are the five things He asks *of* us. Now, if it is true that everything He asks of us, He does so because He wants to give something good *to* us, what are the five good things He wants to give to us in return for our obedience to Him?

These are the five which can be ours:

1. In return for loving Him, He wants to give us a satisfying relationship with Himself, the God of the universe. Everyone would long for spiritual intimacy with God if they knew it were possible. He wants us to be deeply satisfied with life because we are deeply satisfied with Him. (see John 4:24)

2. In return for loving others, He gives us rewarding relationships with others. Our relationships with people influence significantly our quality of life. Everyone wants a lot of friends and a few very close friends. By loving others, we gain many friendships and a few close friends. (see 1 Corinthians 13:4–8)

3. As we see ourselves as He sees us, we gain a satisfying relationship with ourselves. Most of us have a love/hate relationship with ourselves. We instinctively love ourselves, but we hate many things about who we are and what we have done. God wants us to feel good about who we are in Christ, and to be comfortable with being "us," and to experience the joy of seeing ourselves as He sees us. (see Ephesians 1:3–4)

4. In return for being a steward, God frees us from the tyranny of pursuing "things" in the hope that they will satisfy. They won't satisfy, so God tries to free us from the trap of living for them. He wants to free us from the bondage and futility and disappointment of living for this world. (see Ephesians 4:17–24)

5. In return for being a servant, God gives us a satisfying purpose in life. Man was not created to live selfishly, for himself only. He was created to live unselfishly, for others. Just
as an eagle cannot be happy confined to a cage, so we cannot be happy confined to a life consumed with ourselves.
As everyone lives for others, everyone's needs are met in a
context of unity and harmony. (See Ephesians 4:11–16.)

God wants to bring us to maturity in these five areas. He feels
free to do whatever necessary to mature us in these areas, because
He knows that this is where our highest good is found. His goal is
not to make us comfortable in this world. His goal is to give us the
qualities of the next world. If making us uncomfortable in this
world will make us more like Christ, so be it. C. S. Lewis described
it as "severe mercy." It is mercy, but it is severe. It is severe, but it is
mercy.

Personal Love

In this chapter, we will focus on our first task: loving God and
worshipping Him. The heart of what it means to worship is to
value, to follow, and to obey. In the Old Testament, when it talks
of those who worship Baal, it talks of those who believe in him,
who follow him, and who do the things Baal wants them to do.
That is what it means to worship in a general sense. For example,
1 Kings 9:6 reads, "If you or your sons shall indeed turn away from
following Me, and shall not keep My commandments and My statutes which I have set before you and shall go and serve other gods
and worship them, then I will cut off Israel from the land which I
have given them." The key words are: *follow, keep commandments,
serve,* and *worship.* John 14:15 says, "If you love me, keep my commandments." John 14:21 says, "If you keep my commandments,
you love me." There we have it both ways.

These are all aspects of worship in a "life context." For our
relationship with God, it means we believe in Him; we serve Him.
It means we trust Him and obey Him as a result of that trust.
There can be no worship without life commitment. There can be
no worship without obedience from the heart to God's commands.

God does not want obedience with gritted teeth. He wants willing obedience that is rooted in confidence in Him, that what He is asking *of* us is best *for* us.

In a real sense, He says, "you do this . . . and I'll do that. You seek first My kingdom and My righteousness, and I will meet your material needs. You love Me unconditionally, and I'll give you meaning and purpose and satisfaction in life. You serve Me, and I will give you love, joy, and peace."

To achieve our highest good in life, we must closely follow the Bible. It is God's owner's manual for man. God made us. He knows what it takes to make us run smoothly, and what will bring us to a grinding halt. He knows what will help us, and what will harm us. He knows what will exalt us, and what will debase us, what will expand us and what will limit us. His commandments are designed to keep us from the things which harm us, and to take us to the things which help and heal us.

His commandments are very much like an automobile owner's manual. The manufacturers specify what grade of oil and gasoline you must use. They specify which parts must be used as replacement parts, and how the car must be maintained. You may look at that and think they are being very narrow. "Look," you might say, "I can save a lot of money by using regular gasoline instead of high-test. I can save several hundred dollars a year. You are being unrealistically narrow and inconsiderate in my personal budget." But when the fuel injectors clog because of the cheaper gasoline, and it costs you $1500 to repair the engine, you then realize you have not saved any money at all. You have cost yourself much more than if you had simply complied in the first place.

The same is true with God and the Bible. Certainly, you can get away with inferior behavior. But do not be deceived, Galatians 6:7 says. God is not mocked. Whatever a person sows, that shall he also reap. The point is, you will always pay in the end, and in the end, the price will always be higher.

Whenever we have an obedience problem, we must see it for what it really is—a "faith" problem. We're not talking about the areas in which we want to do the right thing, and are trying to do the right thing, but because of weakness, we are not having complete success. We are not talking about a situation in which we have simply not been a dedicated Christian long enough for the

Holy Spirit to work a given "kink" out of our life. Rather, we are talking about the things in which we know what the right thing to do is, and we don't want to do it, or even try to do it.

In these cases, there is something we are not believing, or we would be willing to obey.

If we believe that we will be better off for obeying, then we will obey. If we are not sure, then obedience is a struggle. It's like trying to stick to a diet when we're not confident it is going to work. Full faith and confidence are necessary, or we won't stick it out when the French pastry is offered to us.

Let me summarize, then, what we are saying. We love God and worship Him with our life. There are three things that we must do:

1. We must believe that everything He asks of us, He does so because He wants to give something good to us.

2. When we have a lapse of obedience, we must see it as a lapse of faith. There is something we are not believing.

3. By faith, we must obey God from the heart. Not with gritted teeth, not with fearful heart, but because we understand and agree that His way is best.

Our broad definition of personal love is an active one. We are to believe in, to trust, to follow, and to obey God.

Public Love

While we worship God with our lives, there is a more specific sense in which we must worship God. We must worship Him publicly. Public worship means nothing to God unless we are worshipping Him with our lives. But worshipping Him with our lives alone is not complete. He wants our public and corporate worship also.

By public and corporate worship, we don't necessarily mean a formal worship service. We just mean something more than "living a good life." There are those who feel it is not necessary to go to church or do anything to associate ourselves with God or anything religious. This is an incomplete understanding of Scripture. God wants us to identify with Him. God wants others to know we are His children. He wants to receive our public worship as His many beloved spiritual children gather to praise Him. We must stop and engage in a ceremony, whether modest or grand, in which we give our public worship to God.

In the Old Testament, some of the worship services were on such a grand scale that there is nothing in our culture to compare them with except perhaps the opening ceremonies of the Olympics. They had huge orchestras, double choirs marching toward each other on top of a city wall, elaborate costumes, high liturgy, and great pomp and splendor were all part of the ceremony.

On the other hand, in the New Testament, we see Jesus worshipping with His disciples in the upper room just before He went out to the Garden of Gethsemane. Their ceremony was very simple. They discussed God's Word; the Lord taught His disciples. They had some prayer and sang a few hymns. Nothing elaborate.

Nevertheless, whether it is small and simple, or large and elaborate, God wants our public worship. He wants more than just the worship of our upright conduct. He wants us to worship Him publicly, in ceremony.

What Is Worship?

By studying the examples of worship in Scripture, we can isolate at least four principles of worship.

Participation

Worship is a verb. There are a number of words in the Old Testament and New Testament that are translated *worship,* but they are active concepts—to bow the knee, to do homage, to serve.

A person cannot be passive, distant, merely a spectator of others in a service, and worship. Worship demands involvement—participation. In a church service, many people have the wrong idea of what worship is. They think a program is conducted by people who are being paid to put on a good show for you. If you're lucky, it holds your attention throughout. Perhaps you are even moved emotionally. You grade the worship leaders on how good a job they did. This is not a proper understanding.

The philosopher Soren Kierkegaard once wrote: "People have the idea that the preacher is an actor on a stage and that they are the critics, blaming or praising him. What they don't realize is that they are the actors on the stage; he is merely the prompter standing in the wings, reminding them of their lines."[1]

God is the audience!

With this understanding, we realize that we must mentally participate in everything that is said, sung, and prayed. We must understand that we are the ones "putting on the show" in the right sense of the word. God is watching and receiving our worship.

Structure

The primary elements of worship in the examples we have in the Bible are: prayer, music, Scripture, and offerings.

Actual examples of worship services are not easy to find in the Bible. Four of the clearest are:

1. 1 Chronicles 16, where David brings the ark of the covenant into the tent.

2. Nehemiah 8, where Nehemiah dedicates the walls of Jerusalem.

3. John 13–17, where Jesus worships with His disciples.

4. Revelation 4 and 5, where John sees into the throne room in heaven.

In each of these instances, we see prayer, music, and Scripture being the primary characteristics, all three integrated into a meaningful ceremony. In 1 Chronicles 16, we also see the bringing of financial gifts being specifically mentioned as an act of worship.

If we put the first principle, *participation,* and the second principle, *structure,* together, we see that the worship service must allow people to be active through the media of prayer, music, Scripture, and offerings, all integrated into a meaningful ceremony.

The degree of ceremony depends on the resources and inclinations of the people involved. Some people prefer simplicity. Others prefer grandeur. Some people prefer informality. Others formality. As long as no Biblical principles are violated, each person is free to worship the Lord however it is most meaningful to him. The only hard rule is that you must worship.

Heart Response

What goes on in the heart is important. God takes no pleasure in the externals. Worship is pleasing to God only if what is going on in the inside is the same as what is going on on the outside. One of the most complete examples of a worship service in the Bible is found in 1 Chronicles 16. In this description of worship, we find these verbs: give thanks, make known, sing, speak, glory, seek, remember, proclaim, tell, ascribe, bring offerings, tremble, be glad, rejoice, exalt, give thanks.

Boiled down, these ideas can all be represented by four categories:

1. Praise: Honor Him publicly for who He is and for what He has done.

2. Submission: Accepting His dominion over your life. Forsaking sin, asking forgiveness.

3. Dependence: Making requests of Him, according to His will, and according to the desires of your heart. Trusting His sovereign goodness over your life.

4. Gratitude: Giving thanks. Expressing personal gratitude for who He is and what He has done personally for you.

What Worship Is Not

To further our understanding of what worship is, we must look at some of the things worship is not. Worship is not the pursuit of a warm, fuzzy feeling. You can worship without being emotionally moved. You can be emotionally moved without worshipping. We must be clear on the relationship between worship and emotions, or we risk falling into the imbalance of being either too emotional on the one hand or of precluding emotion on the other.

There is danger in precluding emotion. If we preclude emotions, then worship can become lifeless and meaningless. We become all head and no heart. We can end up straight as a gun barrel theologically and just as empty spiritually.

But if we *depend* on emotions, we must drive ourselves to new highs when the old tricks fail to satisfy. What used to satisfy doesn't anymore, and we must try new things, which can lead to excesses which dishonor God.

We must lead with our minds, but we can allow our emotions to follow—perhaps even encourage our emotions to follow, but not demand that our emotions follow. When we lead with our mind, our emotions will follow.

While it is true that you worship with your mind and not your emotions, if you are *never* moved emotionally it is possible you are not worshipping with your mind. Your mind cannot be *keenly engaged* with the great themes of the ages without them touching the heart occasionally. If these themes do not move you sooner or later, there is something wrong somewhere. Check it out!

If you want a mature relationship with God, you can have it. He wants to give it to you. But you must play by His rules. He won't play by yours. Your satisfaction in life will be directly tied to how closely you follow Him.

A mature relationship means you must worship God. You must show your love for Him by living a life of faithful obedience to Him. In addition, you must worship Him both personally and corporately.

It is not sufficient to say that you try to live a good life, and that *that* is your worship, and, therefore, you don't need to go to church. Nor is it sufficient to say that you go to church on Sunday as your tribute to God, and then live like the devil Monday through Saturday. God wants all of you all of the time.

> O God, Thou art our God; We shall seek Thee earnestly; Our soul thirsts for Thee. Because Thy lovingkindness is better than life, our lips shall praise Thee. So we will bless Thee as long as we live. . . and our mouth offers praises with joyful lips. When we remember Thee on our bed, we meditate on Thee in the night watch, and in the shadow of Thy wings, we sing for joy. (Psalms 63:1–7, paraphrased)

Father, in the words of David, we pledge to You our personal allegiance, and we proclaim publicly the greatness of who You are and what You have done. Touch us now with a sense of true worship as we praise You and honor You in Your very own words and with the song of our heart. Lift up Yourself and exalt Jesus in our hearts now, we pray in our Savior's name. Amen.

REVIEW

1. Personal Love

Our *love* of God is manifested by being *obedient* from the heart to His *commandments.*

2. Public Love

Whether it is small and *simple,* or large and *elaborate,* God wants our *public* worship.

3. What Is Worship?

When we *worship,* we are the *participants,* and God is the *audience.*

4. What Worship Is Not

Worship is not the pursuit of a *warm, fuzzy* feeling. When we lead with our *mind,* our emotions will *follow.*

As a memory exercise, write in the missing words in the paragraphs below. Notice that they are the same words as the italicized words in the paragraph above.

1. Personal Love

Our _____ of God is manifested by being _____ from the heart to His _____.

2. **Public Love**

   Whether it is small and _____, or large and _____, God wants our _____ worship.

3. **What Is Worship?**

   When we _____, we are the _____, and God is the _____.

4. **What Worship Is Not**

   Worship is not the pursuit of a _____, _____ feeling. When we lead with our _____, our emotions will _____.

RESPONSE

Questions for Group Discussion or Personal Exercises

1. Do you agree that a life of worship begins with a life of obedience? Why or why not?

2. Of the three principles of public worship (Participate, Structure, or Heart Response), which do you need more of in order to more genuinely worship?

3. Which of the four heart responses (Praise, Submission, Dependence, Gratitude) is easiest for you following a ceremony of worship? Why might the other three be more difficult for you and/or others?

4. Do you have a tendency to rely on emotion too much or too little in your worship?

5. Other passages, while they are not as complete, still reveal the same general pattern in this chapter. You might want to look them up and read them to gain a fuller first-hand understanding of the attitude of the heart in worship: Psalm 145:1–7; Psalm 25:4–7; Psalm 119:33–40; Revelation 11:17.

FIVE

LOVE OTHERS

We take care of our health, we lay up money, we make our roof tight and our clothing sufficient, but who provides wisely that he shall not be wanting in the best property of all—friends?

Ralph Waldo Emerson

I n his poem *The Thousandth Man,* Rudyard Kipling wrote:

One Man in a thousand, Solomon says,
Will stick more close than a brother.
And it's worthwhile seeking him half your days
If you find him before the other.
Nine hundred and ninety-nine depend
On what the world sees in you,
But the Thousandth Man will stand your friend
With the whole round world agin you.

'Tis neither promise nor prayer nor show
Will settle the finding for 'ee
Nine hundred and ninety-nine of 'em go
By your looks or your acts or your glory.
But if he finds you and you find him,
The rest of the world don't matter;
For the Thousandth Man will sink or swim
With you in any water.

You can use his purse with no more talk
Than he uses yours for his spendings,
And laugh and meet in your daily walk
As though there had been no lendings.
Nine hundred and ninety-nine of 'em call
For silver and gold in their dealings;
But the Thousandth Man he's worth 'em all,
Because you can show him your feelings.

His wrong's your wrong,
    and his right's your right,
In season or out of season.
Stand up and back it in all men's sight—
With that for your only reason!
Nine hundred and ninety-nine can't bide
The shame or mocking or laughter,
But the Thousandth Man will stand by your side
To the gallows-foot—and after.[1]

I admit, it's a *little* corny, and yet, there's something to it. There's a call that it makes to our heart. There's a longing that it evokes in our soul. A longing that will never be satisfied until we see Jesus, because He is who we are longing for. Only Jesus can truly be the "Thousandth Man."

And yet, He has created us to want, to long for, to need friends and to have deep, meaningful relationships with others. God uses people to fill many of the voids in our life. One day, in heaven, God will fill us with Himself so completely that we will have no unfulfilled longings. God wants to give us a foretaste of His ultimate fulfillment now, through other people.

When we love others, it has an obvious benefit to them. But the benefit to them is not the only reason God asks us to love others. In addition, He wants to give us a deep satisfying relationship with others—that intangible "something" without which life is nowhere nearly as satisfying.

It is hard for us to experience that "Thousandth Man" type of relationship with others, because we have lost sight of what it means to love. Our understanding has been warped by movies, music, and television. Our brains have turned to plastic. We have lost our ability to evaluate the sludge that is poured into our minds.

Do you remember what that poor soul sang in *My Fair Lady* after he caught a glimpse of Eliza Doolittle?

My Fair Lady was a musical written many years ago about a Miss Doolittle, who was a beautiful but ignorant, ill-tempered, and loud-mouthed flower girl on the streets of London. Professor Higgins, the male opposite of her, decides to try to make Eliza into a lady. In the end he succeeds. After she has been turned into a beautiful society figure, a young guy gets a look at her and decides after one look that he's (sigh) in love. He has never even met her. Just seen her. He stands outside her house, arms and legs draped around a light pole singing, "Ooohhhh, the towwwwerrring feeling"—just being on the street where she lives.

Herds of little warm fuzzies go stampeding up and down the spine. We think that's love—true love.

But what happens when the towering feeling disappears? Has love disappeared? In America, we've said *yes* because we have equated emotional bonding with love. He gets up one morning. She has curlers in her hair, wrinkles under her eyes, and morning breath—and the towering feeling is gone. Then, like a tomcat, he is gone.

Love and emotional bonding are not the same. You can have emotional bonding without love. Love has been defined as the steady direction of my will toward another's lasting good. Nowhere does Scripture define love, but it does describe love: "For God so *loved* the world that He *gave* His only begotten Son" (John 3:16). "Husbands, love your wives just as Christ also *loved* the church and *gave* Himself up for her" (Ephesians 5:25). "I live by faith in the Son of God who *loved* me and *gave* Himself for me" (Galatians 2:20), (emphasis added).

Love gives. That is its central characteristic. It gives what it can to the welfare of another.

Now we want to apply that definition, elaborated upon by Scripture, to three of life's basic relationships: loving those in need, loving other Christians, and loving our family.

Loving Those in Need

In Luke 10:25–37, Jesus was speaking with a large group of people, and a lawyer asked Him what he should do to inherit eternal life. Jesus asked, "What is written in the law?" The lawyer said, "To love the Lord your God with all your heart and soul and strength, and with all your mind: and your neighbor as yourself." Jesus said, "You have answered rightly. Do this and you shall live." Wishing to justify himself, the lawyer asked, "Who is my neighbor?" To which Jesus gave the story of the Good Samaritan. From that story we get at least three principles of loving those in need. First, they have a legitimate need (we need not fund someone's irresponsibility). Second, you have the resources to meet it (in time, talent, resources, emotional strength, spiritual depth). Third, they come across your life's path. Then you are to help them. That is what it means to love those in need.

Loving Other Christians

In Francis Schaeffer's book *The Mark of the Christian,* he defines what he called a Christian's badge. He appeals to John 13:34–35, "by this all men will know that you are my disciples, if you have love for one another"; and to John 17:21, "by this [unity] the world may believe that Thou hast sent Me." From these two passages, he concludes that the badge or mark of a Christian is his love for other Christians. If the world does not see love and unity among Christians, the world has a right to conclude that we are not true disciples (we are hypocrites), and that Christ was not sent by God (He was only a man).

Therefore, love becomes a priority for the serious Christian. Unity in the bond of love, as Paul puts it in Philippians, is something for which we must all strive. Jesus placed it as the second greatest commandment in Matthew 22:37–40. If we take the Christian life seriously, we must take seriously our responsibility to live in love toward others.

Perhaps 1 Corinthians 13:4–8a has expressed it as succinctly as possible:

> Love is patient, love is kind, and is not jealous; love does not brag and is not arrogant, does not act unbecomingly; it does not seek its own, is not provoked, does not take into account a wrong suffered, does not rejoice in unrighteousness, but rejoices with the truth; bears all things, believes all things, hopes all things, endures all things. Love never fails.

Many times, God gives us the privilege of having very close friends, and the level of our love for them intensifies. In his book *Loving God,* Chuck Colson writes:

It was a quiet December evening on Ward C43, the oncology unit at Georgetown University Hospital. Many of the rooms around the central nurse's station were dark and empty, but in Room 11 a man lay critically ill.

The patient was Jack Swigert, the man who had piloted the Apollo 13 lunar mission in 1970 and was now Congressman-elect from Colorado's 6th Congressional district. Cancer, the great leveler, now waged its deadly assault on his body.

With the dying man was a tall, quiet visitor, sitting in the spot he had occupied almost every night since Swigert had been admitted. Though Bill Armstrong, U.S. Senator from Colorado and chairman of the Senate subcommittee handling Washington's hottest issue, social security, was one of the busiest and most powerful men in Washington, he was not visiting this room night after night as a powerful politician. He was here as a deeply committed Christian and as Jack Swigert's friend, fulfilling a responsibility he would not delegate or shirk, much as he disliked hospitals.

This night Bill leaned over the bed and spoke quietly to his friend. "Jack, you're going to be all right. God loves you. I love you. You're surrounded by friends who are praying for you. You're going to be all right." The only response was Jack's tortured and uneven breathing.

Bill pulled his chair closer to the bed and opened his Bible. "Psalm 23," he began to read in a steady voice. "The Lord is my shepherd, I shall not want. . . ."

Time passed. "Psalm 150," Bill began, then his skin prickled. Jack's ragged breathing had stopped. He leaned down over the bed, then called for help. As he watched the nurse examining Jack, Bill knew there was nothing more he could do. His friend was dead.

Politicians are busy people, especially Senate committee chairmen. Yet it never occurred to Bill Armstrong that he was too busy to be at the hospital. Nothing dramatic or heroic about his decision—just a friend doing what he could.[2]

In its simplest form, loving close friends is not very sophisticated. All you have to do is care, and then do something to show how much. In Proverbs, in the King James Version, it says, "if you want to have friends, you must demonstrate yourself to be a friend." Reach out. Be vulnerable. Be transparent. Drop your guard. There is no need to be heroic or dramatic. Just care, and do what you can to show it. But do it.

Friendships fail because we fail to *express* friendship. The depth of friendship we long for is "out there," but most of us don't taste of it because we ourselves are not willing to meet another potential close friend halfway.

Loving Our Family

Perhaps you have heard of the man who had been married for 20 years. He and his wife still had a very fresh, happy, close relationship. People often asked him the secret of his marriage, and he would tell them that it's really quite simple. Two evenings a week they take time to go out to a restaurant. A quiet dinner, soft music, some candlelight, a slow walk home. She goes Tuesdays; he goes Fridays.

Maybe that worked for them, but I wouldn't recommend it and neither would the Bible. Scripture gives us very helpful and direct information on the secret to good relationships in the family. The key is found in Ephesians 5:18–6:4. It is "mutual submission." As an expression of being filled with the Spirit (v. 18), Paul says, "and be subject to one another in the fear of Christ" (v. 21). Then he specifies three relationships in which people are to be subject to one another: husbands and wives, parents and children, and masters and slaves.

This is not a 50/50 relationship in authority. Rather, those in authority are to be in submission to the needs of those under them, while those under them are to be submissive to the authority of those over them. The wife is to "be subject" and "respect" her husband. But her husband is to "love her as Christ loved the church and gave Himself up for her." The children are to obey their parents, but their parents are to "bring them up in the discipline and instruction of the Lord," and not to "provoke them to wrath." The New International Version says, "do not exasperate them."

The key, then, to family relationships is the same as any other relationships—loving one another, and expressing it effectively; respecting one another and honoring the dignity and worth of one another; treating one another as Christ would if He were in our shoes.

How many close friends do you have? How many people are you intimate with? Ones that you can share deep personal things with? How close are your family relationships? God wants to make your life rich through other people. He wants you to be able to taste the love that He has for you, by tasting the love of a close friend or family member.

If you are married, I hope your spouse is your closest friend. You should have other close friends in addition. If you don't have any, you need to ask the Lord to show you why. Is there something about you that keeps people at a distance? Do you reach out to others? Do you accept it when others reach out to you? Are you pursuing God? Your ability as a Christian to have a deep relationship with others will depend on a deepening relationship with the Lord.

In her book *Up with Worship*, Anne Ortlund writes:

> Every congregation has a choice to be one of two things. You can choose to be a bag of marbles, single units that don't affect each other except in collision. One Sunday morning you can choose to go to church or to sleep in: Who really cares whether there are 192 or 193 marbles in a bag?
> Or you can choose to be a bag of grapes. The juices begin to mingle, and there is no way to extricate yourselves if you tried. Each is part of all. Part of the fragrance. Part of the "stuff."[3]

I hope that wherever we are in our experience of meaningful friendships, that we can begin experiencing even deeper, more meaningful friendships. It is part of the richness of the life which God wants to give to His children here on earth.

> Faithful are the wounds of a friend, but deceitful are the kisses of an enemy. . . . Oil and perfume make the heart glad, so a man's counsel is sweet to his friend. Do not forsake your own friend or your father's friend. (Proverbs 27:6, 9–10)

Heavenly Father, help me to love others consistently. Help me direct the focus of my will toward the good of others. Help me love those in need, love other Christians, love close friends, and love my family. Help me be faithful to You from my heart. And give me the deep richness of family relationships and friendships that give my life a taste of heaven on earth. In the Savior's name. Amen.

REVIEW

1. Loving Those in Need

When someone has a legitimate *need,* and we have the *resources* to meet it, and he comes across our path, we should *help* him.

2. Loving Other Christians

Loving *others* is not very sophisticated. All we have to do is *care,* and then do something to *show* it.

3. Loving Our Family

The key to good family relationships is mutual *submission.* Wives must be submissive to the *authority* of the husbands, and husbands must be submissive to the *needs* of the wife.

As a memory exercise, write in the missing words in the paragraphs below. Notice that they are the same words as the italicized words in the paragraph above.

1. Loving Those in Need

When someone has a legitimate _____, and we have the _____ to meet it, and he comes across our path, we should _____ him.

2. Loving Other Christians

Loving _____ is not very sophisticated. All we have to do is _____, and then do something to _____ it.

3. Loving Our Family

The key to good family relationships is mutual _____. Wives must be submissive to the _____ of the husbands, and husbands must be submissive to the _____ of the wife.

RESPONSE

Questions for Group Discussion or Personal Exercises

1. Which of the three sets of relationships do you find most difficult to love consistently (those in need, others Christians, or family)?

2. What characteristics do you admire in other people who are your close friends, or someone with whom you would enjoy having a close friendship? Is there a characteristic which you feel you should cultivate more?

3. Identify one person that you are going to love more this week. What does that person need from you in order to feel loved?

4. What are three things you could do to show those in your family that you love them?

S I X

ESTEEM YOURSELF

To esteem one's self properly is to think nei-
ther too highly nor too little of one's self. It is
to see one's self as God sees him. No more,
no less. Then, we will recognize that we
have inherent and infinite worth, though we
are worth no more than anyone else.

M any of us have a love/hate relationship with ourselves. We
naturally love ourselves. We want and hope the best for ourselves, but at the same time we have a nagging sense of inferiority,
insecurity, and inadequacy. We often try to cover up these feelings.
Usually we just get in trouble. I read of a newly promoted army
colonel who moved into his new and impressive office. As he sat
behind his new big desk, a private knocked at his door. "Just a
minute," the colonel said, "I'm on the phone." He picked up the
phone and said loudly, "Yes sir, General, I'll call the President this
afternoon. No, sir, I won't forget." Then he hung up the phone
and told the private to come in. "What can I help you with?" the
colonel asked. "Well, sir," the private replied, "I've come to hook
up your phone."

Someone once said that at twenty, we worry about what people
think about us. At forty, we don't care what people think about us. At
sixty, we find out that people haven't been thinking about us at all!

Our self-image has a dramatic impact on how we act. Our self-
image is determined not by how we see ourselves, nor by how oth-

ers see us. It is determined by how we think others see us. If we think others see us positively, it helps us act positively. If we think others see us negatively, it makes it hard to act positively.

This puts tremendous power in the hands of other people. Usually, they don't want this power. Probably, they don't even know they have it. It limits our ability to achieve our own potential. It limits our ability to give of ourselves to others. The only way out is to begin to see ourselves as *God* sees us—no more and no less. When that happens, our spirit stabilizes, our mind expands, and the sky's the limit!

Seeing Ourselves as God Sees Us

Mankind is created in the image of God. Because of that, he has infinite worth. Our worth does not lie in the value of who we are, but in the value of who God is. It is not we who determine our worth. It is God. Man is the apple of God's eye. All of creation was created for us. All that God is doing now, He is doing to restore us. Jesus, the Son of God, came to earth to die for our sins. We are central to everything God is doing. In the eyes of God, we have inherent and infinite value. However, no one person is worth any more to God than any other person. We are of infinite but equal value!

This truth is important because the quality of our own lives is directly affected by how we view ourselves. If we think too highly of ourselves, we alienate ourselves from other people and from God. If we think too little of ourselves, we alienate ourselves from other people and from God. Both extremes limit our personal satisfaction in life, limit our ministry effectiveness, and diminish the degree to which our lives can glorify God. One of the keys to happiness in life, then, is to see ourselves as God sees us—no more and no less.

The curse of our culture is a shattered sense of self-worth. A Gallup poll has revealed that two-thirds of the people in America suffer from poor self-esteem. James Dobson polled over 5000 women to ask them what was the number one problem they had that caused depression. The majority of women listed low self-esteem as the number one problem.

A struggle for worth is inherent within the fall of man, but the explosion of it in our generation, I am convinced, is part of an overall satanic strategy to deceive and destroy men. For the previous generation, the Depression Era generation, Satan had one strategy for his spiritual warfare. His goal included getting man to disbelieve in God, and to believe in evolution and scientific reason as the basis for viewing the world. We had the residual personal and social stability of a Biblical background, so we did not feel the immediate impact of the defection.

Now, having accomplished that, for the next generation, the Baby Boomer generation, Satan's strategy has evolved, and includes the shattering of our sense of self-worth, a consequence of severing ourselves from God. The result is a generation of people utterly self-absorbed, trying desperately to find meaning in "externals," now that "internal" meaning has been destroyed. The most devastating consequence to the church is to produce a generation of Christians who may believe the right thing, but who appear incapable of living it out because of our own internal battle with a shattered sense of self-worth.

Our society was originally founded upon a belief in God and on Biblical principles. Our value system derived totally from this foundation. This brought prosperity. Then, in our prosperity, we forgot God, thinking that we had gotten ourselves all our wealth, power, and cultural scientific advancement. God became a relic from another era for a people too sophisticated to take Him seriously any longer.

In the 60s, we finally killed God (the God-is-Dead movement). Now man was cut loose to fend for himself. However, that has been like a kite being cut loose from a string. It was the string that gave the kite the ability to fly. Mankind clumsily started wobbling down out of the sky which he once ruled so magnificently.

The death of God also brought with it the death of truth. Now, truth floats. Nothing is absolute. The Bible isn't true. Now, we have no right and wrong. You cannot say that anything is right and anything is wrong. If one man says something is right, and another says it is wrong, they cancel each other out. They have no higher authority to which to appeal. So if one person says it is wrong to kill babies before they are born, and another person says it is right, they cancel each other out. How do you make decisions then? Those in power make the decisions. In a dictatorship, the dictator decides what is right. In a democracy, the majority decides what is right.

Man now has lost his meaning. He is no more than an animal or a machine. Children's cartoons and adult movies are now blurring the distinction between man, and animals, and machines. If man sees himself as no more than an animal or machine, it should come as no surprise that he begins to treat others as animals or machines—hence abortion, euthanasia, genetic engineering, and so on.

Man now has no basis for giving himself any more worth or value than a rock, or a cactus, or a dolphin. He has no supreme worth. The problem is man *has* been made by God, to know and understand that he has been created in God's image and has infinite worth. He cannot function normally without a sense of self-worth.

He subsequently tries to find meaning wherever he can. He pursues the gold medal of beauty, the silver medal of brains, and the bronze medal of talent. Those who cannot win these medals feel hollow, as though they have missed out on success. For those who win all three, they still feel hollow. They know that that is not where meaning and worth are to be found. It is as Oscar Wilde once said: "There are only two tragedies in life. One is not getting what one wants, and the other is getting it."

Man cannot tolerate the weight of his existence if he does not have meaning. So he takes cocaine, he drinks alcohol, he immerses himself in sex, materialism, music, movies, and anything else that will provide diversion. When that doesn't satisfy, he begins killing himself. People can't understand why teenagers are committing suicide in unprecedented numbers. It is because they understand the utter hopelessness of life without God. They are simply acting consistently with their presuppositions.

Christians have a different world view: They believe in God, and they believe in the worth of man in God, but they still have the self-worth problems. Why? Many Christians have been saved as adults, and their mind was programmed according to the world's value system. Just becoming a Christian doesn't completely re-program the mind overnight. So we find ourselves saying we believe we have infinite value, and wanting to believe it, but we don't believe it. Believing it is not just an isolated act of the will. The mind must be transformed.

Another reason why Christians struggle with poor self-image is that while they may have been brought up in Christian homes, the homes did not live out Biblical principles consistently. As a result, the value system of the world creeps in. If our parents nurtured us, steeped us in the values of the Lord, modeled Jesus before us, we see ourselves as having value. If that didn't happen, we look at beauty, brains, and talent, see our deficiencies, and assume we are of no worth.

A third reason Christians struggle with poor self-worth is that this whole process is fostered by the media. Television, music, movies, magazines, and books all directly implant the values of beauty, brains, and talent into our minds, unless we guard our minds carefully. We must guard the quantity as well as quality of what we put into our minds. We must mentally reject that which is contrary to a Biblical world view.

Our minds are being transformed according to the value system of the world. We become worldlings. We know that we don't belong to the world; yet, we don't feel like we belong to God. Because we tend to act consistently with how we see ourselves, we are hampered in living out a healthy Christian experience. We are confused as to who we are and have difficulty believing and acting like who the Bible says we are.

Lifting the curse, as it were, is simple in concept but difficult in practice.

1. We must accept by faith that we are children of inherent and infinite worth, and ask God to reveal to us what that means.

2. We must repent of any sin we have allowed ourselves to stray into, and be cleansed and restored to fellowship with God.

3. We must accept responsibility for having our minds transformed.

- Memorize Romans 12:1–2.

- Carefully control media exposure.

- Expose yourself to positive input (books, seminars, speakers).

- Establish spiritual accountability relationships with other like-minded Christians: pray for each other, study Scripture together, read books together and discuss them, give each other emotional support, hold each other accountable.

I know what you're thinking. I want to believe all this, but I'm having trouble. I don't feel like I have infinite worth. How could I have inherent worth? I may have started out with infinite value, but look at all the things that have happened to me. Look at all the things I've done. How can God love me with all my faults and all my inherent deficiencies?

God can love you the way you are now the same way you can love a gold mine. Suppose with me for a while that you inherit a gold mine. You would be overjoyed. But the gold says, "how can you love me? Look! I'm all dirty. I'm all mixed up with that awful iron ore, and I have that rotten clay all over me. I'm contaminated through and through with boxite and mineral deposits. I'm ugly and worthless."

But you say, "O, but I do love you. You don't understand. You don't recognize your inherent worth. You don't realize that your worth to me isn't destroyed by the impurities. You see, I understand what you really are. I know you have all these imperfections now, but you see, I have plans for you. I am not going to leave you the way you are now. I am going to purify you. I am going to get rid of all that other stuff. You see, I understand what you really are. I see your inherent worth. I know that the iron ore, clay, and mineral deposits are not part of the true you. You are just temporarily mixed up with them for now. However, I know how to rid you of the impurities. I know how to change you from what you are now to what you can be."

"I must warn you, it won't be easy. You will go through a lot of heat and refinement. However, look at this gold jewelry which has already been purified. Isn't it beautiful? That's what you are. Left to yourself, you would not become like this, but I know how to complete your beauty. I will make you beautiful, and you will make me rich."

This is how God sees us. He is not blind. He knows about our imperfections. But, you see, God has plans for us, both now and in eternity. He understands and sees our inherent worth more than we do. He knows how to change us from what we are now to what we can be. The fulfillment of this refinement process is not completed until we join Him in heaven. There, God will have completed our beauty, and we will have made Him rich.

The first step in pursuing a proper relationship with yourself is to dare, by faith, to see yourself as God sees you—no more, no less.

Pursue the Image of God Within

Now we look at the second step of properly esteeming ourselves: pursuing the image of God within. By image of God, we do not mean that we are exactly like God or that God is exactly like us in all respects. Rather, it means that we bear characteristics of God. God has intellect, emotions, and will. We have intellect, emotions, and will. God is creative. We are creative. God is a moral being, and we are moral beings, and so on.

The image of God within has been weakened and tarnished by sin. Yet the image remains. We are like Him, in terribly imperfect ways, but like Him. The redemption that He offers us through Jesus Christ will restore that image.

To nurture this image of God within means to strive to become as much like God as we can, beginning now—not waiting until heaven. The image of God is moral, for certain, and one task is to become more and more like Him in our daily actions. But, I want to assume that for now, because we will be dealing with that in great detail later. For now, let's go beyond the moral image of God to pursue the image of God within in areas that transcend the moral arena.

We want to look at the talents and callings which He has given us, and see how, under His leading, we take the *seeds* He gives us, and we develop, nurture, and cultivate them into full-blown *plants* and give them back to God as an offering of praise.

David is perhaps the most complete example in the Bible of someone who pursued the image of God within. There is a captivating verse in 1 Samuel 16:18: "I have seen a son of Jesse the Bethlehemite who is a skillful musician, a mighty man of valor, a warrior, one prudent in speech, and a handsome man; and the Lord is with him."

In analyzing the verse, we see six things that characterized David. He was (a):

1. skillful musician—an artist

2. mighty man of valor—physically strong

3. warrior—skilled as a military man

4. prudent in speech—had presence of mind

5. handsome man—well groomed

6. the Lord was with him—spiritually mature

All of these six characteristics were things that David had cultivated to such an extent that he was *known* for each characteristic. Not one of these characteristics can be neglected if it is to be well developed. Each one of them takes commitment and patience, over time. It takes time and commitment to become a skillful musician. It takes time and commitment to become a mighty man of valor. It takes time and commitment to become a skilled warrior, prudent in speech, well-groomed, and spiritually mature. These things did not happen by accident. They happened because David pursued them, with great commitment over time.

Pursuing the image of God within involves taking the abilities and interests God has given us, developing them under His guidance and leading, and offering the fruit back to the Lord as a sacrifice of praise and worship. Of the many areas in which we could focus in the pursuit of the image of God within, I want to focus on two areas: our *work* and our *play*.

Our Work

In Snow White and the Seven Dwarfs, the seven dwarfs go marching off to work each morning singing, "Hi ho, Hi ho, it's off to work we go." There is a lilt in their step and merriment in their voice. There would be a lilt in your step and merriment in your voice, too, if you were going to the same job they were going to. They owned and worked in a diamond mine.

Today, our attitude toward work has shifted significantly. There is a bumper sticker which reads "I owe, I owe, its off to work I go." For many people, work is a drudge. It is utterly without meaning. There is little connection between their workplace and the rest of their life. Yet, God intends for work to have meaning for us, as Doug Sherman declares in the title of his book *Your Work Matters to God*. In that book, we see that our work matters to God for three reasons:

1. Because work is part of the image of God. God works. In Genesis 1, God labored for six days, and on the seventh day, He rested, not because He was tired—an omnipotent being doesn't get tired—but because He wanted to model the pattern He wanted man to follow. Work has inherent value because it is an attribute of God. God is a worker, and He enjoys it!

2. Because we are co-workers with God in exercising dominion over the earth. We extend original creation. God created trees, but He didn't create cabinets. We create cabinets. God created rubber, but He didn't create tires. We create tires. God created electricity, but He didn't create light bulbs or ovens or computers. We create light bulbs, and ovens, and computers. And I am convinced that God wants light bulbs and ovens and computers, so it is an honorable thing to make them and sell them and use them. God established original creation, but fully intended man to further that creative work and create a society through it.

We have done a disservice to suggest that if a person is totally committed to the Lord, he will go into vocational Christian work. The highest calling in life, and the only calling in life, is to be faithful at what God calls you to do. If that is a great matter in the eyes of men, or if it is a little matter in the eyes of men, it doesn't matter in the eyes of God. If it is the vocational ministry or another vocation, it matters not. Faithful obedience to what God wants you to do is the only thing that matters.

3. Because it accomplishes five significant purposes. First, you serve other people. Your work serves other people, and other people serve you. God intended us to all work together to form

an efficient society. We all play a part by serving others. None of us does everything. We just do our part. But our part is important.

Second, you meet your own needs. Third, you meet your family's needs. Fourth, you earn to give money to others. Fifth, you love and serve Christ. "Whatever you do, do your work heartily, as for the Lord rather than for men; knowing that from the Lord you will receive the reward of the inheritance. It is the Lord Christ whom you serve" (Colossians 3:23, 24).

If we serve Christ in our work, we must work as Christ would if He had our job. What are the marks of Christ in the marketplace? First, we must be morally distinctive. We must be ethical and honest. We must not be morally camouflaged. Second, we must do our work as well as we are able. We must serve an excellent God with excellence. Third, we must express love toward others. How we treat the people we work with must be distinctive. People must see that we treat others with dignity and respect . . . that we treat them the way Christ would if He had our job.

As people in the marketplace see our moral standards, our commitment to excellence, and the dignity with which we treat others, they will see the thumbprint of God.

Everything that is said of a worker in the marketplace can be said of the homemaker. Giving birth and nurturing new life is part of the image of God, because God gives birth and nurtures new life. You are co-workers with God in extending His dominion over the earth. You are accomplishing very important purposes in the world. You are shaping the future of the world. The hand that rocks the cradle does rule the world. It rarely seems so, but life is like that. The significant things of life are often made up of seemingly insignificant things. If you raise a child to love you, to love others, and to love the Lord, you have done one of the most significant things possible.[1]

Our Play

Those things which God has given you in which you find inherent pleasure can be cultivated and pursued to your own personal pleasure and the glory of God (assuming it doesn't keep you from fulfilling a higher obligation). God is the ultimate creative person, and we are created in His image. If we are to be like Him, we are free to be creative, and we are free to enjoy it.

Art in the form of music, painting, photography, sculpting, etc., can be expressions of the image of God. Physical activity, such as walking, tennis, fencing, jogging, and other sports nurture the temple of the Holy Spirit and can be done as an offering to God. The talent and aptitudes of music, athletics, mathematics, engineering, mechanical aptitude, architecture, etc. can be expressions of the image of God within. Special interests like gardening, animals, different kinds of collections and so forth (I had a friend who memorized plane and train schedules for the fun of it) can all be expressions of the image of God within.

It is my conviction that God has given us these things to make life more enjoyable, and we please God by nurturing them in ways that give Him glory.

Zechariah paints a picture of the coming Kingdom in Zechariah 8:5: "The streets shall be full of boys and girls playing in the streets." In Ecclesiastes, we read that there is a time to laugh, a time to dance, and a time to embrace (3:8).

Arthur Holmes in *Contours of a World View* writes:

> Like Tevye in "Fiddler on the Roof," we can play and sing even in a strange land. Scripture begins with life in a garden and ends with a city at play; so play—art and celebration and fun and games, and a playful spirit—is part of our calling, part of the creation mandate. It is not the play of self-indulgence, nor of shed responsibility, but of gladness and celebration in responsible relationship to God. Play requires a free spirit, rather than free time, a spirit freed from thinking and acting as if life itself depends altogether on me. It is an attitude that carries over into all of life, finding joyful expression in whatever we do, productive or not. At the appropriate times, then, the Christian can afford to play.[2]

Enjoy What God Has Given You to Enjoy

I enjoy poetry. For example:

> There was a little girl,
> And she had a little curl
> Right in the middle of her forehead.
> When she was good she was very, very good,
> And when she was bad, she was horrid.

That poem will never win a Pulitzer Prize. That isn't the point. The point is that someone enjoyed writing that poem. It brought pleasure to him. And I enjoyed reading the poem. It brought pleasure to me. If you enjoy something, it is worth doing. God has given us things we enjoy doing, simply because we enjoy doing them. If it doesn't violate the will of God, there is no need to justify it. We just like it, because God made us that way. We all have a right to be happier than many of us are.

Imagine a gourmet cook who creates a culinary work of art as a special gift to us. And we sit down and smother it with salt and pepper, drown it with ketchup, turn on the news, and bolt it down without tasting it. Sure, it's an affront to him, but we miss out, too.

That's what we do with life. We smother it with work and over commitment; we drown it with television and bolt it down without tasting it. We need to fast, to cleanse our palate and sharpen our senses. Then we need to focus on the feast—the presentation as well as the flavor. Then eat slowly in gentle, quiet conversation with the Master Chef.

So much of life is punctuated with pain. I feel it as well as you do. But with every stem of thorns, there's a rose. If you look only at the thorns, you'll never see the roses. Look at the roses, drink in their color and their fragrance. Pursue the image of God within.

> There is an appointed time for everything. And there is a time for every event under heaven—A time to weep, and a time to laugh; a time to mourn, and a time to dance. (Ecclesiastes 3:1, 4)

Father in Heaven, thank You for investing each of us with infinite and inherent worth. Help us to see ourselves as You see us, so that we may enjoy the security and worth we have in Christ. Thank You for giving us good things to enjoy and for giving us the freedom to enjoy them. Help me never to enjoy them at the expense of being obedient to You. Amen.

REVIEW

1. **Seeing Ourselves as God Sees Us**

   We each have *inherent* and *infinite* worth in God's eyes, be-cause we have been created in His *image.*

2. **Pursue the Image of God Within**

   God has given us His own *characteristics,* which, when we pursue at *work* or at *play,* will enhance our enjoyment of that which He gives us to do.

3. **Enjoy What God Has Given You to Enjoy**

   In order not to miss much of what God intends for us to enjoy, we must *slow down* and *notice* that God has put it there for us to *enjoy.*

As a memory exercise, write in the missing words in the para-graphs below. Notice that they are the same words as the italicized words in the paragraph above.

1. **Seeing Ourselves as God Sees Us**

   We each have _____ and _____ worth in God's eyes, because we have been created in His _____.

2. **Pursue the Image of God Within**

   God has given us His own _____, which, when we pur-sue at _____ or at _____, will enhance our enjoy-ment of that which He gives us to do.

3. **Enjoy What God Has Given You to Enjoy**

   In order not to miss much of what God intends for us to enjoy, we must _____ _____ and _____that God has put it there for us to _____.

RESPONSE

Questions for Group Discussion or Personal Exercises

1. Read Romans 12:3 and Philippians 2:3–4. What do these verses say about pride as well as false humility?

2. Someone has said, "There is nothing you can do to make God love you more. And, there is nothing you might do that would cause God to love you less." Do you see yourself this way? Why do we rely on the measuring stick of performance rather than to just accept the worth which God says we have?

3. What are some of your inner passions? What are some of the "bents" God has created within you? Do you feel free to pursue them without feeling guilty?

4. Are you a part of a spiritual accountability group that upholds one another? If not, why not form one and use this book as your starting point? Who among your friends might respond to the challenge of joining you? Why not give them a call?

S E V E N

BE A STEWARD

Your vocation is not to work for lepers . . .
your vocation is to belong to Jesus.

Mother Teresa

I n his book *Loving God,* Chuck Colson writes of Mother Teresa, who came to a Washington, D.C., ghetto of hunger, crime, drugs, and hopelessness to establish an outpost for nine of her Sisters of Charity. The power brokers, politicians, and press were there.

"What do you hope to accomplish here?" a reporter shouted.

"The joy of loving and being loved," she smiled, her eyes sparkling in the face of camera lights.

"That takes a lot of money, doesn't it?" another reporter asked.

Mother Teresa shook her head. "No, it takes a lot of sacrifice."

Her message? Do something . . . for someone else . . . for the sick, unwanted, crippled, heartbroken, aged, or alone. The world cannot understand the source of Mother Teresa's power. Though her words sound naive, something extraordinary happens wherever she goes.

A few years ago a brother in the order came to her complaining about a superior whose rules, he felt, were interfering with his ministry. "My vocation is to work for lepers," he told Mother Teresa. "I want to spend myself for the lepers."

She stared at him a moment, then smiled. "Brother," she said gently, "your vocation is not to work for lepers, your vocation is to belong to Jesus."[1]

Colson goes on to write that Mother Teresa is not in love with a cause, noble as her cause is. Rather, she loves God and is dedicated to living *His* life, not her own. This is holiness. It is the complete surrender of self in obedience to the will and service of God.

As Christians, we exchanged the right to self-determination when we asked Jesus to save us. Not in a trade: not, "I'll give you all my rights if You'll give me salvation." That is not the way salvation works. But we did say, "Jesus, forgive me of my sins, come into my life and be my Lord and God." You received Him, by faith, as your Savior and as your Lord. If *He* is your Lord, you no longer have the right to self-determination. Your life now belongs to Him. Paul says, "Do you not know that your body is a temple of the Holy Spirit who is in you, whom you have from God, and that you are not your own? For you have been bought with a price: therefore glorify God in your body" (1 Corinthians 6:19–20). You exchanged the temporal for the eternal, death for life, darkness for light, fear for love, doubt for faith, physical for spiritual, despair for joy, confusion for purpose, self for God!

Our joy, our meaning in life, comes not by pursuing happiness, but by pursuing God, who then gives us joy and meaning as a consequence.

This changes everything! Before, we thought we were owners of our resources and the authorities of our lives. Now we see that neither one of those is true. Now we see that we are stewards, not owners, and ambassadors, not authorities. A steward is one who manages the *property* of another. An ambassador is one who manages the *affairs* of another. In both cases, they never act independently, but always for the interests of their master. Therefore, as stewards, we have no possessions. All that we have belongs to God. As ambassadors, we have no personal agenda in life. We are here to do His will. Now, we will look specifically at each of these two responsibilities.

The Role of a Steward

First, the stewardship requirement is faithfulness: " . . . it is required of stewards that one be found trustworthy" (1 Corinthians 4:1–2). It is not required of a steward that he be found successful. It is not required of a steward that he be found clever. It is not required of a steward that he be found lucrative. It is only required of a steward that he be found trustworthy, or faithful. This is a requirement that everyone has an equal ability to fulfill. The main areas of stewardship are below.

Time

Franklin Field wrote: "The great dividing line between success and failure can be expressed in five words: I did not have time." Paul Meyer wrote: "Most time is wasted, not in hours, but in minutes. A bucket with a small hole in the bottom gets just as empty as a bucket that has been deliberately kicked over."[2]

In the Scriptures we read: "Be careful how you walk, not as unwise men, but as wise, redeeming the time for the days are evil" (Ephesians 5:15–16). "Conduct yourselves with wisdom toward outsiders, redeeming the time" (Colossians 4:5). "Lord, make me to know my end, and what is the extent of my days. Let me know how transient I am" (Psalm 39:4). "Teach us to number our days that we may present to Thee a heart of wisdom" (Psalm 90:12).

It matters to God how we use our time. It is something which He has given us. We don't own it. We are responsible to manage it for Him. It doesn't mean we must always work. Part of our time should be used in recreation and rest, the development and enjoyment of relationships. But we must be aware of how we use our time, and use it wisely.

Talent

A missionary teaching in Africa, just before Christmas, had been telling his national students how Christians, as an expression of their joy, gave each other presents on Christ's birthday. On Christmas morning, one of the nationals brought the missionary a seashell of lustrous beauty. When asked where he had discovered such an extraordinary shell, the national said he had walked many miles to a certain bay, the only spot where such shells could be found.

"I think it is wonderful of you to travel so far to get this lovely gift for me," the teacher said.

His eyes brightening, the national replied, "Long walk part of gift."

It isn't the value of the gift, the degree of talent, but the attitude of the heart. In the eyes of God, there are no little people, there are no little places, there are no little jobs, there are no little talents. To each of us, God has given talents. We can use them with great satisfaction in the service of God and man.

Treasure

A little boy went to Sunday school for the very first time, and when he came home, he started unloading his pockets which were absolutely stuffed full of money—$10 bills, $5 bills, $1 bills. His parents gasped and said, "Where did you get all that money?"

The little boy said, "In church . . . they've got buckets of it!"

If that church had buckets of it, it is because some in that church had come to grips with their stewardship responsibility in the area of his treasures. "Let each one do just as he has purposed in his heart; not grudgingly or under compulsion; for God loves a cheerful giver. And God is able to make all grace abound to you, that always having all sufficiency in everything, you may have an abundance for every good deed" (2 Corinthians 9:6–8).

You can tell how spiritually mature a person is by how he uses his money. If he contributes money to the purposes of God, you are probably looking at a person who has accepted spiritual values. If he doesn't, he has not come to that point yet. Giving of money is often the last thing to "fall" as a person matures, because if you are living for this world, you won't give your money to the next world.

One out of every four verses in the book of Luke talk about money. Jesus spoke of money more than heaven and hell combined. Why? Because it is a litmus test of commitment to Christ.

The areas of stewardship are time, talents, and treasures. The rewards of stewardship are spiritual. You may prosper financially if you handle your money carefully. However, giving to the Lord does not mean that He will bless you financially. There are no monetary promises to us as Christians for giving to the Lord. There are promises in the Old Testament, but we no longer live in the Old Testament.

The rewards of the steward are spiritual and are based on "intent of the heart." First Corinthians 3:10–15 states that God judges the thoughts and intentions of the heart. It is not our actions that are rewarded; it is not our results that are rewarded; it is our motives!

This takes the pressure off of serving Christ, because we are judged on our motives, and everyone can be faithful.

There are some things that just don't work out well on earth, but will be rewarded in heaven. A man rushed into a pharmacy and said, "Quick, do you have a cure for severe hiccups!?!"

The pharmacist had just been to a seminar on the debilitating effects of severe and chronic hiccups, and his heart went out to this man. So suddenly, he screamed at the top of his lungs, reached across the counter, grabbed the man by the lapels, pulled him onto the counter, and slapped him on both cheeks. Then with deep satisfaction he said, "There, do you still have the hiccups?" And the man said, "Actually, it is my wife in the car who has the hiccups."

That didn't work out very well on earth, but our pharmacist friend will get a reward in heaven for that.

The Role of an Ambassador

A steward manages the possessions of God. An ambassador manages the affairs of God. Like the monk who came to Mother Teresa and said, "I want to give my life for the lepers." And Mother Teresa said "Your job is not to give your life for the lepers. Your job is to belong to Jesus." That is what it means to be an ambassador. It means not to move through life according to your own agenda, but to move through life with God's agenda.

This poses a great challenge, however, because we all have our hands full with domestic responsibilities. We go to school, we marry, we work, we raise children. So how do we say we can have no agenda? We can't ignore these domestic responsibilities.

True. The answer is that these responsibilities are part of God's agenda. He intends for us have domestic responsibilities. He just asks that we handle them His way. Ideally, His agenda and our agenda will be identical, but anytime God's agenda and our agenda are in conflict, we accept His agenda.

The Role of Discipline

One story I heard relates to this very well. The person told of the first time he went out for football. The varsity head coach had been a Marine drill instructor. He had a thick neck and a crew cut. His voice was graveled from all the shouting he had done. He was a very successful coach.

> He slammed his clipboard down on the table, scowled at all of us, and announced that he was going to talk to us about the three "D's" of winning football: Desire, Dedication, and Discipline.
>
> There was absolute silence as he took each of these words and told us what they must mean to us if we expected to play football on his team. When he got to the last "D", he told us about what had happened to the team the first year he coached. Football had been a failure up until then. But a number of very talented seniors were on the squad. When they heard his speech about the three "D's," he could tell they all thought it a bit amusing, especially the part about discipline. Discipline for him included no late nights during the week and no drinking alcoholic beverages.
>
> The team was three games into the season and undefeated when he learned that all the seniors had gone to a party and gotten drunk after the game. He kicked everyone of them off the team and moved sophomores and juniors into the starting line up. They proceeded to lose every one of the remaining games that year. But the next year he had a team with discipline and experience. They finished second in the league. And from that year on, they were the team to beat.

It isn't easy to live out our roles as stewards and as ambassadors. It takes discipline. If you struggle with it, don't think you are alone. We all struggle with it. It is utterly unnatural to act as though we have no possessions and no personal agenda. It is not only unnatural, it is supernatural. To help us, we must remember the lesson of Mother Teresa. We aren't called to give ourselves to "things" or "tasks." When we do, we can be continuously frustrated. We are called to give ourselves to Christ. Our vocation is to belong to Jesus. Completely. When that is our call, nothing can thwart us.

> As each one has received a special gift, employ it in serving one another as stewards of the manifold grace of God. . . . We are ambassadors for Christ. (1 Peter 4:10, 2 Corinthians 5:20)

> *Heavenly Father, I offer myself to You as a steward and an ambassador. I recognize that, in Christ, I have no personal possessions nor personal agenda. I willingly serve You in all that I have and all that I do. Give me grace and strength to remain consistent in my commitment. In our Savior's name. Amen.*

REVIEW

1. **The Role of a Steward**

   The steward owns *nothing*. He *manages* the *possessions* of another.

2. **The Role of an Ambassador**

   The ambassador has no personal *agenda*. He *manages* the *affairs* of another.

3. **The Role of Discipline**

Discipline is required to be consistent in our *perspective* on personal matters. Our *vocation* is to belong to *Jesus*.

As a memory exercise, write in the missing words in the paragraphs below. Notice that they are the same words as the italicized words in the paragraph above.

1. **The Role of a Steward**

The steward owns _____. He _____ the _____ of another.

2. **The Role of an Ambassador**

The ambassador has no personal _____. He _____ the _____ of another.

3. **The Role of Discipline**

Discipline is required to be consistent in our _____ on personal matters. Our _____ is to belong to _____.

RESPONSE

Questions for Group Discussion or Personal Exercises

1. What are several practical ways you can demonstrate that all you possess really belongs to God?

2. Does your checkbook reflect an investment in what God is doing in the world?

3. Do you agree that the one who is faithful using a non-public gift is just as important to God as one who faithfully uses a more public gift? Who is someone you can encourage in the use of his gifts that might not be being recognized?

EIGHT

BE A SERVANT

Our souls are not hungry for fame, comfort, wealth, or power. . . . Our souls are hungry for meaning.

Rabbi Harold Kushner

I n his poem, "Richard Cory," Edward Arlington Robinson wrote:

Whenever Richard Cory went downtown,
We people on the pavement looked at him:
He was a gentleman from soul to crown,
Clean favored, and imperially slim.

And he was always quietly arrayed,
And he was always a human when he talked.
But still he fluttered pulses when he said,
    "Good morning,"
And he glittered when he walked.

And he was rich—yes richer than a king,
And admirably schooled in every grace.
In fine, we thought he was everything,
To make us wish that we were in his place.

So on we worked and waited for the light;
And went without meat and cursed the bread.
And Richard Cory, one calm summer night,
Went home and put a bullet through his head.[1]

Put a bullet through his head? Why? He had everything! But did he? Rabbi Harold Kushner wrote:

> Our souls are not hungry for fame, comfort, wealth, or power. Those rewards create almost as many problems as they solve. Our souls are hungry for meaning, for the sense that we have figured out how to live so that our lives matter, so that the world will be at least a little bit different for our having passed through it.[2]

Our Drive for Meaning

Meaning. This is one of the great hungers, one of the great motivating forces in mankind. Who am I, and what shall I do with my life? God has created us with this hunger. He intends this hunger to be satisfied by our living a life of service to others. Therefore, when God asks us to become a servant, He is asking us to do the very thing which will bring us satisfaction.

Everything God asks *of* us, He does so because He wants to give something good *to* us. He asks us to become a servant because He wants to give us meaning, because He wants to satisfy one of the deepest hungers of the human heart.

By being a servant, we do not mean that we don an imaginary black tuxedo or formal gown and commit our lives to fulfilling the wishes of others. Rather, it means that we commit our lives to doing that which helps others, rather than live only for self.

One of the great joys of life is meeting a need for a grateful person. This can actually release endorphines in the blood stream, a natural substance that makes you feel good, takes away pain, heals the body, and strengthens the immunological system. We were made to be kind to others.

This is a simple example of a larger truth. We don't always get endorphine rushes by living a life for others, but we do get a basic sense of meaning and purpose in life. When we live for others, it will have mattered to others that we lived, and the world will be a little better for our having passed through. In addition, we will have the satisfaction that our actions were pleasing to God.

You may be tempted to say, "You want me to be a servant? I'm already a slave! My life is not my own. I'm selling my whole life to those around me—my kids, my boss, school, commitments to other people. I am giving everything I have, and it's the pits. I am getting nothing in return. I don't agree that you 'get' by 'giving.' All I've done is give, give, give, and now I'm dry. I am now giving consideration to 'taking' a little. I'm considering something drastic, like quitting school, or getting a divorce, or quitting my job. I'm thinking of doing something to make me feel good, let me have a little fun, and salvage what time I have left."

The problem with this kind of "escapist" thinking is that the "escape hatch" leads to more and greater problems. You jump out of the frying pan, where it is hot, into the fire, where it is hotter. If you cannot get your life in balance with present commitments, there is little hope that you will solve the problem by trying to flee them. True, you may need to quit school or change jobs. But it must be done in a controlled, thoughtful, decision-making process. And it must not include anything which is sin.

The old cliché "two wrongs don't make a right" is true even if it is a cliché. The secret is learning how to bring one's life into balance with the responsibilities God has given you, not chuck the whole thing and try to start over. You will simply reproduce the problems in the next situation.

The world tells us that if you want to get, you have to take. And we've believed it. We've been deceived, hoodwinked, flim-flammed. In the Sunday paper, I read in the column "It Happened Today in History" about a man earlier in our century who wanted to set a transcontinental flight record. He took off in his airplane from New York City late one evening for California. He landed the next morning in Dublin, Ireland. Understandably, it earned him the nickname "Wrong Way Riley."

There are times in life when we go the wrong way. We *think* that joy will come from "people," "possessions," and "positions." We *think* that the way to get meaning in life is to accrue, accumulate, acquire, amass, stash, store, and stockpile—when just the opposite is true. Meaning in life comes from giving, from serving, and from helping. We have taken off for California, but we've landed in Dublin.

We "get," not by taking, but by giving. In Acts 20:35, we read, "It is better to give than to receive." In Mark 10:45 we read, "Even the Son of Man came, not to be ministered to, but to minister, and to give His life as a ransom for many."

God wants to give to us. He wants to deeply satisfy us, to fill us with Himself so that we will not choose cheap substitutes. It is not that we desire too much. We desire too little. We are willing to settle for shallow and fleeting things, rather than pressing through the resistance to spiritual depth and finding true meaning in God.

We were created to console. We were made to minister. One of the great challenges of our lives, then, is to recognize that the world is askew, to re-orient ourselves; to dare to believe that down is up, that out is in, that far is near, and that giving is getting and take the great step of courage; to start giving our life away.

This does *not* mean that we self-destruct. This does not mean to give ourselves away in a careless, thoughtless pattern that ends up in self-inflicted ruin. There is no virtue in killing geese that lay golden eggs. There is no nobility in flaming out. So we are not talking about a blind, kamikazie raid on life. We are talking about a reasoned apportioning of our resources toward the needs of others, taking into account our own needs.

We are not talking about a mindless flinging of ourselves at the feet of others to use as they see fit, regardless of the wisdom of it. We're not talking about letting others determine for us the course of our lives. We are responsible before God for the judicious use of our time, talents, and treasures, and we must not waste them or give them where they ought not to go.

The point is that, under the wisdom of God and the guidance of the Scriptures, we are to direct our life energies, in reasonable measure, in the direction of others.

Our Natural Tendency

A number of years ago, a team of white-robed scientists marched with clipboards in hand into the barnyard and sat down outside the chicken coop. They were there to observe the chickens. They saw many things they expected to see—some chickens clucked, some crowed, all scratched and pecked around in the dirt. But they saw some things they didn't expect to see. For example, in the barnyard, there was a top chicken, and there was a bottom chicken, and all the other chickens were aligned in a great poultry hierarchy between the top chicken and the bottom chicken. The top chicken could peck any other chicken he wanted to without fear of reprisal. The bottom chicken could not peck any other chicken without certain reprisal. So in the "pecking order," there were lower chickens, middle chickens, and upper chickens. One of the dominant features of barnyard life was a constant "jockeying" for a higher position in the pecking order. Constant squabbles and posturing and faking went on as chickens tried to carve out a higher pecking order position. Occasionally, there were serious fights in which the chickens sometimes actually got hurt.

Very interesting! So the team of scientists picked themselves up, dusted themselves off, and left the barnyard. Then, they walked out into the business world of America and sat down to observe humans. They saw some things they expected to see. Some humans were tall, some were short, some were outgoing and others quiet. But they saw something that they didn't expect to see. In the business "coops" of the world, there were top humans and there were bottom humans. And all the other humans were aligned in a human "pecking order" in between. And one of the dominant features of life in the business world was "jockeying" for a higher position in the pecking order. Constant squabbles and posturing and faking went on as humans tried to carve out a higher pecking order position. Occasionally, there were serious fights which broke out in which humans sometimes actually got hurt. Perhaps not physically but emotionally. Life in the corporate world was little higher than life in the chicken coop.

This is what Jesus was driving at when He said to James and John, who were jockeying for a higher position in the Kingdom pecking order in Mark 10:42–45:

> You know that those who are recognized as rulers of the Gentiles lord it over them; and their great men exercise authority over them. But it is not so among you, but whoever wishes to become great among you shall be your servant; and whoever wishes to be first among you shall be slave of all. For even the Son of Man did not come to be served, but to serve and to give His live as a ransom for many.

Our Need to Serve

Whom do we serve? We serve all men. But perhaps we serve them differently. We are to show love to other Christians and to serve them with our spiritual gift. Ephesians 4, Romans 12, and 1 Corinthians 12 indicate that we have each been gifted by God to minister to other Christians, and that as we do, the entire body of Christ grows to maturity in Him. First Peter 4:10 says, "Therefore, as each one has received a special gift, employ it in serving one another."

As far as non-Christians are concerned, their primary need is the gospel. Therefore, our great concern is to bring to them the message of the gospel. However, there are times when they also need food, clothing, shelter, or medical attention—or they may have spiritual or emotional needs. It is legitimate to help meet these needs out of respect for the dignity of Man. However, it also earns a hearing for the gospel.

When men see our good works, performed as a body unified in Christian love, they glorify, not us, but our Father in heaven: "Let your light so shine before men that they may see your good works and glorify your Father who is in heaven" (Matthew 5:16).

So we minister, to Christians with our spiritual gifts in love, unity, and kindness; and to the world, being salt and light, and carrying the message of salvation to them.

If we were talking about ministering to other Christians with our spiritual gift, and of taking the message of salvation to the lost, this chapter would have to be much longer as we went into much greater depth. However, that is not the point of this chapter. This chapter is simply to make the case that we are not created to live life solely for ourselves. We are made to minister. To live life for any other purpose than to give ourselves away to others in love is to fall short of the joy and purpose which we long for.

When we insist on living for the moment, it pulls us away from a life of meaning. It keeps us from putting together the hard experiences that add up to a sense of purpose and satisfaction in what we do. The significant things in life are usually a compilation of small things that don't seem significant at the time. A life of meaning is achieved not by a few great immortal deeds but by a lot of little ones.

For even the Son of Man came not to be ministered to, but to minister, and to give His life a ransom for many. (Mark 10:45)

> *Father in Heaven, work in me the supernatural transformation of living for others rather than self. Fill me with a sense of meaning and purpose, because I have found them in Christ. May I have His attitude in me, to look not to be ministered to, but to minister. In His name. Amen.*

REVIEW

1. Our Drive for Meaning

Everything God *asks* of us, He does so because He wants to *give* something good to us, and in the process, *satisfy* the deep longings of our soul.

2. Our Natural Tendency

Instead of naturally serving *others*, we usually are looking for ways of getting *them* to serve *us*.

3. Our Need to Serve

We are *made* to *minister*. We are not created to live life solely for *ourselves*.

As a memory exercise, write in the missing words in the paragraphs below. Notice that they are the same words as the italicized words in the paragraph above.

1. Our Drive for Meaning

Everything God _____ of us, He does so because He wants to _____ something good to us, and in the process, _____ the deep longings of our soul.

2. **Our Natural Tendency**

Instead of naturally serving _____, we usually are looking for ways of getting _____ to serve _____.

3. **Our Need to Serve**

We are _____ to _____. We are not created to live life solely for _____.

RESPONSE

Questions for Group Discussion or Personal Exercises

1. What are some evidences that all mankind has a built-in desire for a sense of meaning in life?

2. Have you ever felt like you have been giving, giving, giving, and it was finally your turn to "take?" That the world owed you one? Did you quit giving? If you did, did you really find satisfaction in waiting for someone to "give you your due?"

3. Where, within your sphere of influence, could you give your life away in order to make a difference? What is one step of involvement you could commit to this week in order to begin exploring that possibility?

WHAT HAS TO HAPPEN FOR ME TO BE HOLY?

*There is a process through which
God takes each Christian to bring him
to maturity in the five areas
of responsibility. Leave one step
of this process out, and the Christian
will not be spiritually mature.
Combine all five areas, and
the Christian will be spiritually mature.*

WkG + WdG + PC + OB + T&T = Spiritual Maturity

N I N E

THE WORK OF GOD

WkG + WdG + PC + OB + T&T = Spiritual Maturity

(WkG = Work of God)

C. S. Lewis, the British intellect, who earlier in this century became one of Christendom's most articulate spokesmen, taught at both Oxford and Cambridge Universities during his academic career. The story of his spiritual journey from atheist, to agnostic, to Christian is a captivating and reassuring one. He began to be overwhelmed by the historical credibility of the resurrection account.

Finally, the intellectual reality pressed down on him so completely that he began to yield. In his book *Surprised by Joy*, he wrote:

> You must picture me alone in [my room at Cambridge] night after night, feeling, whenever my mind lifted even for a second from my work, the steady, unrelenting approach of Him whom I so earnestly desired not to meet. That which I greatly feared had at last come upon me. In the Trinity term of 1929 I gave in, and admitted that God was God, and knelt and prayed: perhaps, that night, the most dejected and reluctant convert in all England. I did not then see what is now the most shining and obvious thing; the Divine humility which will accept a convert even on such terms. The Prodigal Son at least walked home on his own feet. But who can duly adore that Love which will open the high gates to a prodigal who is brought in kicking, struggling, resentful, and darting his eyes in every direction for a chance of escape? The

words, in the Gospels, "compel them to come in," . . . properly understood, plumb the depths of the Divine mercy. The hardness of God is kinder than the softness of men, and His compulsion is our liberation.[1]

Oh, the work of God in the affairs of men—how wonderful and glorious it is. In the mysteries of time and space, the affairs of men march on, oblivious, either in part or the whole, to the fact that a sovereign God is guiding the world toward His predetermined destiny.

In the age of scientific ultra sophistication, with micro-chips, semi-conductors, and freeze-dried food, the path to spiritual maturity has finally been reduced to an equation. I can say, without fear of contradiction, that if you follow this formula, you will become spiritually mature. I can also say, without fear of contradiction, that if you omit even one of these elements, you will not be spiritually mature. The equation:

WkG + WdG + PC + OB + T&T = Spiritual Maturity

The first element of the equation, WkG, stands for the Work of God. As the equation unfolds, we must keep very clear what is the work of God and what is the work of man. To that end this little paradigm is helpful:

> God does the work of God,
> Man does the work of man.
> Man cannot do the work of God, and
> God will not do the work of man.

We will make major headway in the Christian experience if we can get this straight. We have a flamboyant drive to reverse the process—to insist on assuming responsibility for the work of God while at the same time neglecting the work of man.

Like each wing of an airplane, the work of God and the work of man must both play a role. Spiritual growth is a mysterious exchange between God and man in which each plays a part. Spiritual growth begins with a work of God. There are a number of passages which point this out. Paul states, " . . . work out your own salvation with fear and trembling, for it is God who is at work in you, both to will and to work for His good pleasure" (Philippians 2:12–13). He also says, "It is God who is at work in us to will His good pleasure." In 1 Corinthians 3:6, we see a similar concept, where Paul writes that, "Paul may plant and Apollos may water, but it is God who must give the increase."

In a companion passage, we learn that salvation begins with a work of God. "No man can come to me unless the Father who sent me draws him. . . ." (John 6:44). We learn also that spiritual growth is a work of the Holy Spirit: ". . . the fruit of the Spirit is love, joy, peace, patience, kindness, goodness, faithfulness, gentleness, self-control . . ." (Galatians 5:22–23).

Also, we see in 1 Corinthians 2:12 and 14 that it is the Spirit who gives us the capacity to understand and embrace the truth of Scripture, which is the basis of spiritual growth.

Finally, we read in John 15:5: "I am the vine, you are the branches; he who abides in Me, and I in him, he bears much fruit; for apart from Me you can do nothing."

These examples reveal the unambiguous and abundant testimony that our spiritual maturity begins with a work of God. Yet, we will see in subsequent chapters that we are also responsible to respond. It is a mystery, but we cannot generate our own spiritual growth. God must do it. But God won't do it unless we are pursuing our own spiritual growth.

Maintaining Our Balance

We must be balanced between what the Bible says God must do and what it says we must do. When carrying two weighty truths, one in each hand, the challenge is to keep the balance. Like two milk buckets on a broomstick, the tendency is to fall to one side or to the other. The tendency is to emphasize the work of man to the exclusion of the work of God, or to emphasize the work of God to the exclusion of the work of man.

In his book, *True Spirituality*, Francis Schaeffer has coined the phrase "active passivity." The point is that we must be active in the pursuit of our spiritual growth, but at the same time, we are passive—God brings the growth about in our lives. In that book, he writes about Romans 6:6, 11: "our old self was crucified with Him, that our body of sin might be done away with, that we should no longer be slaves to sin; . . . consider yourselves to be dead to sin, but alive to God in Christ Jesus."[2]

Schaeffer paraphrases this idea as follows:

> In our thoughts and lives now, we are to live as though we had already died, been to heaven, and come back again as risen. . . .
>
> What would the praise of the world be worth when one had stood in the presence of God? The wealth of the world, what would it look like beside the treasures of heaven? Man longs for power. But what is earthly power after one has seen the reality of heaven and the power of God? Our Christian calling is moment by moment to be dead to all things, that at this moment, we might be alive to God.[3]

Activity: We make all decisions in light of our death, resurrection, and return.

Passivity: We rest in the sovereignty of God . . . in His agenda and in His timetable.

"When we do this," Schaeffer writes, "we are now ready for the war. We are now ready to be used. We can now keep our balance."

Maintaining Our Perspective

In addition to maintaining our balance in life, we must also maintain our perspective. We must understand that God is patient with us. One of the great challenges in the Christian life is reconciling the presence of sin and weakness in our lives with the holiness of God. The serious student will sooner or later stumble over the fact that God wants him to be holy, and he is trying as hard as he can to be holy, but he is not holy.

If that is all you understand, you can come to only one conclusion: God is not pleased with you.

The serious Christian will then try harder. Then he will re-assess himself and realize he is still not holy. So he will try harder, and harder, and harder, and harder. But he cannot keep that up.

Sooner or later, he will do one of two things. First, he will quit. He will check out of the serious Christian life. He may quit his job, get a divorce, perm his hair, buy a sports car, and move to the beach in Southern California. Second, he may keep going through the motions on the outside, but on the inside, something has died.

I'm going to say something that we seldom hear. We fear saying it in public because we are afraid that if we do, people will rush out of the pews and into the world and start sinning like crazy: If you are not living in rebellion against God, then God is satisfied with you even with the weaknesses and sins in your life.

Now let me clarify what I mean by saying some things that I don't mean.

1. I don't mean that God doesn't care if you sin. He does. He wants you to be holy. He knows that sin hurts you, and He loves you, so He hates sin. It is just that He takes into account your weaknesses. He will love you unconditionally even with the sin.

2. It doesn't mean you don't have to be concerned about sin and weakness. You do. You need to be in relationship with God for the purpose of growth *through* the sin and weakness.

3. But the fruit of the Spirit is the fruit of the *spirit,* not of self-effort, and even if you are cooperating with God the best way you know how, you do not achieve instant maturity. That means you will have to take time to grow through some of your weaknesses. That means you have some weaknesses right now that you cannot be rid of because God has not had the time to rid you of them. God has not done the work of grace yet to free you of them. So you must be willing to accept yourself even with the weaknesses, because God does.

A comforting passage teaching this is Psalm 103:8–14:

> The Lord is compassionate and gracious,
> Slow to anger and abounding in lovingkindness.
> He will not always strive with us;
> Nor will He keep His anger forever.
> He has not dealt with us according to our sins,
> Nor rewarded us according to our iniquities.
> For as high as the heavens are above the earth,

So great is His lovingkindess
        toward those who fear Him.
As far as the east is from the west,
So far has He removed our transgressions
        from us.
Just as a father has compassion on his children,
So the Lord has compassion
        on those who fear Him.
For He Himself knows our frame;
He is mindful that we are but dust.

The Lord has compassion on those who fear Him. If you are trying to live the Christian life the best way you know how, but you keep stumbling and falling, God does not get sick and tired of you. He knows that you will require some time to grow, and He will be patient with you.

On the other hand, God deals very harshly with rebellion. He deals decisively with someone who knows what the right thing to do is but doesn't care or makes no attempt to do it. But He deals compassionately with weaknesses.

So we see that God is patient with our weaknesses. On that basis, we must be patient with ourselves.

To illustrate this truth, and to highlight what I perceive to be the importance of it, allow me a personal illustration. I became a Christian while a student in college, and I immediately threw myself into living the Christian life with great zeal. However, in spite of my zeal, I found myself riddled with the same inconsistencies and failures which had plagued me before I became a Christian. I remember very distinctly praying one day, "God if you want me to be holy, and if I want to be holy, then I have one question for you. Why am I not holy?" I knew that somehow God saw me as holy and righteous through the cross, but I was struggling with personal righteousness on a daily level.

Finally, I decided that I was not trying hard enough. I was not reading my Bible or praying enough to achieve the spiritual progress I longed for. So I began to read my Bible for an hour a day, and I began to pray for another hour a day. I continued that practice for the remainder of the semester. And at the end of that semester, I had never been more out of fellowship.

I would get angry or selfish and do things I knew I shouldn't, but when I came to my senses, I would repent. I wanted to not be angry, I wanted to not be proud, I worked against them in my good moments, but just let the wrong person or circumstance come up, and bingo, off I went again.

I came to hate myself. I would sin and then repent, sin and repent. "O God, I'm sorry. *Help* me not to do that again." Then I'd sin the same sin again. "O God, I'm sorry. I *won't* do that again." Then I'd sin again. "O God, I said I wouldn't sin again, and I did. I'm sorry, but I *promise* I won't do it again." Then I'd sin again . . . and again . . . and again. Each time I asked God to help me, give me strength. Each time I failed.

I finally was too embarrassed to come to God again. I was angry at Him for not coming to my rescue. Finally, I said, "Okay, God, I quit. I have done my absolute best, and it isn't good enough, so I quit. If you ever want to do anything with my life, just let me know, but until you do, see you later. I've had it."

I lived for the next two years a frustrated, defeated, angry young man. No one ever told me that I couldn't do it all myself. No one ever told me that I couldn't do it all simultaneously. No one ever told me that if I was earnest in my desire to live a righteous life, God was satisfied with me, even with my sins, that He recognized weaknesses and accepted me anyway, and that therefore, I should accept myself.

If someone had told me that, it wouldn't have made me want to run out and start sinning like crazy. It would have made me drop to my knees in gratitude to God for His grace and would have given me the strength to keep on trying. Properly understood, God's grace *never* encourages us to sin. It only ever encourages us to righteousness.

A breakthrough came when I went to seminary and one of my seminary professors in theology class said, "Be patient with yourself. You can't be holy in a hurry!" My heart *jumped!* My mind swelled with hope. Then, as I transitioned from a context of legalism to a context of grace, my true spiritual development began.

Patience in the Process

I believe that all of the big things in this physical world of ours are designed to picture the big spiritual truths. The infinite size of the universe pictures the infinity of God. The transition from summer to fall to winter to spring pictures death, burial, and resurrection.

Have you ever stopped to think about why humans grow up physically the way they do? I think it is for the purpose of picturing spiritual birth and spiritual growth.

A child is born knowing very little and being able to do very little. He needs constant care and attention from a loving provider. He grows both slowly and quickly at the same time. At each stage of growth, we take into account age level characteristics and accept behavior which is not ideal but which is normal.

If a six-month-old child wants you to hold it, and then squirms around in your lap, stands up, and spits up on your shoulder, you do not consider that ideal behavior. You wish that he wouldn't have done it, but you accept it, because he is only six months old. But if a thirty-year-old person squirms around in your lap, stands up, and spits up on your shoulder, you'd want an explanation!

The six-month-old child turns one year, and he is ready to take his first step. He takes one death-defying step, weaves dangerously to the right, spins around 90 degrees, and collapses to the floor. You don't say, "Listen you rotten kid, if you are gonna walk, walk! And if you're gonna sit down, then sit down. But stop this falling business." On the contrary, you probably have a spontaneous celebration. Whoops and hand clapping and "attaboy's" fill the air. Then you prop him up and encourage him to do it all over again, knowing that he is going to fall down again.

Falling down isn't ideal behavior, but you expected it from the age of the child. You focus, not on the fall, but on the step.

And take the child who wants to be a basketball player. He feels as though he will never grow up. He asks you to measure him each day to see if he has gotten any taller. You know he hasn't. He hasn't had the time to grow. But he can't stand it, so you humor him. These things take time, and not enough time has passed.

The same thing is true of spiritual growth. It takes time. How much time? It depends on a million variables. But it almost always takes more time than you think it should. But God will grow you up if you will grow His way.

So don't live in rebellion. God will deal decisively with that. Earnestly live for the Lord. But when you do, accept that you can't be holy in a hurry, and give yourself time. Then, in the meantime, accept yourself, because God does.

Trust in the Lord with all your heart, and do not lean on your own understanding. In all your ways acknowledge Him, and He will make your paths straight. (Proverbs 3:5–6)

Our Heavenly Father, work in my heart. I am powerless, and sightless without You. Make my spirit sing with longing for You. Shed light into every corner of my soul, chase out the darkness, and may I live only for You all my life. Amen

---

REVIEW

1. Maintaining Our Balance

We must be *active* in the pursuit of spiritual growth, while at the same time being *passive*, recognizing that God gives the *growth.*

2. Maintaining Our Perspective

We must not hate ourselves. God is *patient* with our *weakness.* If He *accepts* us in Christ, we must accept ourselves.

3. Patience in the Process

We must be patient in our *process* of *growing* spiritually, knowing that we cannot be *holy* in a hurry.

As a memory exercise, write in the missing words in the paragraphs below. Notice that they are the same words as the italicized words in the paragraph above.

1. **Maintaining Our Balance**

   We must be _____ in the pursuit of spiritual growth, while at the same time being _____, recognizing that God gives the _____.

2. **Maintaining Our Perspective**

   We must not hate ourselves. God is _____ with our _____. If He _____ us in Christ, we must accept ourselves.

3. **Patience in the Process**

   We must be patient in our _____ of _____ spiritually, knowing that we cannot be _____ in a hurry.

RESPONSE

Questions for Group Discussion or Personal Exercises

1. Up to this point in your spiritual life, has the pendulum swung to the side of relying on self-effort for your spiritual growth or the side of relying totally on God?

2. What Scriptural references can you find that demonstrate that God is committed to direct your spiritual growth?

3. Identify the areas in your life where you may have had the tendency to identify the sin as weakness when actually it was an area of rebellion?

TEN

THE WORD OF GOD

$WkG + WdG + PC + OB + T\&T = Spiritual\ Maturity$

(WdG = Word of God)

L et me share with you about the last flight of the "Lady Be
Good." She was a massive bomber during World War II. She
had flown many successful missions, and tonight was just another
mission. She pierced the enemy air space, dropped her cargo of
destruction, and turned around to head home.

This night was different, however. As she reversed course for
the return flight, she was pushed along by a powerful tail wind,
causing her to travel much faster than normal. When the instruments told the pilots to land, they looked at their watches and
knew that it was much too soon. They faced a critical decision. If
they believed their instruments, they would come down out of the
clouds and prepare to land. However, if they believed their watch,
they would keep flying.

To come down too soon might expose them to enemy anti-air-
craft fire. On the other hand, if they didn't come down now, and
the instruments were right, they would overshoot the airfield, and
perish in the desert, since they had no excess fuel. Life and death
was in their own hands. Do they trust their instruments, or do they
trust their own judgment?

They had to make a decision. They chose to ignore the instruments and believe their gut-level hunch. They stayed up. They *overshot* the airfield. Their plane was found days later, out of fuel, crashed in the desert. All crewmen had died.

The story of the "Lady Be Good" is presented as one of the Moody Science Films and portrays a microcosm of life. We are *all* on the "Lady Be Good," and we are all in flight. In deciding where and when to land as our final destination, we must choose whether we look within ourselves for the answers, or whether we look outside ourselves, whether we trust our gut-level hunches, or whether we look for an instrument panel.

The Bible presents itself as the great, cosmic instrument panel. It tells us where we came from, where we are, and where we are going. It is up to us to decide whether or not we accept the "readings" we get from it. But, like the "Lady Be Good," the choices are serious—safe landings or death in the desert.

Truth Doesn't Change

The Bible is not a book of philosophy, though it is philosophical. It is not a scientific treatise, though it is consistent with science. It is not a book of history, though it is accurate whenever history is recorded. The Bible was given to man by God, revealing the purpose of God in the world, and establishing how man can know God and grow spiritually.

> The Word of God is living and active and sharper than any two-edged sword, and piercing as far as the division of soul and spirit, of both joints and marrow, and able to judge the thoughts and intentions of the heart. (Hebrews 4:12)

The Living Bible reads:

> [God's Word] is full of living power: it is sharper than the sharpest dagger, cutting swift and deep into our innermost thoughts and desires, exposing us for what we really are.

The Scripture has an inherent power as it is energized by the Holy Spirit in our lives. Reading the Scripture is not like reading Shakespeare. It is a body of absolute truth which penetrates our thought life to its very core. Paul points out, "All Scripture is inspired by God and is profitable for teaching, for reproof, for correction, for training in righteousness, that the person of God may be adequate, equipped for every good work" (2 Timothy 3:16–17).

The Word of God is profitable for what you need to *know* (profitable for teaching), for what you need to *be* (for reproof, for correction and training in righteousness), and for what you need to *do* (that the man of God may be adequate, thoroughly equipped for every good work).

"The Word is a lamp unto our feet and a light unto our path" (Psalm 119:105). The picture here is of walking in darkness and not being able to see. When you are walking in the dark, you cannot tell if you are going in the right direction; you cannot tell if you are going to walk into something dangerous; you cannot tell if you are going to get sidetracked and delayed; you cannot tell if you are going to get lost altogether.

But if you do one simple thing—put a flashlight on your feet— the entire situation is corrected. The same is true with life. We are walking in the dark. We cannot tell if we are going in the right direction, if we might be in danger of an injurious misstep, if we might be going astray, or be lost altogether. If we look into the Scripture, it throws light on the path of our life and saves us from the perils of darkness.

As King David says, "Thy word have I hidden in my heart that I might not sin against Thee" (Psalm 119:11). Hiding (the NASB says "treasure") the word in your heart renews your mind and contributes to the transformation process which we all long for.

Perhaps you have heard the story of the airplane which was flying across the continent and encountered a violent thunderstorm. It was struck by lightening, which knocked out all its navigation equipment. The captain came on the intercom and said, "Ladies and gentlemen, I have good news and bad news. The bad news is that our navigation equipment has been knocked out. The good news is that we have a tremendous tail wind, and we are way ahead of schedule."

Without the Bible, our navigation equipment is knocked out. Many of our natural inclinations take us 180 degrees in the opposite direction from truth. We might be making great time, but we have no idea where we are. The Scriptures play a crucial role in the spiritual maturation process.

We Need Absolute Truth

For us to have a proper respect for the Bible and a proper regard for its value and importance, we must catch a glimpse of what happens when we lose absolute truth. When one person argues with another person over a given matter, they cancel each other out. One person says something is right; another says that it is wrong. They are on the same authority level, and they cancel each other out. When that happens, they have to appeal to a higher authority.

For example, this is seen at the earliest experience when two siblings want the same thing. One says, "I want the blue truck." The other retaliates, "No, I want the blue truck." They are deadlocked. So they holler, "Mom!" They appeal to a higher authority for a decision.

In a second example, when two people are in business, and they disagree, they appeal to a higher authority. One takes the other one to court, and the court decides which one was right and which one was wrong, and the higher authority of the court is imposed on the situation.

If two entities are deadlocked in determining right and wrong, and there is no higher authority immediately available, the stronger one usually imposes his will on the weaker one. If mom isn't around, then the bigger kid takes the blue truck away from the smaller kid. When that happens, right and wrong have died. The law of the jungle becomes the law of the land—the survival of the fittest rules.

In the larger context of life, if two nations disagree, they go to war. There is no higher authority to which they can appeal.

When it comes to moral issues, the only higher authority you can appeal to is God. If two men disagree on a moral issue, you can go to God's word and settle the issue there. However, if the people involved do not believe in God, then that eliminates the "higher authority." When that happens, right and wrong are destroyed. You can no longer talk about right and wrong. You can only talk about preferences. You can say, "I prefer that you not cheat on your income tax," but you cannot say, "it is wrong to cheat on your income tax." If you say it is wrong to cheat on your income tax, and someone else says it is not wrong, and if you have no higher authority, such as God, to determine it, then you cancel each other out.

In an *extreme example*, you may feel that it is wrong for a person to come into your home, rob you, violate your wife and daughter, kill you, and then burn your house down to conceal the evidence. All that *sounds* wrong, doesn't it? But if you do not appeal to a higher authority, then you have no basis upon which to call those acts wrong. You can be violently opposed to them personally, but you cannot call them wrong. You might say, "This is wrong." But the criminal says, "No, it isn't. For me, it is right." So the criminal imposes his view on you with no consideration for absolute truth.

An excellent historical case in point is the extermination of the Jews by Hitler. If there is no absolute truth, then by what authority does anyone say what Hitler did is wrong? You say it was wrong, but Hitler says it was right. You are two human beings. You cancel each other out.

The same thing is true with less heinous examples, but which still have a major destructive impact on society. Take, for example, white collar crime on Wall Street. If there is no absolute truth, then the only thing wrong is getting caught. Also, selling drugs is a very lucrative profession. If there is no absolute truth, then the only wrong is getting caught. Again, padding defense contracts and milking the government out of millions of dollars—if there is no absolute truth, then the only wrong is getting caught. Also, adultery and marital infidelity—if there is no absolute truth, then the only wrong is getting caught. And on and on we could go!

Now we begin to catch a glimpse of the magnitude of the importance for society of accepting absolute truth. With a respect for absolute truth, you can build relationships and a society in which the innocent are protected. Without it, you cannot.

In an editorial in his newsletter, "Jubilee," Chuck Colson wrote:

> I have argued that we are living in an age advancing backwards. Where once stood a standard of truth and authority is now a fearsome freedom and autonomy. Modern men and women, hav-

ing elevated the individual above all else, hold no principles except their passions to plot their paths—nothing above themselves
to respect or obey, nothing to live or die for.

And, as I've argued, such egoism destroys individual character, in turn undermining the very institutions upon which our
society depends.

Our crisis, at root, is one of individual character. Therefore,
our principle task must be to reawaken those internal restraints
on passion and self-interest that are the very substance of character. Our task is moral education.[1]

There can be no moral education without moral absolutes.
The term, "moral," is obsolete, unless we can appeal to God for
His absolutes.

It is obvious that the disintegration of moral absolutes has a
destructive influence on society. It also has a major destructive impact on an individual's personal world view. Without absolute
truth, we have no certain knowledge of God. Without absolute
truth, we have no assurance of eternal life. Without absolute truth,
we have no hope.

There is a dire necessity for accepting absolute truth. In a free
society, it forms the basis for all civilization. For the individual, it is
the only thing which allows a world view that includes hope.

Our Response to Absolute Truth

We can see the terribly destructive nature of disobeying God's absolutes in the broad strokes of society, but disobedience in the
subtle things of the Christian life is also detrimental to our Christian experience.

There are two tasks of obedience on the road to happiness: the
elimination of the negatives and the introduction of the positives.
We must eliminate those things which we must stop doing—lying,
cheating, stealing, immorality, drunkenness—the glaring sins of
commission. But that only puts us half of the way there in experiencing the life which God wants us to experience. The other half
involves the introduction of the positives—that is, consistently loving God and others, even in the small things.

For example, it is one thing to stop beating your wife. It is another to love her as Christ loved the church and gave Himself up for her. It is one thing to stop yelling at your child. It is another to bring him up in the nurture and instruction of the Lord. It is one thing to stop swearing. It is another to "let no unwholesome word proceed out of your mouth, but only such a word as is good for building up others, according to the need of the moment, that it may give grace to those who hear" (Ephesians 4:29). It is one thing to stop spending your money carelessly. It is another to begin investing heavily in eternal things. It is one thing to stop being selfish. It is another to start loving others compassionately and giving your life for them.

All of God's truth is absolute truth. It is all intended by God to be followed. There are consequences for all of it when it is not followed. As Christians, our response to absolute truth is to be total. We will fail, but we will be better off for trying and failing than if we never tried at all.

The Bible is God's owner's manual for man. He knows how man works. He knows what will work well for man and what will harm man. If we operate according to the manual, our machinery will run well. If we violate the machinery, things break down. And that goes for the big things as well as the little things. That goes for new Christians, and that goes for mature Christians. Each of us has areas in which God is working in us, and we must respond as best we can to the truth, as we understand it. We must take the Bible seriously, from beginning to end!

The first step in responding to absolute truth is to understand that there is a price to be paid for ignoring it.

Second, we must catch a glimpse of the glorious goodness of absolute truth. There is a very close tie between the written Word and the Living Word. The written Word is a revelation of the Living Word. In John 1:1, Jesus is called the Word of God. "In the beginning was the Word, and the Word was with God, and the Word was God."

In Revelation 19 verses 6–11, we read:

> And I saw heaven opened; and behold, a white horse, and He who sat upon it is called Faithful and True; and in righteousness

He judges and wages war. And His eyes are a flame of fire, and upon His head are many diadems; and He has a name written upon Him which no one knows except Himself. And He is clothed with a robe dipped in blood; and His name is called The Word of God. And on His robe and on His thigh He has a name written, KING OF KINGS AND LORD OF LORDS.

To uphold the Word is to uphold God; to learn of the Word is to learn of God; to believe the Word is to believe God; to obey the word is to obey God. We must see the unfathomable riches of the Word of God! It brings us truth; it brings us light; it brings us love; it brings us life.

Chuck Swindoll writes in his book, *The Seasons of Life,* about the caveman in the comic strip "B.C." The man is leaning over the ever-present boulder, and on the rock is inscribed "Trivia Test," and B.C. is administering the exam to one of his deadpan prehistoric buddies.

"Here's one from the Bible," he says. "What were the last words uttered by Lot's wife?"

Without a moment's hesitation his fur-clad friend replies: "Fooey on your fanatical beliefs. I'm going to take one last look."

Whether or not that is what she really said, the bottom line of Mrs. Lot's philosophy of life could have been etched on her tombstone:

THERE'S NO NEED TO TAKE GOD SERIOUSLY.

I know of no philosophy more popular today. It's the reason we're caught these days in the do-your-own-thing syndrome. What a subtle web the spider of self has woven! Millions are stuck—and instead of screaming "I'm caught," they shout, with a smile, "I'm free!"

If you don't take God seriously, then there's no need to take your marriage seriously . . . or the rearing of children . . . or such character traits as submission, faithfulness, sexual purity, humility, repentance, and honesty.[2]

On the road to spiritual maturity, we must have the *Work of God,* and we must have the *Word of God.* We must hold to a high view of Scripture. God has given us absolute truth in the Bible. We must heed that absolute truth. We must respect it. We must understand the consequences of ignoring it. And we must catch a glimpse of its glorious goodness.

> All scripture is inspired by God and is profitable for teaching, for reproof, for correction, for training in righteousness; that the man of God may be adequate, equipped for every good work. (2 Timothy 3:16–17)

> *Father in Heaven, I believe that the Bible is Your Word. I commit myself to learning it well, so that I may be adequate, equipped for every good work. Bless me that from Your Word, I may know what I need to know, become what I need to be, and be able to do what I need to do. I pray to Your glory in Jesus' name. Amen.*

REVIEW

1. Truth Doesn't Change

The Bible is God's permanent record to us, telling us what we need to *know, be,* and *do.*

2. We Need Absolute Truth

Without absolute truth, we have no basis for *morals,* no knowledge of *God,* and no hope of *eternal* life.

3. Our Response to Absolute Truth

There are *bad* consequences for violating truth and *good* consequences for following it. Therefore, the only logical thing to do is *follow* it.

As a memory exercise, write in the missing words in the paragraphs below. Notice that they are the same words as the italicized words in the paragraph above.

1. **Truth Doesn't Change**

   The Bible is God's permanent record to us, telling us what we need to _____, _____, and _____.

2. **We Need Absolute Truth**

   Without absolute truth, we have no basis for _____, no knowledge of _____, and no hope of_____ life.

3. **Our Response to Absolute Truth**

   There are _____ consequences for violating truth, and _____ consequences for following it. Therefore, the only logical thing to do is _____ it.

RESPONSE

Questions for Group Discussion or Personal Exercises

1. Do you accept completely that the Bible is God's revealed, authoritative truth for the world?

2. What is an experience where God's Word served as a light for your path, giving you direction in a decision?

3. Identify an event from the newspaper where man was "doing what was right in his own eyes" and got caught.

4. What are some areas in your business or home life that are common practice among non-Christians but in which you won't participate because of Biblical convictions?

5. Name a benefit that being obedient to Scripture has brought you.

ELEVEN

PERSONAL COMMITMENT

$WkG + WdG + PC + OB + T\&T = Spiritual\ Maturity$

(PC = Personal Commitment)

I n his autobiography, Benjamin Franklin writes about his attempt to become morally perfect. He consulted himself and decided upon thirteen qualities which he felt embodied moral perfection. He decided to work on one quality for a week to perfect it, then move to the second, third, fourth, and so on. At the end of thirteen weeks, he expected to be morally perfect.

But, at the end of the thirteen weeks, he was not morally perfect. So he tried again for another thirteen weeks. At the end of that time, he was not morally perfect, so he tried again . . . and again, and again, and again.

At the end of his life, he had to admit that he never became morally perfect. He is reported to have commented, very astutely, however: "Though I never became morally perfect, I became a much better man for trying and failing then if I had never tried at all."

This is of interest to us because, as Christians, we too all long for moral perfection. God places that desire in our heart when we become a Christian. We want to lay aside, to leave behind the sins and weakness of the past, and to become a whole person. God then starts to work in us to begin to experience the process.

As the process begins, we must keep very clear what is the work of God and what is the work of man. To that end, let's review our opening premise:

> God does the work of God,
> Man does the work of man.
> Man cannot do the work of God, and
> God will not do the work of man.

As we said, we will make major headway in the Christian experience if we can get this straight, but we tend to reverse the process—to insist on assuming responsibility for the work of God while at the same time neglecting the work of man.

Our Actions

If God does the work of God and man does the work of man, then we must determine what is the work of man and stick with it!

The Scripture establishes this in Philippians 2:12–13: "Work out your own salvation with fear and trembling, for it is God who is at work in you both to will and to work for His good pleasure." God is at work in us, placing new desires, new longings, new values in our heart. He expects us to pick up on that—to feed those new desires, to reorder our lives to pursue the new life He has created in us. God is planting seeds in our heart. He asks *us* to water them, to fertilize the soil, and to tend and husband the new life.

We can kill the new desires by lack of attention, by failure to cultivate. Or we can strengthen the life and growth of the new desires by nurturing and feeding them. So we see it is God's will that we act on our new life.

Experiencing the will of God requires commitment on our part:

> I urge you, therefore brethren, by the mercies of God, to present your bodies a living and holy sacrifice, acceptable to God, which is your spiritual service of worship. And do not be conformed to this world, but be transformed by the renewing of your mind, that you may prove what the will of God is, that which is good and acceptable and perfect. (Romans 12:1–2)

To get the full impact of this verse, it can be helpful to look at it backwards. If we want to be a living demonstration of the fact that God's will is good and perfect and acceptable, we must not be conformed to this world. If we don't want to be conformed to this world, we must have our mind transformed. If we want to have our mind transformed, we must present our bodies as a living sacrifice to God. Experiencing the will of God requires total commitment on our part.

Taking the next step, we see that commitment requires ongoing attention.

> Do you not know that those who run in a race all run, but only one receives the prize? Run in such a way that you may win. And everyone who competes in the games exercises self-control in all things. They do it to receive a perishable wreath, but we an imperishable. Therefore I run in such a way, as not without aim; I box in such a way, as not beating the air; but I buffet my body and make it my slave, lest possibly, after I have preached to others, I myself should be disqualified. (1 Corinthians 9:24–27)

We see from this passage that Paul had spiritual goals (not without aim) and self-discipline (make my body my slave). In this we see the Biblical mandate for the third element in our equation: Personal Commitment.

The next question might be, "To what do we commit ourselves?"

Of course, there are the obvious things. We must read, study, and memorize the Bible. Ignorance is darkness. Knowledge is light. Falsehood is darkness. Truth is light. The Scripture says "the entrance of Thy word bringeth light," and "thy Word is a lamp unto my feet and a light unto my path."

The picture is of us walking along a path in darkness where the possibility of stumbling or getting lost is very real unless we can see where we are going. The Scripture shines light on our feet and on our path so that we do not stumble and do not get lost. We cannot hope to avoid stumbling; we cannot hope to avoid taking wrong turns; we cannot hope to avoid getting lost, unless we are shining the light of Scripture on the path of our life.

Another obvious thing we must do is pray. There are many reasons to pray: because God answers prayer (ask, and you shall receive, seek, and you shall find, knock, and it shall be opened to you); because it drives us to deeper spiritual understanding (if you ask anything according to My will I will answer). We must learn about the will of God, because prayer drives us to a deeper spiritual relationship with God.

God doesn't need our prayers. He wants our heart. But the only way He can have our heart is to require our prayer. God wants to live in close fellowship with us. If prayers are answered easily, then we tend to treat God as a vending machine—request in, answer out—and our depth of relationship with God is little closer than a relationship with a vending machine. With a vending machine, we expect the product when we put in the quarter. If the product doesn't come out, we kick or slam the door demandingly. "*Where's* our answer?!" God now serves man, rather than man serving God.

God doesn't need our prayers. He wants our heart, and the only way to have our close attention and affection is through prayer.

A third obvious thing we must do is worship the Lord. In the Gospel of John, we read, "God seeks those who will worship Him in spirit and in truth." In the Psalm 147:1 we read, "Praise the Lord! For it is good to sing praises to our God; for it is pleasant, and praise is beautiful."

Also, we are to develop a rich community with others who are committed to the Lord. We are not made to be able to make it alone. We need a support group—a place where we can belong.

However, the goal at this point is not to exhaust all the practical areas of Christian commitment, but rather to give a representative sample of the types of commitments a Christian must make. The main goal is to drive home the point that a Christian must make a commitment to his spiritual journey if he is to experience the depth of joy which God intends for His children.

However, reading your Bible, praying, going to church, memorizing Scripture, sharing your faith with others, helping others—all these things are good things, but in and of themselves, they are insufficient.

We all know people who do these things, and yet whose lives do not draw us to Christ. They have no compelling spiritual reality that creates in us a thirst to know God better. And worse, sometimes, they are cold and rigid, distant and legalistic. Not only do they not draw us to Christ, they nudge us away from Him.

There is no magic in fulfilling these responsibilities. A chapter a day doesn't keep the devil away.

You can have Bible reading, prayer, church attendance, and ministry without experiencing compelling spiritual reality, though you cannot have compelling spiritual reality without Bible reading, prayer, worship, and spiritual fellowship. We must see the total picture; otherwise, we will be tempted to think that if we go through these motions, that is all there is. That is not all there is.

That leads us to our final major consideration, and that is that our attitude and our perspective as we pursue God are all important. Attitude and perspective are what can keep us from "going through the motions" without any spiritual reality.

Our Attitudes

When we do these things (Bible study, prayer, etc.), we must probe below the surface of life. Our temptation is to live life on the surface. We want, by nature, two things from life: peace and prosperity. We want God to help us gain peace and prosperity. We want to know just enough of the Bible to make our lives go smoother, but not so much as to make us change our priorities. We don't want to get too serious, or it erodes our peace and prosperity. We may realize we need to give more money, or get involved in evangelism, or reach out to hurting people.

In his book, *When I Relax I Feel Guilty*, Tim Hansel quotes Wilber Rees:

> I would like $3 worth of God, please, not enough to explode my soul or disturb my sleep, but just enough to equal a cup of warm milk or a snooze in the sunshine. I don't want enough of Him to make me love a black man or pick beets with a migrant. I want ecstasy, not transformation; I want the warmth of the womb, not a new birth. I want a pound of the Eternal in a paper sack. I would like to buy $3 worth of God, please.[1]

We come to church and keep everything on the surface. News, weather, and sports. "Hot out, isn't it?" "Cowboys going to be any good this year?" "Who do you think is going to get elected?" And that may be okay at Sunday morning worship service where the emphasis is on our vertical relationship with God. But somewhere, sometime, we must be willing to get involved in the other ministries that get us below the surface of each others' lives.

Here is the main reality: Satisfaction in our spiritual life cannot be found on the surface. The very thing we want in life, meaning, is the very thing we are trying to get by pursuing peace and prosperity. However, peace and prosperity won't give meaning. So we are in a self-defeating circle.

Our Goals

We must be aware of what we're living for. I have deep longings. I feel their pull constantly. I long for deep, intimate relationships with God and with people. And I long for a life of significance.

I have pain, because those longings are not fulfilled completely or consistently. I give and receive love so imperfectly. I do not have the depth of relationship that I long for with God or with people. And I am so limited in my time, my talents, my treasures, that I do not sense the depth of significance that I long for in what I do.

Therefore, I am tempted to try to manipulate God and people to give me a greater sense of loving and being loved. I am tempted to manipulate circumstances to make me look better than I do to heighten my sense of significance. I try to take life into my own hands and be responsible for meeting my own needs.

We think, *Oh, if I only had that job, or that house, or that car, or that girlfriend, or that spouse, or that bank account, or that "whatever-it-is," I would be happy.* Then we get it, and it satisfies for a while, but pretty soon the longing comes back, and like a donkey after the carrot, we set off after the next thing thinking . . . *well, the last thing didn't satisfy for long, but this will be different . . . this will satisfy.*

But I deceive myself, because the depth of what I long for cannot be tasted here on earth. This world is fallen, and I cannot get out of it what I long for. What I really long for is heaven. But sometimes, I lose sight of that, and I am like the two-year-old who must get a vaccination shot for childhood diseases. I don't understand about disease and vaccination. All I know is that it hurts, and I want the pain to stop.

So what do we do when life hurts and we want the pain to stop?!? First, we must accept life's limitations. It is *okay* to long: God has given us longings, and has structured life so that *He* is the only thing that will satisfy those longings fully or permanently. So it is *okay* to long, but we must be patient and wait for heaven.

Next, accept that it is *okay* to hurt: Many different things in life may bring us pain. It may be very personal, such as family relationships, professional circumstances, financial calamity, lost personal goals, physical pain, spiritual frustration. Or it may be more global, such as moral disintegration in Western culture, famine, war, drugs, crime, prisons. With many of us, it is a combination.

It is not unspiritual to hurt. Read the Psalms—David hurt! Read the prophets—Elijah hurt! Isaiah hurt! Jeremiah hurt! Read the gospels—Jesus hurt! Read the epistles—Paul hurt! We need not paste on an artificial wax smile. Joy and pain are not mutually exclusive.

After we accept life's limitations, we must rest in God's love for us. We must let the longing and let the pain drive us to God. We must focus our lives on the only thing that matters anyway—loving God. The value of God's severe mercy is that when God rips everything out of our hands that we ever wanted, if we turn to Him with nothing left but Jesus, we find that Jesus is enough.

Most of the things I wanted out of life when I was a young man, I now realize I cannot have. When I realized that, I had a very important choice to make. I could either drop out of the ministry, get a divorce, buy a sports car, curl my hair, open my Hawaiian shirt to the navel and start living on the beach in southern California. Or, I could come to grips with what really satisfies and put all my hopes in that: loving God and loving others—living for the *only* two things that satisfy—and looking to heaven when all longings will be satisfied and all pain will cease.

So, when we're reading the Bible, when we're praying, when we're worshipping, when we're fellowshipping, when we're ministering, we must do it honestly! Not with a mindset of manipulating people, possessions, and positions to try to get momentary relief from our longings and our pain. But with a mindset of clinging to God for the only meaning that there is in life, and waiting for heaven when the longing will be completely fulfilled in Jesus and when the pain will cease.

Also, we must deal with the real issues of life—not putting on a "happy face," but with sincerity and transparency and tenacity, pursuing God!

However, in the meantime, don't let the disappointments of life keep you from enjoying what's pleasurable about life. There is much joy available in life. We can take joy in relationships with loved ones and friends, with music and literature, with athletic activity, with helping others, with beautiful scenery, with the color of flowers, with watching kittens play, with bass fishing, with woodworking, and with a hundred other things.

These things do not completely or permanently remove the deep longings and pain that provide so much basic motivation in life, but God has given us these things to enjoy. And we can enjoy them.

Allow yourself to be driven to God. What He wants more than anything from you is a relationship with you, fellowship with you.

He doesn't *need* your Bible study.

He doesn't *need* your money.

He doesn't *need* your prayers.

He *wants you,* a deep meaningful relationship with you. We have trouble imagining that.

Imagine that you adopt a child that has been physically and emotionally abused, left alone most of the time, and when the parents were around, they just wanted him out of the way. You long for a close relationship with this adorable, pathetic little child, but the child's perception of relationships is so distorted, he is incapable of receiving the amount of love and acceptance you want to give him. So he remains distant and aloof, playing with his own broken toys in his own little world, while all along, you want to love him, sit him in your lap, and tell him you are going to fly with him to Disney World.

So what do you do? You just love him, unconditionally, and wait for him to realize the type of relationship that you want to have with him.

It is not that we want too much in life. It is that we want far too little. We are far too willing to settle for the incomplete and temporary meaning that the world has to offer, rather than to turn them aside for the deep meaning and satisfaction in a relationship with the Creator of the universe.

He wants you to bring glory to Him by enjoying Him, forever. And if you can dare to believe this, the things which He pulls from your hands can be seen accurately as an act of great love, so He can fill your hands with Himself.

> I count all things loss in view of the surpassing value of knowing Christ Jesus my Lord, for whom I have suffered the loss of all things, and count them but rubbish in order that I may gain Christ. . . . That I may know Him, and the power of His resurrection. (Philippians 3:8, 10)

Our Father in Heaven, help me to care about my relationship with You. Draw me to Yourself. May my spiritual pursuits not be with gritted teeth, but a willing and consistent longing for You. Help me believe that all I long for is found in Christ, for when I believe that, I will seek Him faithfully. O Lord, strengthen me to draw near to You, and then, according to Your Word, draw near to me. Amen.

REVIEW

1. Our Actions

Spiritual *goals* and personal *commitment* are an essential part of the spiritual *growth* process.

2. Our Attitudes

As we commit ourselves to spiritual *disciplines*, a sincere and honest *attitude* is essential to keep us from "just going through the *motions*."

3. Our Goals

Our *goal* is *spiritual.* It is a *relationship* with God.

As a memory exercise, write in the missing words in the paragraphs below. Notice that they are the same words as the italicized words in the paragraphs above.

1. **Our Actions**

   Spiritual _____ and personal _____ are an essential part of the spiritual _____ process.

2. **Our Attitudes**

   As we commit ourselves to spiritual _____, a sincere and honest _____ is essential to keep us from "just going through the _____."

3. **Our Goals**

   Our _____ is _____. It is a _____ with God.

RESPONSE

Questions for Group Discussion or Personal Exercises

1. Has there been a point in your life at which you dedicated yourself to a lifetime pursuit of the goal of "knowing God?" If not, why not make that personal commitment to Him right now.

2. Choose one of the spiritual disciplines mentioned in the chapter and nurture it this week (for example, memorize a verse, read through a section of Scripture, set aside a specific time of prayer, etc.).

3. Do you agree that the practice of the spiritual disciplines at the surface level is not sufficient for spiritual growth? Why or why not?

4. Have you ever set "spiritual" goals for your life? Where would you like to be one year from today in your relationship with God?

TWELVE

OTHER BELIEVERS

WkG + WdG + PC + OB + T&T = Spiritual Maturity

(OB = Other Believers)

T he sea gull, on the surface, is a beautiful bird. They are like dazzling, white feathered kites sailing serenely against a brilliant blue background. Since the early seventies, with the publication of the book *Jonathan Livingston Seagull,* the sea gull has been immortalized as a symbol of freedom, grace, and beauty. Beneath the surface, however, the sea gull does not live up to its initial impression. In reality, it is a nasty, dirty little bird. Sea gulls scavenge on garbage and refuse. They will often eat the unprotected young of other sea gulls. They are loners, and if other gulls get too close to them, they attack. If a white gull happens to rub up against a bright color of wet paint, and become different in marking from the rest of the birds, the other birds may attack it and kill it. They have been unaffectionately referred to as "water pigeons." Underneath the surface of their dazzling beauty, they are aggressive, selfish, dirty, nasty, disgusting little birds.

Canadian geese, on the other hand, stand out in sharp contrast to the sea gulls. On the surface, they are not beautiful birds. They are short, squat, dumpy, brown, black and gray waddlers. But look below the surface, and you see a much different picture. Below the surface, the Canadian geese are marvelous birds. They mate for life. They are devoted to their young, never leaving them exposed to danger. Both the male and female care for the young, sharing the nesting duties and trading off on the responsibilities of feeding and guarding the young.

All the geese get along. In fact, some mothers will babysit for geese of another family. When it is time to fly south, the flock will not leave until all the young are strong enough to fly. If a very young goose or an older goose is unable to keep up the pace of the main flock and needs more rest, some other geese will stay behind with them until they are strong enough to make the flight. Then, as they travel, they fly in a "V" formation with the lead bird breaking the air for the others, and they trade off lead positions so that no one goose gets too tired. Though they are not streamlined and beautiful, beneath the surface, Canadian geese are marvelous, admirable birds.

As Christians, we need to ask ourselves, if we were birds, what kind of a bird would we be? Would we be a sea gull, or would we be a Canadian goose? In the great Audubon Society of life, God calls upon us to be not sea gulls but Canadian geese.

All Christians Need Other Christians

God does not want us to be able to make it alone. In fact, He has stacked the deck against us so that we *cannot* make it alone. We need others. We must have others. He does not want us to be sea gulls, but Canadian geese. He does not want us to be the Lone Ranger, but the Three Musketeers. He does not want us to be a rock or an island, but a bridge and an oasis. I need you, and you need me! God has seen to it.

In the pursuit which each of us undertakes to become like Christ, as each of us walks down life's road toward spiritual maturity, we must dispel the notion that we can do it alone. We must abandon the thought that we are self-sufficient. We must relinquish the impression that we do not need others.

We *need* others, and others *need* us. We will never become spiritually mature unless we open our lives to the ministry of others, and commit ourselves to developing community and involvement with other believers in Christ.

Let's look at the Biblical evidence for this requirement. In Ephesians 4:11–13, 15–16, we read:

> It was [Christ] who gave some to be apostles, some to prophets, some to be evangelists, and some to be pastors and teachers, to prepare God's people for works of service, so that the body of Christ may be built up until we all reach unity in the faith and in the knowledge of the Son of God and become mature, attaining to the whole measure of the fullness of Christ. . . . Speaking the truth in love, we will in all things grow up into him who is the Head, that is, Christ. From him the whole body, joined and held together by every supporting ligament, grows and builds itself up in love, as each part does its work. [NIV]

The body of Christ is built up as each individual part makes its contribution to the welfare of the whole. The more people who are contributing to the welfare of the whole, the healthier the body is. The fewer people who are contributing, the less healthy the body is.

In his remarkable book, *Fearfully and Wonderfully Made,* Dr. Paul Brand has written:

> Chemically, [the cells in my body] are almost alike, but visually, and functionally they are as different as the animals in a zoo. Red blood cells, discs resembling Lifesaver candies, voyage through my blood loaded with oxygen to feed the other cells. Muscle cells, which absorb so much of that nourishment, are sleek and supple, full of coiled energy. Cartilage cells with shiny black nuclei look like bunches of black-eyed peas glued tightly together for strength. Fat cells seem lazy and leaden, like bulging white plastic garbage bags jammed together.
>
> Bone cells live in rigid structures that exude strength. The aristocrats of the cellular world are the nerve cells.
>
> I believe these cells in my body can teach me about larger organisms: families, groups, communities, villages, nations—and especially about one specific community of people that is likened to a body more than thirty times in the New Testament. I speak of the Body of Christ, that network of people scattered across the planet who have little in common other than their membership in a group that follows Jesus Christ.

My body employs a bewildering zoo of cells, none of which individually resembles the larger body. Just so, Christ's Body comprises an unlikely assortment of humans.[1]

That's the body. A host of individuals, vastly different from each other, and each one playing an important part in giving life and purpose to the whole.

In another passage dealing with the inter-relatedness of Christians, we read: "Let us consider how we may spur one another on toward love and good deeds. Let us not give up meeting together, as some are in the habit of doing, but let us encourage one another . . ." (Hebrews 10:23–25).

We are to get together regularly to help one another live godly lives, and this mutual encouragement is not optional. It is essential. If we are to grow to maturity in Christ, we must have the ministry of mutual encouragement to one another. The Bible is filled with references to "one another."

- Romans 12:5—we are members of one another.
- Romans 12:10—be devoted to one another in brotherly love.
- Romans 12:10—honor one another above yourselves.
- Romans 15:5—be of the same mind with one another.
- Romans 15:7—accept one another.
- Romans 15:14—admonish one another.
- Romans 16:16—greet one another.
- Galatians 5:13—serve one another in love.
- Galatians 6:2—bear one another's burdens.
- Ephesians 4:2—bearing with one another in love.
- Ephesians 5:21—submit to one another out of reverence for Christ.
- 1 Thessalonians 5:11—encourage one another and build each other up.

One can see that we need other believers in order for us to prosper spiritually. We cannot make it alone. Our response to this reality, then, is twofold. First, we must give of ourselves to others, and second, we must be willing to receive from others when appropriate. No one can give unless someone is willing to receive.

We Must Be Willing to Give to Others

What should we be willing to give? First, we must give our spiritual gifts. Galatians 6:10 reads, "While we have time, let us do good to all men, but especially to those who are of the household of faith." Also 1 Peter 4:10 says, "as each one has received a special gift, employ it in serving one another, as good stewards of the manifold grace of God. And finally, Ephesians 4:11–16 says, as we saw earlier, that we must make our individual contribution in order for others to be able to grow effectively.

For example, when someone stands up in front of people and preaches, or teaches, or if someone disciples or counsels, it is obvious the contribution that they are making to the body of Christ. But the people who are gifted in this way are a minority. What about the majority of people who are not gifted in this way? We have allowed an elitist mentality to sneak into our churches in which, if we cannot preach, teach, disciple, or counsel, we think we can't do anything.

This is terribly unfortunate and has very harmful effects throughout the church. First, it keeps those who are not gifted in these ways from understanding their importance to the body of Christ and creates a feeling of insignificance. The second harmful effect it has is that the body of Christ does not benefit from their ministry. Both the individual and the body suffer.

Everyone is gifted to do something, and we need them desperately. Take, for example, the people necessary to conduct a normal weekly church service. Those who show love and mercy to children in the church nursery each Sunday morning, they are heroes. Those who teach the children, and make them feel important and wanted in the Sunday School classes, they are heroes. Those who unlock the doors on Sunday morning, and lock them up again on Sunday afternoon, they are heroes. Those who come here on Saturday evening to make sure the air conditioning is on and that everything is working, they are heroes. Those who cut the grass so that we can have an attractive facility, they are heroes. Those who stuff the bulletins and put mailing labels on the newsletter, they are heroes. Those who babysit the children so that the mothers of pre-schoolers can be ministered to, they are heroes. Those who are greeters, come early to set up your classroom, prepare communion elements, help in VBS and children's musicals, look out for visitors each Sunday to make them feel welcome, fix meals for families of new mothers, provide roses on the pulpit, take flowers to those in the hospital, write to the missionaries, open homes for youth parties, provide transportation for youth events, organize sports teams and events, operate the tape ministry, and scores of others—*they are heroes!*

Of course, this says nothing of all those who have ministries outside the church. You must see that what you do is serving God by serving men. You are needed. If all of you stopped doing your ministry Saturday night, the church would shut down Sunday morning. It is true: you *do not get* the recognition you deserve. Nevertheless, many people know and appreciate. And God knows and appreciates. And your reward in heaven will be just as great as Billy Graham's, because God only rewards faithfulness—nothing else. And you are what makes the church function.

In addition to giving our spiritual gifts, we must give our resources, our time, talents, treasures to those in need. These resources are not our own. They belong to the Lord for use as He sees fit.

Next, we must give our encouragement. Let me give you just one example to help us appreciate the power of encouragement. In his book entitled *Encouragement,* Larry Crabb tells this story:

> As a young person, I developed the humiliating problem of stuttering. I was elected president of my class in the ninth grade, and was called upon in a large assembly to be inducted during a ceremony. The principle said, "I, Larry Crabb, of Plymouth-Whitemarsh Junior High School, do hereby promise . . . etc." I said, "I L-L-L-L-Larry Crabb, of P—P—P—Plymouth-Whitemarsh Junior High School, do hereby p-p-p-p-promise . . . etc."
>
> The principle was sympathetically perplexed, my favorite English teacher wanted to cry, a few students laughed out loud, most were awkwardly amused, some felt bad for me—and I died a thousand deaths.

A short time later, I was called upon to pray during communion. Filled less with worship than stark terror, I became confused to the point of heresy. I remember thanking the Father for hanging on the cross, and praising Christ for triumphantly bringing the spirit from the grave. Stuttering throughout, I finally thought of the word "amen," (perhaps the first evidence of the Spirit's leading), said it, and sat down. I recall staring at the floor, too embarrassed to look around.

When the service was over, I darted for the door, hoping to escape before someone came to correct my twisted theology. I was too late. Jim Dunbar intercepted me. I recoiled as he put his arm around me. "Just endure this, and then get to the car," I said to myself. I then listened to this godly gentleman speak words that I can repeat verbatim today, more than twenty years later.

"Larry," he said, "there's one thing I want you to know. Whatever you do for the Lord, I'm behind you one thousand percent." Then he walked away.

Even as I write these words, my eyes fill with tears. Those words were life words. They had power. They reached deep into my being. They encouraged me![2]

We must give, serve, minister to others. We can give them our spiritual gift. We can give them our resources. And we can give them our encouragement.

We Must Be Willing to Receive from Others

We began this discussion by saying that there were two ways for us to respond to the reality that Christians need each other. First, we must be willing to give of ourselves to the needs of others. Second, we must be willing to receive from others when appropriate.

When you are in physical need, if someone offers to help in a time of need, accept it. They are offering because they care. They are doing what they have been gifted and prompted by God to do. If you are a new mother, and someone offers to bring you meals for a few days, accept it. If you are in financial need, and someone offers a gift of money, accept it. If you are in need of counsel, and someone offers to help, accept it. Unless there is some other reason not to accept it, that is the way things are supposed to work.

As it relates to your spiritual growth, if someone is offering something you need, accept it. If it is Bible knowledge, discipleship, training, and you don't know where to get what you need, start asking and looking around. Somewhere there is probably someone gifted to give you what you need spiritually.

As it relates to encouragement, if someone says something nice to you, don't deny it. Don't deprecate yourself, run yourself down, or invent a story showing that you don't deserve the encouragement. Accept it. Say, "thank you." In order for the body to work as it is intended to work, we must be willing to give, and we must be willing to receive.

John Donne, early in the seventeenth century, captured the spirit of the unity of the body of Christ when he wrote:

> No man is an island, entire of itself; every man is a piece of the continent, a part of the main; if a clod be washed away by the sea, Europe is the less, as well as if a promontory were, as well as if a manor of thy friends or of thine own were; any man's death diminishes me, because I am involved in mankind; and therefore never send to know for whom the bell tolls; it tolls for thee.[3]

We, in the body of Christ, are part of one another. We are not entire of ourselves. We were made by God to love and be loved, to give and receive ministry. The Bible gives us the mandate: other believers—we need them if we have any hope of growing to greater spiritual maturity. We must accept the mandate. We must give to others our spiritual gifts, our resources, our encouragement. And we must be willing to receive that which others have to give us. We must be willing to live together in mutual ministry and love.

> [Be] of the same mind, maintaining the same love, united in spirit, intent on one purpose. Do nothing from selfishness or empty conceit, but with humility of mind let each of you regard one another as more important than himself; do not merely look out for your own interests, but also for the interests of others. (Philippians 2:2–4)

Father in Heaven, help us to be kind to each other, in mutual ministry and love, so that we might all grow to maturity in Christ. Build into our hearts a care and a concern for others, that we might regard others as more important than ourselves. And as a result, may others see Jesus in us, and know that He is the reason for our love. In His name we pray. Amen.

REVIEW

1. All Christians Need Other Christians

We will never become spiritually mature unless we *open* our lives to the *ministry* to *others.*

2. We Must Be Willing to Give to Others

We can give others our spiritual *gift,* we can give them our *resources,* and we can give them our *encouragement.*

3. We Must Be Willing to Receive from Others

If we are in *need,* God may move *others* to meet our needs, but we must be willing to *receive.*

As a memory exercise, write in the missing words in the paragraphs below. Notice that they are the same words as the italicized words in the paragraph above.

1. All Christians Need Other Christians

We will never become spiritually mature unless we _____ our lives to the _____ to _____.

2. We Must Be Willing to Give to Others

We can give others our spiritual _____, we can give them our _____, and we can give them our _____.

3. We Must Be Willing to Receive from Others

If we are in _____, God may move _____ to meet
our needs, but we must be willing to _____.

RESPONSE

Questions for Group Discussion or Personal Exercises

1. Have you ever gone through a period in your Christian life where you tried to "go it alone?" What is your status today?

2. Why do you think God made us to need each other? What are the benefits of having to give and receive as it relates to personal growth?

3. Where are others contributing significantly to your spiritual growth right now? Make sure to thank them this week through a note or phone call.

4. Whom do you know that needs your involvement in his life? What is one thing you could give them this next week (time, advice, listening ear, helping hand)?

5. Sometimes it is easy to forget that serving others is also actually serving God. Have you ever quit helping someone because they weren't responding or appreciating your help? Would God want you to recommit some time to them, because it is actually service to Him?

THIRTEEN

TIME AND TRIALS

WkG + WdG + PC + OB + T&T = Spiritual Maturity

(T&T = Time and Trials)

E very fall the monarch caterpillar crawls out to the end of a twig, fashions a meticulously fabricated cocoon around itself, slams the door, and goes to sleep for the winter. The following spring something utterly miraculous happens—out crawls a butterfly! Somehow, by some power hidden deep in the mysteries of nature, a fat, low-slung, many-legged, ugly little creature of the earth is changed into a light, sleek, brightly-colored, beautiful little creature of the sky. *How* it happens and *that* it happens is one of the true glories of nature.

As we look closer at this mystery, however, to probe its secrets, we learn some startling truths. For example, if you happened to be walking past the low tree limb where the cocoon was attached, at just the precise moment the butterfly chose to emerge from its magic chamber, you would see quite a struggle going on—a struggle that would rend your heart and make you fear for the butterfly's life. The butterfly pushes and pulls and wiggles. Then falls back, exhausted. Then pushes and pulls and wiggles and falls back exhausted. And pushes and pulls and wiggles and falls back exhausted. And finally, after an agonizing struggle, pulls itself out of the cocoon.

As you watched this struggle for life—and indeed it is, for if the butterfly does not get out within a certain length of time, it will die in the cocoon—you would be tempted to come to the butterfly's rescue. You would be tempted to take some tweezers and pull back the opening ever so slightly to let the butterfly out of its potential coffin.

Well-meaning as such a gesture would be, that very kind gesture would seal the doom of the butterfly. For it is the very struggle to get out of the cocoon that gives the butterfly the developed strength in its wings to fly. If the butterfly does not struggle to get out of the cocoon, it is condemned to crawl the twigs, unable to fly, until it starves to death or becomes dinner for a neighboring bird.

Both time in the cocoon and trials struggling to get out of the cocoon are essential to transform the ugly little caterpillar into a beautiful little butterfly. Time and trials are both necessary to transform a worm, condemned to inching its way along the underbrush of life, to a lovely winged creature able to take to the heavens.

Just as it is in the natural realm with butterflies, so it is in the spiritual realm with children of God. God wants us to undergo continuous transformation, from creatures of the physical realm to creatures of the spiritual realm, from creatures of the world to creatures of the heavens, from creatures of time to creatures of eternity. With our bodies on earth, God wants us to live with our minds on heaven.

And, just as it takes "time and trials" to transform a caterpillar into a butterfly, so it takes time and trials to transform a child of God from one whose interests and values and affections are on earth, to one whose interests and values and affections are on heaven.

There is a teaching afoot that says if you are in God's will, you will not have trials. You will not have physical problems, or financial problems, or relationship problems. It teaches that if you have enough faith, God will heal you of those things. It teaches that if you claim what you want as though it were already true, it will become true. Yet, is this teaching true?

Time and Trials in Scripture

As we look at some of the fundamental passages in Scripture, we will see that is not true. In Psalm 119, we read:

> Before I was afflicted I went astray,
> But now I keep Thy word. (v. 67)
>
> It is good for me that I was afflicted,
> That I may learn Thy statutes. (v. 71)
>
> I know, O Lord, that Thy judgments
> are righteous,
> And that in faithfulness Thou hast
> afflicted me. (v. 75)

This passage teaches very clearly that the Lord allowed David to be afflicted for the purpose of maturing him. We see also in 2 Corinthians 4:8–11, 16–18 that Paul suffered tremendously:

> We are afflicted in every way, but not crushed; perplexed, but not despairing; persecuted, but not forsaken; struck down, but not destroyed; always carrying about in the body the dying of Jesus, that the life of Jesus also may be manifested in our body. For we who live are constantly being delivered over to death for Jesus' sake, that the life of Jesus also may be manifested in our mortal flesh. . . . Therefore, we do not lose heart, but though our outer man is decaying, yet our inner man is being renewed day by day. For momentary, light affliction is producing for us an eternal weight of glory far beyond all comparison, while we look not at the things which are seen, but at the things which are not seen; for the things which are seen are temporal, but the things which are not seen are eternal.

Again, in James 1:2–4, we see, "Consider it all joy my brethren when [not if] you encounter various trials, knowing that the testing of your faith produces endurance. And let endurance have its perfect result, that you may be perfect and complete, lacking in nothing." Trials produce endurance, endurance produces maturity.

Finally, we see in 1 Peter 2:18–21:

> Servants, be submissive to your masters with all respect, not only to those who are good and gentle, but also to those who are

unreasonable. For this finds favor, if for the sake of conscience toward God a man bears up under sorrows when suffering unjustly. For what credit is there if, when you sin and are harshly treated, you endure it with patience? But if when you do what is right and suffer for it you patiently endure it, this finds favor with God. For you have been called for this purpose, since Christ also suffered for you, leaving you an example for you to follow in His steps.

God's will includes suffering, and Christ suffered, leaving us an example of how we are to suffer. Verse 17 says that we may suffer for doing right. Christ suffered, we read in 1 Peter 4:1, and we should arm ourselves for the same purpose. Chapter 4:12–16 indicates that we can glorify God in our suffering, and finally in 5:10–11, we see that suffering will be used for strength and maturity.

We must dispel the notion that the Christian life does not include suffering. Otherwise, it will distort our perspective, it will confuse us, it will frustrate us, it will cause us to think there is something wrong with us. Not only does the will of God include trials, it includes trials over time. You cannot have one bad day, and wake up the next day spiritually mature.

In his book, *Principles of Spiritual Growth,* Miles Sanford writes:

A student of his school asked the President whether he could not take a shorter course than the one prescribed. "O yes," replied the President, "but then, it depends upon what you want to be. When God wants to make an oak, He takes a hundred years, but when He wants to make a squash, He takes six weeks."[1]

If you want to be a spiritual squash, you can make it in a hurry. But if you want to be an oak, you must sink your roots deep and lay in for the long haul.

In Luke 2:52, we read that Jesus kept increasing "in wisdom and stature, and in favor with God and men." He waited until He was thirty to minister. He experienced growth over time.

In a similar vein, in Romans 12:1–2, we read, "Do not be conformed to this world, but be transformed by the renewing of your mind." Growth over time. In 1 Corinthians 3:6, Paul writes, "I planted, Apollos watered, God gave increase." Growth over time.

One of the qualifications for an elder, a spiritual leader in the church, is that he not be a new convert (1 Timothy 3:6). Growth over time.

You cannot be holy in a hurry!

Biblical Examples

Perhaps the most vivid and heartening way to grasp this truth is to see it fleshed out in the lives of some of the giants of the Scripture. Joseph, for example, was given by God reason to believe that God was going to use him in an extraordinary way. Yet each time he tried to do something right, it backfired on him, circumstantially, and he paid dearly for it.

He tried to get his brothers to shape up, so he told them about the dreams he had. He shared his vision of sheaves of grain bowing down to him, and the sun, moon, and stars bowing down to him, indicating God was going to cause Joseph to rule over them. They didn't like it, and Joseph paid for it. They considered killing him, though they finally just sold him as a slave.

He tried to do the right thing by resisting the advances of Potipher's wife. She didn't like that, and Joseph paid for it. She had him imprisoned. He tried to do the right thing in prison, but the man he befriended forgot about him, and Joseph paid for it, staying in prison for another two years.

Finally, God plucked him out of the prison and set him over the entire nation of Egypt.

God gave him promises, but between the time that Joseph received the promises and the time they were fulfilled was probably at least ten years—easily more. During that time, God was putting him through the types of experiences he would need in order to gain the strength of character, the sense of right and wrong, the compassion for others, and the vision for the future that he would need in order to be a leader.

In a second example, David was anointed by Samuel to be king over Israel. But between the time he was anointed until he sat over all of Israel was fourteen years. During that time, rather than living like a prince, he was running from cave to cave like a common criminal, trying to keep Saul from lopping his head off.

During that time, God was putting him through the types of experiences he would need in order to gain the strength of character, the sense of right and wrong, the compassion for others, the vision for the future that he would need in order to be a leader.

In the New Testament, Paul was spoken directly to by Jesus. He told him that He was going to use Paul to take the message of salvation to the Gentile world. From the time Paul was given that promise until the time that he went even on his first missionary journey was fourteen years. And during that time, Paul sewed tents, lived in the desert, and had unsatisfying experiences with Jewish Christians in Jerusalem.

During that time, God was putting him through the types of experiences he would need in order to gain the strength of character, the sense of right and wrong, the compassion for others, the vision for the future that he would need in order to be a leader.

If it is true of the spiritual giants of the Bible, it must be equally true for us. Growth takes time, and it takes trials. We cannot be holy quickly or easily.

Our response to these realities, then, must be a cultivation of patience. Patience isn't one of the stronger virtues for most of us. I'm afraid my ultimate character was revealed at an early age when someone told me that the pit of a peach was a seed, and that if I planted it, it would grow into a peach tree. So I raced out to the sand box outside my home and planted the peach pit. I waited anxiously until the next day when I raced out to see my peach tree. There was no peach tree. In a fit of anger, which I remember clearly to this day, I ripped the peach pit out of the sand and threw it as far into the adjoining field as my little arm could throw it. I have been struggling since then to be patient.

The writer to Hebrews says that we must run with patience (endurance) the race that is set before us (12:1).

In addition to patience, we must persevere. Passive patience is not what is called for. Active patience fits the need. We *will* fail. And when we do, we must get back up and try again. The person is not a failure who falls down, but who refuses to get up. How many times? Seven times seventy, as many times as it happens, that is how many times God will forgive you, so that is how many times you must forgive yourself.

No one enjoys failure, but God can make failure the back door of success. He did for Joseph, He did for David, He did for Paul, and He can for us.

We Need an Eternal Perspective

In *30 Days to Understanding the Bible,* I describe an event which is appropriate to describe here. My wife, Margie, and I went to a professional dog show once. There was competition for looks and breeding, and best of show, but the competition which captured our attention was the obedience trials.

These trials, which took place within a large, square green of closely mowed grass, were particularly interesting. Several tests of obedience were displayed. One at a time, the dogs had to start running, stop, change directions, sit, stay, and return to their master, following a prescribed course that took them all over the lawn, without any verbal commands, only hand signals.

The dogs had to select, out of a pile of "dumbbells," one wooden dumbbell which their master had handled. The dumbbell was identical to all the others except for its identification number. On command, the dogs had to jump back and forth over a high, solid wooden hurdle; again, only hand signs were used. The dogs were required to lie down in the center of the lawn, and upon being told to "stay," were required to remain there for a number of minutes, while being totally ignored by their master, who was out of sight behind a canvass.

Two dogs in particular stood out. One was a large, white German Shepherd. He was an eager, grinning, fun-loving dog, but not fully trained. While enduring one of the "sit-stay" commands, he spied a cottontail rabbit hopping at leisure around the back edge of the lawn. With eyes riveted in utter absorption on his rodent treasure, he began whining absent-mindedly and started to tremble.

As though deliberately baiting him, the rabbit began cavorting playfully around the base of a mesquite bush.

One final tantalizing hop was more than the shepherd could endure, and, as though shot out of a cannon, he exploded in the direction of the rabbit. Both disappeared into the bush, not to be seen in public again. While entertaining to watch, the dog was a flamboyant failure.

Untrained, he did not yet attain to that marvel of harmony and communication that exists between skillful trainer and well-trained dog.

In contrast to the white German Shepherd was a glorious, silky Golden Retriever. The retriever's excellence was as great as the shepherd's failure. Obedience to every command was instantaneous and perfect. Before, during, and after each command, the eyes of the retriever were fixed devotedly on the young girl who was his owner and trainer. After each drill the dog would return to her side, and with head up, tongue hanging out, panting, stare into her eyes for the next command.

After all the dogs had gone through the trials, all the trainers and canines lined up for the awards. Fourth prize went to a Springer Spaniel, third to a German Shepherd, and second to a black Lab. All during this time, the Golden Retriever sat obediently beside his master, looking up into her eyes.

Finally, first prize went to this marvelous dog and the girl who trained him. A polite ripple of applause washed through the audience. Then crowd and contestants began to disperse. As they did, a marvelous thing happened. The girl wheeled to face her dog, squealed with delight, and began clapping her hands together excitedly. At this, the dog lunged up toward the girl's face in a desperate attempted to lick her in the mouth. She laughed and pushed him back. He tried again. She began running toward her car, laughing, clapping in unbridled joy as her dog barked and jumped and circled around her all the way, sharing completely in her joy.

Chills played up and down my spine as I watched in undisguised admiration, the joy, the intimacy, the trust, the devotion, and the adoration that flowed between dog and girl.

The intelligence, athletic ability, courage, and personality latent within this dog was developed to a higher degree, and displayed more effectively, than any other dog I have ever seen. I thought, *this is the highest good to which I have ever seen canine life elevated.* He was a marvel—a tribute to himself. But everyone knew that the skill, intelligence, insight, patience, and personality of the owner were also on display. A lesser trainer could not have gotten so much from her charge. Glory to the dog! Glory to the owner!

Had that dog been left to his own world, he would have been just a dog, an ignorant slave of his basic instincts to eat and bark.

There were surely times in the training process when the dog was unhappy. He wanted to quit, to run away. There were times when the owner wondered if he would ever learn. Before the training process was completed, the dog would gladly have been dismissed. But after the training process, the dog was happier and more fulfilled at its master's side than anywhere else in the world. The dog received that which it most wanted out of life from its relationship with its master.

How like God and man this is! If we cast ourselves in utter devotion on our "heavenly master," He will enlarge, expand, and develop us so that we achieve our highest good as a human being—to the satisfaction of man and the glory of God.

But the opposite is true. If we don't, life is frustrating and confusing.

The whole point in obedience trials is to have the dog show instantaneous and total obedience, even when it doesn't accomplish anything inherently significant. Then, when the dogs have proved themselves in the trials, the owner can take them out into a real situation and know that they can be trusted.

The same thing is true in our spiritual lives. God puts us to the test in little things, which don't always make any sense at all. If we prove ourselves faithful, He knows He can use us in the bigger things.

In the course of training, the dog can become confused, bewildered, sometimes even frightened. But finally, he learns, and each new thing learned elevated the dog to a higher existence and deepened its relationship with its master.

So it is with God. He wants to elevate us to a higher existence and deepen our relationship in the process. Many of us forfeit a deeper relationship with God because we won't be obedient in the little things over the long haul. And many of us forfeit being used by Him in a significant way because we refuse to be faithful to Him in the little things over the long haul. There's no trick to being a squash. But God wants you to be an oak.[2]

C. S. Lewis paints another image:

Imagine yourself a living house. God comes in to rebuild that house. At first, perhaps, you can understand what He is doing. He is getting the drains right and stopping the leaks in the roof and so on . . . But presently, He starts knocking the house about in a way that hurts abominably and does not seem to make sense. What, on earth, is He up to? The explanation is that He is building quite a different house from the one you thought of . . . throwing out a new wing here, putting on an extra floor there, running up towers, making courtyards. You thought you were going to be made into a decent little cottage: but He is building a palace.[3]

This is the process which God takes us through to make us mature in the five key areas: God, others, self, perspective, and purpose. It takes personal commitment, the work of God, the word of God, other believers, and time and trials. If all of these are present in sufficient quantity, the believer will become spiritually mature. Leave one of them out, and the believer will not be spiritually mature.

Consider it all joy, my brethren, when you encounter various trials, knowing that the testing of your faith produces endurance. And let endurance have its perfect result, that you may be perfect and complete, lacking in nothing. (James 1:2–4)

Help me, Dear Lord, to see time and trials as You see them. May I be strong, and go through trials Your way. And may they have their intended result, that I may be perfect and complete, lacking in nothing. In Jesus' name. Amen.

REVIEW

1. Time and Trials in Scripture

The Bible teaches that *trials* over a period of *time* are used by God to bring us to spiritual *maturity*.

2. **Biblical Examples**

The spiritual *models* in the Scripture developed mature *character* through the "time and trials" *process*.

3. **We Need an Eternal Perspective**

We must see "time and trials" as God sees them, as producing spiritual *benefits* and heavenly *reward* that cause them to be *justified* in comparison with the suffering.

As a memory exercise, write in the missing words in the paragraphs below. Notice that they are the same words as the italicized words in the paragraph above.

1. **Time and Trials in Scripture**

The Bible teaches that _____ over a period of _____ are used by God to bring us to spiritual _____.

2. **Biblical Examples**

The spiritual _____ in the Scripture developed mature _____ through the "time and trials" _____.

3. **We Need an Eternal Perspective**

We must see "time and trials" as God sees them, as producing spiritual _____ and heavenly _____ that cause them to be _____ in comparison with the suffering.

RESPONSE

Questions for Group Discussion or Personal Exercises

1. Is it hard for you to accept that the will of God for you includes trials?

2. Relate an experience in your life where, after the struggle, you could see spiritual growth which was created by it. (Think of areas such as athletics, discipline of children, an exercise program, musical practice, etc.)

3. Have you lived long enough to see an area in your life where your faithfulness in "the little things" led to God's increasing your opportunities and responsibilities?

4. Which of your current daily routines appears to be an example of "little things"? What might God have in store for you if you continue to faithfully carry out those tasks?

5. Has this issue of time and trials been a particular "sticking point" between you and God? If so, what would be a practical way to express to God your acceptance of a trial or a prolonged delay?

SPIRITUAL SNARES

*As the Christian travels along the road
to spiritual maturity
in the five main areas,
there are six predictable snares
that he will step into
if he is not on guard for them.*

FOURTEEN

INTELLECTUAL INTIMIDATION

Men occasionally stumble over the truth,
but most of them pick themselves up and
hurry off, as if nothing had happened.

Winston Churchill

Some Christians silently worry about whether or not Christianity is true. I vividly remember making a serious attempt to defect from the faith a few years after I had become a Christian. When I first became a Christian, it was during a time of personal turmoil, and like a drowning man, I grabbed at the closest thing that I thought had a chance of saving me—that was Christianity. I had grown up going to church every Sunday until I got tall enough to look my mother in the eye. It was the only thing I knew. Later, however, I began to wonder if I had made the right decision. I began to fear that maybe Christianity wasn't true. After all, I had not analyzed all the alternatives before making my decision. Could Christianity really stand up to the test of severe scrutiny?

In his book, *Answering the Tough Ones,* David Dewitt has written:

"Could you be wrong?" Joe asked as he sipped a cup of coffee. His half-open eyes were trying both to examine me and screen

151

out the steam from his coffee at the same time. "I mean about Jesus—could you be wrong about Jesus being God and all that?"

As my mind scanned the evening's events, I wondered if Joe was asking an honest question. Our group had just completed an exciting discussion about life and God.

And it was quite a group! About seventy people had packed themselves into one of Baltimore's finest homes. There were Catholics, Protestants of various denominations, some Jewish people, and several agnostics. There were even some who believed in reincarnation—one told me he remembered my being a saloon keeper in Baghdad 2,000 years ago!

Joe (not his real name) cornered me at the coffee pot after the discussion. We had barely exchanged introductions when he asked me if I could be wrong about a statement I had made claiming that Jesus was God.

"Sure," I answered.

"Really?" His head jerked back. I wondered whether it was because of my answer or the hot coffee he had just swallowed. Joe's next question convinced me it was not the coffee.

"How about the Bible? Could you be wrong about it being God's word?" He straightened into a posture that seemed to say, "I dare you to answer that one." His eyes, wide open now, examined me like those of a trial lawyer. I wondered if the answer I had in mind would get me into trouble, but I barged ahead anyway.

"Of course I could be wrong about the Bible," I said. "Everything we know begins with some sort of faith. So, no one can be absolutely sure he's right." I paused to gauge Joe's response.

Because the February weather made the coffeepot corner a crowded place, Joe and I made our way back into the living room while we talked.

"You know something?" Joe continued as we sat down on an empty sofa. "I've never met a Christian who would admit that he could be wrong. I'm an evolutionist," he went on, "and I've decided that Jesus was wrong and so is the Bible. What do you think about that?"

Our Lord had a way of encouraging communication by answering a question with a question. So I tried it. "Tell me something, Joe. Could you be wrong—I mean about Jesus and the Bible? Could you be wrong about Jesus not being God and the Bible not being God's word?"

Joe's expression froze. Apparently caught off guard, he sat silent, his coffee cup leaning between his fingers and his teeth. After a few seconds, he answered, "Well . . . uh . . . of course, I could be wrong. As you say, nobody can be absolutely sure he's right . . ." His voice trailed off.

"Well, then," I suggested, "if I could be wrong and you could be wrong, are you willing to look at this with me and see if we can figure out what's right?"

Before we were finished, Joe invited me to have dinner with him and his wife. We set a date. After several exciting discussions, both Joe and his wife received Jesus Christ as their personal savior.

I recognized again that something almost mysterious happens in people when they are willing to consider the real issues.[1]

The Christian does not have to fear any intellectual scrutiny. The Christian need not sit in a corner, eyes dark, cheeks sunken, wringing his hands, wondering if Christianity is really true, and dreading the possibility that somebody might ask "The Unanswerable Question." After 2,000 years, no one is going to ask a question that will bring Christianity crashing down. The Christian faith will stand up in the face of all evidence, no matter how hard it is pressed to the wall. In fact, the harder it is pressed to the wall, the brighter the light shined on it, the better Christianity comes out. Truth need fear no examination. Rather, truth welcomes examination, and Christianity is no exception. The halls of heaven are lined with people who set out to prove Christianity false and ended up bowing their knees and crying out, "Lord Jesus, save me!"

But it is a snare nevertheless—unless we understand how solid the Christian faith is—that someone will ask us a question that seems reasonable and logical, and will plant seeds in our minds that will cause doubt to grow, and bear the fruit of rejection—perhaps against Christianity as a whole, or some part of it essential to a satisfying spiritual experience. This need never happen, and we will see why in this chapter.

The Intellectual Attack

The Attack on Creation

There are several predictable questions which people will ask which, if we are not prepared, could catch us off guard.

Question: "How can you believe in Creation in the face of all the scientific evidence to the contrary?"

Answer: There isn't "all the scientific evidence to the contrary." There is plenty of evidence to suggest that the currently accepted theory of evolution is impossible—unworkable. There are so many problems with evolution that scientists are having to stand on their heads to cover the academic, scientific, and intellectual holes in it. There is a tremendous problem with the fossil records supporting evolution. The testimony of mutations upon which evolution rests is terribly suspect. No mutation has ever proved beneficial, and no mutation has ever produced another kind of thing—just a variation of the same thing.

And there is not enough time for evolution to have occurred. At first scientists speculated that it took "X" number of millions of years for certain progress in evolution to have been made, but now the studies are suggesting that "X" isn't anywhere near enough time. Now scientists are talking about spontaneous evolution, in which a frog gave birth to a duck instead of a tadpole. That is an overstatement, of course, but regular evolution demands more time than we can defend, so evolutionists are having to come up with some explanation to validate their conclusions.

When you hear the academic community and the so-called specialists on public television, and elsewhere, they will lead you to believe that evolution is virtually airtight. In fact, educators are even going so far as to talk about the "fact" of evolution, rather than the "theory" of evolution. However, when you listen to "leading edge" scientists, you see that the academic community is lamentably and embarrassingly behind on their thinking. Cutting-edge scientists are now trotting out a "Rose Bowl Parade" of lethal problems with the theory of evolution.

The goal at this point isn't to show all the problems with evolution. It is simply to say that evolution isn't fact . . . it's theory. It has monstrous problems within it. You may ask, "Well then, why do all the scientists believe it?" The answer is, first, that not all scientists do believe it. Second, those who do must either believe evolution or they must believe divine creation. Since they have already made up their mind that they do not want to believe in divine creation, the only alternative available to them is evolution.

It is as Winston Churchill said at the start of this chapter: "Men occasionally stumble over the truth, but most of them pick themselves up and hurry off, as if nothing had happened."[2]

D. M. S. Watson, a zoologist, once wrote, "Evolution is a theory universally accepted, not because it can be proved to be true, but because the only alternative, special creation, is clearly impossible."[3]

Why is it impossible? Because the scientific evidence renders it impossible? Absolutely not! There is credible scientific explanation for all the scientific data from a "creationist" viewpoint. The evolutionists reject creation, not because of the incontrovertible evidence, but because they have decided ahead of time that they do not believe in supernatural creation. Therefore, they must come up with another explanation for "what is." Evolution is the best current explanation, therefore, they believe evolution.

It is as Paul wrote in Romans 1:19–22:

> That which is known about God is evident within [men]; for God made it evident to them. For since the creation of the world His invisible attributes, His eternal power and divine nature, have been clearly seen, being understood through what has been made, so that they are without excuse. For even though they knew God, they did not honor Him as God, or give thanks; but they became futile in their speculations, and their foolish heart was darkened. Professing to be wise, they became fools.

Back home, during basketball season, most of the schools in the part of Indiana where I am from root against each other during the post-season tournaments. Whenever Warsaw High School plays, most of the schools root for whomever is playing against Warsaw. It isn't that they are "for" that other team. It is that they are "against" Warsaw. That is much the same phenomenon that exists in the scientific community. It isn't that all the scientists are "for" evolution, so much as they are "against" creation, and evolution is the only present alternative.

A brilliant scientist, Robert Jastro, is a geologist, astronomer, and agnostic. Nevertheless, he said:

> Perhaps the appearance of life on earth is a miracle. Scientists are reluctant to accept that view, but their choices are limited. Either life was created on earth by a being outside the grasp of scientific understanding, or it evolved on our planet spontaneously through chemical reactions in non-living matter lying on the surface of the planet. The first theory places the question of

the origin of life beyond the reach of scientific inquiry. It is a statement of faith in the power of a supreme being not subject to the laws of science. The second theory is also an act of faith. The act of faith consists in assuming that the scientific view of origins is correct without having any evidence to support that belief.[4]

If you believe in creation, you believe it by faith. If you believe in evolution, you believe it by faith!

Dr. Fred Hoyle, a highly regarded British scientist wrote an article entitled, "The New Scientist, The Bang in Astronomy." In it he says, "The latest data differ by so much from what theories would suggest as to kill the big bang cosmologies, but now because the scientific world is enamored by the big bang theory, the facts are ignored."[5]

In another article entitled "The Tailor-made Universe," P. C. W. Davies asks, "Why does it fit so well? It looks like someone made the universe. I don't believe it was made, but it sure looks that way."[6]

Another newspaper article reads:

Intergalactic Ribbons of Blue Tie Up Astronomers in Knots

Two brilliant blue arcs stretching for hundreds of trillions of miles across distant galaxies have been discovered by astronomers who are puzzled by the discovery. What are these discoveries? They are arcs, portions of a circle, so geometrically perfect that there is no known or even conceivable explanation. "It looks like God created something like a long rope, cut it into a circle, and placed it in the heavens."

You have two options. The universe has a naturalistic explanation (and to take that approach violates the known laws of physics and gives no explanation from some of our observations most recent), or creation.[7]

We simply do not have to be intimidated by the intellectual community on scientific issues.

The Attack on the Bible

Question: "How can you believe the Bible when it has so many contradictions in it?"

Answer: The Bible doesn't have any contradictions in it. It has some variations that may appear on the surface to be contradictions, but upon further investigation, it is demonstrated that they are not contradictions. To solve most of the supposed contradictions, realize that two statements may differ from each other without being contradictory.

In his book, *Answers,* Josh McDowell writes:

> For example, the case of the blind men at Jericho. Matthew relates how two blind men met Jesus, while both Mark and Luke mention only one. However, neither of these statements denies the other, but rather they are complementary.
>
> Suppose you were at city hall talking to the mayor of your city and later, the chief of police. Later, you see your friend, Jim, and tell him you talked to the mayor today. An hour later, you see your friend John, and tell him you talked to both the mayor and the chief of police.
>
> When your friends compare notes, there is a seeming contradiction. But there is no contradiction. If you had told Jim that you talked only to the mayor, you would have contradicted yourself.
>
> Other passages appear contradictory because the translation of the original text is not as clear as it could be. Other times, they appear contradictory because we do not understand historical or cultural factors.
>
> While not all apparent discrepancies have a simple answer, there is no reason to accept that the Bible has any discrepancies.[8]

In most cases, if someone were to say to you, "How can you believe the Bible when it has all those contradictions?", if you were to respond, "Oh, really? I'm not aware of any. If you could give me an example, I'll get the solution for you," you would stop the person in his tracks. Most people know of no contradictions from first-hand experience. They have just heard somewhere along the line that there were contradictions, and because they wanted to believe it, they grabbed hold of it. If you don't realize how flimsy their attack is, you can be intimidated by it. Just a little knowledge can give you great security.

The Attack on Miracles

Question: "How can you believe in miracles? I mean, the story of Jonah and the whale, for example, is pretty hard to . . . uh, swallow, so to speak!"

Answer: The real questions with miracles are whether God exists and whether He is active in people's lives.

If there is a God, what good is He if He can't do miracles? The very definition of God is that He is greater than man. Either you must say that there is no God, or you must admit that He can do miracles. Just because miracles do not commonly happen, does not mean that they cannot happen.

Miracles did not occur regularly throughout the Bible as most people suppose. They were concentrated in several historical periods. The vast majority of believers throughout history have never seen a miracle. So it is no breach of normality for us, today, never to have witnessed a miracle on the scale of Jonah and the whale. The real issue isn't miracles; it's the existence of God. If you're going to have a God, then what is the problem with a miracle or two? If you want to throw away miracles on the basis that they simply can't happen, you are throwing away God without adequate support from the evidence.

In summary, my purpose is not to bring up all the difficult questions about Christianity and answer them fully. My purpose is to bring up sample and typical questions which, on the surface, can appear intimidating. But once investigated, they disappear like the morning dew.

You hear horror stories of professors in colleges destroying the faith of students. In a nearby college which was founded by a major denomination, the Bible professor asked how many students actually believed that the Bible is true. A few brave souls raised their hands. The professor then announced that his goal was, that at the end of the course, they would no longer believe it.

The stories may be true, but not because Christianity is intellectually inferior. If the stories are true, it is simply because the professor has studied his side very thoroughly, and the student hasn't. Add to that the intimidation factor in the classroom, and the professor has a profound advantage. Nevertheless, the professor, in that instance, is like the town bully. He is always picking on those smaller than himself. Let him pick on someone his own size, and you would see quite a different result and a much humbler professor.

There is no intellectual threat to Christianity. Period.

Our Intellectual Response

When you discuss specific issues, Christianity stands up against all attacks. The secularists, the evolutionists, and the atheists have no answers for the most fundamental questions of life. Their philosophical foundation is inadequate. Why not put the burden of proof on them?

The secularist has no adequate explanation for the existence of the universe. The secularist has no adequate answer to man's longing for a sense of purpose in life. The secularist has no satisfying response to the fundamental questions which sooner or later everyone asks, "Who am I? Where did I come from? Why am I here? Where am I going?"

What are some examples of the kinds of problems the secularist faces with his own position? First is the existence of the universe. The secularists say that the universe began with a big bang. Several things cooked for a few billion years, and life started. It has been evolving ever since.

Oh, yeah? Well, answer this: Where did the "matter" that exploded in the beginning come from? Are you saying that "matter" is eternal? That "matter" always existed? If that is what you are saying, don't ask me to believe it. It simply isn't adequate. When you boil it down, the secularist is saying that the universe as we know it today is explained by this formula: *Nothing + the impersonal + time + chance = everything we see today*

This formula is presented by Francis Schaeffer in his writings. There are several key questions we need to ask. How can something come from nothing? How can the personal come from the impersonal? There's not enough time to explain everything, and the odds against the complexity of our universe being accounted for by time and chance are too great.

In his book *The Church at the End of the Twentieth Century*, Francis Schaeffer tells of Murray Eden at MIT who was working with a high speed computer to answer this question: "Beginning with chaos at any acceptable amount of time up to eight billion years ago, could the present complexity of the universe come about by chance? So far the answer is absolutely NO."[9] And very few scientists think the earth is older than 8 billion years.

To get a feel for the odds against our universe coming about as the result of "nothing + impersonal + time + chance . . .," there is as good of a chance that a monkey sitting at a typewriter, hitting the keys at random, could accidently produce the complete works of Shakespeare, as there is that the universe can be explained by chance.

When the secularist attacks Christianity, he is not doing so from a position of strength. The only strength the secularist has is that most scientists agree with him. That doesn't mean he is right. But it strengthens his position in society, nevertheless.

The second problem the secularists have is explaining away the divine link to God. By giving up a divine link from man to God, the secularist destroys any basis for meaning to life and to mankind. Man is reduced to an animal or a biomechanical machine. He has no inherent meaning greater than a rock or a cactus. As a result, we have begun treating each other like animals and like biomechanical machines. There is no moral structure to which people hold, since they have thrown off God, and now the law of the jungle is becoming the law of the land: the survival of the fittest. The result is a disintegration of the things which hold society together and a diminishing of the quality of life for everyone.

Now, I do not want to suggest that there are simple answers to every question raised by the non-Christian. There are some very difficult problems with the Christian world view. We want a flawless body of belief—a perfect "something" to believe. We want something to believe where all the answers are reasonable and logical, and where we have all the answers. However, we do not have that option. There are difficulties and questions about the complexities of this life that are not easy to deal with. But there are even greater difficulties outside of Christianity.

We want a world view (an understanding and explanation of things) that doesn't have any major problems or difficulties with it. But every world view has problems and difficulties associated with it. To say that Christianity has inherent difficulties does not at all suggest that you will solve them by rejecting Christianity. The problems with the atheist's world view are ten times as hard to deal with as the problems with Christianity.

Our Personal Response

Now, we come to the really important conclusion. If all this is a matter of intellectual curiosity, we can debate it until the cows come home, end in a stalemate, shrug our shoulders and say, "Well, that was interesting, but I guess there's no way to know for sure." Then we can go home and think about something else.

But it is certainly more than an intellectual debate to me. I want to know if it is safe to die. I want to know if there is a God. I want to know if there is something I can do to make everything okay when they lay me six feet under and throw a shovel full of dirt in my face. I'm not content to dismiss all this as an interesting intellectual debate. I'm not content to leave this as a stalemate. I want to press through the stalemate, and if it is not possible to prove things, then I want to know what the probabilities are. If we cannot prove God or disprove Him, I want to know what the probabilities suggest as to whether or not He exists. If we cannot prove that the Bible is the Word of God, then I want to know what the probabilities are that it might be the Word of God.

I'm not going to jeopardize my eternal destiny by deciding ahead of time that there is no God, and then interpreting all the evidence in light of that presupposition. I'm going to hold out the possibility that there is a God. Then I am going to look at the evidence with an open mind and let the evidence tell me whether or not there is a God. There are no certainties, but there are probabilities. And when I go with the probabilities, I end up kneeling at the cross, and saying, "Lord Jesus, save me. Lord Jesus, I'll live for you." There isn't a single logical flaw in that decision, and there isn't a single body of information or evidence to suggest convincingly that it isn't probable.

Of course, we understand that "probabilities" don't convince anyone to become a Christian. The Bible says that the Holy Spirit must illumine our minds to understand spiritual truth (1 Corinthians 2:9–16), and that no one comes to Christ "unless the Father who sent me draws him" (John 6:44). Nevertheless, the Holy Spirit uses truth, and the truth is, probabilities can be used by the Holy Spirit to lead us to God.

Winston Churchill once said: "Truth is incontrovertible. Panic may resent it; ignorance may deride it; malice may distort it; but there it is."

We need not fear walking down the path of life and have someone jump out of the intellectual bushes and say, "Aha! . . . I bet you never thought of this!" We are secure. We have truth. And truth will stand any test. Don't worry about the strength of your faith. It's plenty strong enough to hold up against the closest scrutiny. Don't be intimidated by those who attack or ridicule your belief. You are secure in what you believe. It will stand up against any attack. Relax, rest, and enjoy the security which you have.

> How blessed is the man who finds wisdom,
> And the man who gains understanding.
> For its profit is better than the profit of silver,
> And its gain than fine gold.
> She is more precious than jewels;
> And nothing you desire compares with her.
> Long life is in her right hand;
> In her left hand are riches and honor.
> Her ways are pleasant ways,
> And all her paths are peace.
> She is a tree of life to those
>   who take hold of her,
> And happy are all who hold her fast.
> My son, let not [wisdom] depart from your sight;
> Keep sound wisdom and discretion,
> So they will be life to your soul,
> And adornment to your neck.
> Then you will walk in your way securely,
> And your foot will not stumble.
> When you lie down, you will not be afraid;
> When you lie down, your sleep will be sweet.
> Do not be afraid of sudden fear,
> Nor of the onslaught of the wicked
>   when it comes;
> For the Lord will be your confidence,
> And will keep your foot from being caught.
>   (Proverbs 3:13–26)

*Father in Heaven, thank You for making the truth under-
standable and believable. Thank You that we do not have
to commit intellectual suicide to be a Christian. Thank
You that it all makes sense. Help me to be secure and
confident in my faith, and help me to be eager to share it
with others. Amen.*

REVIEW

1. **The Intellectual Attack**

   Creation, the *Bible*, and *miracles* will all stand up under the attack of intellectuals.

2. **Our Intellectual Response**

   No world view is without *difficulties*. However, if you have not already made up your mind, there are *fewer* problems with the *Biblical* view than with the secular view.

3. **Our Personal Response**

   In the absence of proof, if we press through the *difficulties* to the *probabilities*, we end up kneeling at the cross of *Christ*.

As a memory exercise, write in the missing words in the paragraphs below. Notice that they are the same words as the italicized words in the paragraph above.

1. **The Intellectual Attack**

   _____, the _____, and _____ will all stand up under the attack of intellectuals.

2. **Our Intellectual Response**

   No world view is without _____. However, if you have not already made up your mind, there are _____ prob-lems with the _____ view than with the secular view.

3. Our Personal Response

In the absence of proof, if we press through the _____ to the _____, we end up kneeling at the cross of _____.

RESPONSE

Questions for Group Discussion or Personal Exercises

1. Have you ever had your faith in the Scriptures challenged by a fellow student, professor, co-worker, or family member? Did you feel prepared to respond?

2. Does it surprise you to hear evolution talked about as a theory rather than a fact? Why are scientists fearful of discussing evolution in terms of a theory?

3. Are there any areas in which you still feel intellectually intimidated about your faith?

FIFTEEN

MATERIALISM

Possessions weigh me down in life;
I never feel quite free.
I wonder if I own my things,
Or if my things own me?

Anonymous

S omeone said that Americans often spend money they don't have on things they don't need in order to impress people they don't like. Such is the bondage of materialism. If this were a purely secular affliction, we would not have to deal with it. Unfortunately, it afflicts believers and unbelievers alike. It clutches at our ankles and drags us to a stop in our spiritual walk unless we have the courage to stomp its twisted fingers into the soil. In the cover story of a financial magazine entitled *The Money Society*, we read:

> Money, money, money is the incantation of today. Bewitched by an epidemic of money enchantment, Americans in the eighties wriggle in a St. Vitus's dance of materialism unseen since the Gilded Age or the Roaring Twenties. Under the blazing sun of money, all other values shine palely . . .
> "I think people are being measured again by money rather than by how good a journalist or social activist or lawyer they are," says an investment banker.
> As a result, this banker is continually comparing himself with others to make sure he's okay. He schmoozes about compensa-

tion to try to determine if he makes more or less than the person he's talking to. But such conversations can be inconclusive, so when he visits friends or business acquaintances, he's continually sizing up the towels, the cars, the silver, with practically an auctioneer's eye, to see what he's worth by comparison.

"It frightens me to be sensitive to the idea that my neighbor just got a big-screen TV that's three inches bigger than mine," says the banker. "But that's something I look at."[1]

Money, money, money—the incantation of the day. The flame is personal desire, the fuel is a consumer society, and the wind is Madison Avenue and television, whipping us into a firestorm of materialism.

As mentioned earlier, Christians are not immune. When one falls into a pool of ink, he has difficulty not turning blue. We are in the ink bottle of a materialistic society, and we have difficulty not turning blue with materialism.

Have you ever noticed that someone born in Germany acts just like the Germans? Those born in Russia act just like the Russians. Those born in Egypt act just like Egyptians. And those born in America act just like Americans. We are all children of our society, products of our environment. Each different culture affords some benefits and some liabilities to a healthy Christian life. Our task as Christians, wherever we are from, is to take on the benefits and resist the liabilities of the culture in which we live.

In America, with the liability of materialism, one of the ultimate tests of a person's character is how he spends his money. The problem of money is summed up by Jesus. "No one can serve two masters. Either he will hate the one and love the other, or he will be devoted to one and despise the other. You cannot serve both God and money" (Matthew 6:24). Keying on the teachings of Jesus, Howard Hendricks of Dallas Theological Seminary has said, "teaching Biblical principles of giving is one of the greatest needs of the evangelical world. If you do not confront the issue of money, you are selling a person down the river in terms of discipleship. It is the acid test of a person's commitment to Christ."

In his book, *The Man in the Mirror*, Patrick Morely writes:

It is not a question of advisability, "You should not serve both God and money." That would be a priority choice.

It is not a question of accountability. "You must not serve both God and money," That would be a moral choice.

Rather, it is a question of impossibility. "You cannot serve both God and money." There is no choice; we each serve one, and only one, master. We are either a slave to God or a slave to money.[2]

Materialism is a disease—a potentially fatal disease for the Christian's spiritual life. It is particularly tricky for the Christians in America, because we often don't have to choose between material blessing and following the Lord, the way we might have had to in other times or other places. But money can trap us and rob us of our priorities, of our sense of purpose, and of our spiritual satisfaction, all the while we are pursuing an outwardly Christian lifestyle. We need to be aware of the danger of materialism. We need to understand what it is, what are the symptoms, the causes, and the cure.

Webster defines materialism as: "The tendency to be more concerned with material than with spiritual or intellectual values."

Christian materialism might be defined as the belief that satisfaction in life is most completely achieved when the Christian can possess the things he desires. It is not that he wants material possessions rather than Christ, but that he wants material possessions in addition to Christ. And at certain points in his life, he is willing to sacrifice obedience to Christ for the sake of material possessions.

That is a reasonable "working definition." Now, we need to go to the symptoms, to see if we might have the disease ourselves.

The Symptoms of Materialism

Here are some tell-tale signs of Christian materialism:

1. A sign of Christian materialism is, "getting into unmanageable debt." I'm not talking about a person perhaps having a loophole in his insurance and getting caught unexpectedly with very high hospital bills. I'm not talking about someone who has been out of work. I'm not talking about someone who is in the middle of circumstances beyond his control. I'm talking about unmanageable debt because of consumerism. It is a sign of materialism.

2. Another sign is "buying things you don't need or can't afford." When we purchase things we don't need or can't
   afford, rather than to live within our means or to look for
   higher ways of using our money, that is materialism.

3. Next, is "buying things for show—because of how it makes
   you look in the eyes of others." Clothes for show, a car for
   show, a house for show, jewelry for show. Motive is everything
   in the matter of materialism. Why do we buy what we buy?

4. Again, "buying things too soon." We make the decision to
   put off doing something right and good, so that we can
   buy something you want now. I know a gentleman who
   bought his wife a 12-gauge shot gun for her birthday. You
   talk about "thinly disguised!" You may say, "I know I should
   take the family on a real vacation, but I would like a new
   bass boat." You could perhaps supply your own illustration.
   Any time you put off doing something you should do instead, in order to buy something you want, it is a sign of
   materialism.

5. Finally, and perhaps the most insidious, is "thinking that
   you will be happy if you can just buy _____." (You
   fill in the blank.) If I could just . . . buy that house, buy
   that car, buy that stereo, buy those clothes, go to that
   school, get that job, join the country club . . . *then I'd be
   happy.*

That is materialism. It is part of the Cinderella Syndrome. You
will be happy when . . . when your prince comes and makes everything right. Or part of the Baby Boomer Syndrome. "I'll be happy
if . . . my investment portfolio pays off."

The Causes of Christian Materialism

The root cause of materialism is a breakdown in faith. There is a
failure to know, or understand, or believe what the Bible says
about a meaningful life. The Bible teaches that Christ has come

that we might have life, and have it more abundantly (John 10:10). Abundant life is found in Christ, not in material possessions.

We don't believe that. And, on the *surface*, we don't believe it for a good reason. Perhaps your experience was like mine. I became a Christian when I was in college. Upon my conversion, life's problems were solved. Circumstances smoothed out. I felt like E. Stanley Jones, the great missionary, who said that when he met Christ, he felt he had swallowed sunshine. Life was a joy—for probably, oh, two months. Then, reality set in; the old problems began resurfacing. Instead of being a non-Christian with problems I couldn't handle, now I was a Christian with problems I couldn't handle. The Christian life was no longer satisfying.

All of us, from time to time, come to the very vulnerable point at which the Christian life is not satisfying. At that very crucial and vulnerable point, we have a choice to make. We can believe that Christ is still the source of meaning in life and press through the difficulties to find peace on the other side (but not without struggle), or we can conclude that the Christian life is not all it was cracked up to be and try to create our own fulfillment outside of Christ.

Many people, perhaps most people, choose a subtle blend of the two. They continue their Christian activities but combine it with a subtle strategy of self-determination to take what they find meaningful from Christ and try to get from someplace else the rest of the meaning they seek.

Our deepest longings are for love, and for a sense of purpose and meaning in life. We want to be secure knowing that someone loves us totally and indefinitely. We want to feel that we belong. And, we want to know that our life has meaning and purpose— that it matters that we have lived.

These are our deep personal longings, and it is not wrong to have these longings. God gave them to us. Then, He constructed the world so that He and only He could satisfy those longings. Oh, yes, fame and fortune and reputation and busyness can mask it for a time, but let the adrenaline slow down, and there's a hollowness that cannot be denied. There is a God-shaped vacuum in each of us, and we will not have our peace until we find our peace in Him.

We don't believe that God and only God can satisfy those deep longings, can soothe the deep burning, can ease the fundamental ache. So we take what we can of Him and look for the rest in other people, in possessions, and in circumstances. We become materialistic.

The breakdown in faith is this: God has made us for Himself, and we will be restless until we find our rest in Him. The straightest line between me and satisfaction in life is total obedience to God. Any disobedience detours us from the fulfillment of the deepest longings of our soul. There is greater pain in sin than in righteousness. There may be pain in righteousness (Hebrews 11), but there is greater pain in sin than in righteousness. This is what we must believe if we are to break the hold of materialism.

Review what the Scriptures say:

- I have come that you might have life, and have it more abundantly. (John 10:10)

- Come unto me all you who labor and are heavily burdened, and I will give you rest. Take my yoke upon you and learn from me, for I am gentle and humble in heart, and you shall find rest for your souls. For my yoke is easy, and my load is light. (Matthew 11:28–30)

- I pray that He would grant you, according to the riches of His glory, to be strengthened with power through His Spirit in the inner man; so that Christ may dwell in your hearts through faith; and that you, being rooted and grounded in love, may be able to comprehend with all the saints what is the breadth and length and height and depth, and to know the love of Christ which surpasses knowledge, that you may be filled up to all the fullness of God. (Ephesians 3:14–18)

- I will not lose heart, but though my outer man is decaying, yet my inner man is being renewed day by day. For momentary, light affliction is producing for me an eternal weight of glory far beyond all comparison, while I look not at the things which are seen, but the things which are not seen. For the things which are seen are temporal, but the things which are not seen are eternal. (2 Corinthians 4:16–18)

What more could be promised? The question is, "Do we believe it?" This leads us to the next point.

The Cure for Materialism

The word *cure* is perhaps too strong a word. However, there are at least two fundamental things we must do to get free from materialism. First, we must scale down what we want and bring it into balance with the will of God. We must give up on that which the will of God does not give us. Not wanting something is as good as possessing it.

Second, we must take a radical leap of faith and believe that God will do what He said He would do: He will satisfy us—and only He will satisfy us. We must take Him at His word. Then, we can be satisfied by God, and God receives the glory. Others see our satisfaction in our relationship with God and are attracted to God because of what He has done in our lives.

But there is a price to be paid. It means that when we are having difficulties relating to our wife or husband, we don't take the easy way out, but we dig into the Scripture, and we commit ourselves to prayer, and we get others to help us be faithful to the teachings. It means we hang in there and go through it God's way.

It means that when we have financial desires that aren't fulfilled, rather than taking the easy way out, we dig into the Scripture and commit ourselves to prayer, and we get others to help us be faithful to the teachings. It means we hang in there and go through it God's way.

It means that when we are stuck in a job we don't like, or we are lonely and wish we were married, or our kids are a disappointment to us, or someone has spread a rumor that hurt us professionally, or that we get an opportunity to make money at someone else's expense, that we don't bail out and start handling the situation the way the world would. At that very point, it must make a difference that we are a Christian. The whole point is that we act like a Christian at the very point at which we are most tempted not to. Then, Christ is free to bless us and fill our lives with the richness that He promises.

We must believe Him when He speaks and do things His way. It is after the test that the blessing comes, not before it, and not in the middle of it to give us an easy way out.

God humbles us . . . to see whether we will keep his commandments or not. Otherwise, we may say in our heart, 'My power
and the strength of my hand made me this wealth.' But you must
remember the LORD your God, for it is He who is giving you
power to make wealth. (Dueteronomy 8:2, 8:17–18)

His goal is to do good for us in the end—to bring us into a good
land. Our requirement is to go through the tough times His way.

Conclusion

Self-determination and materialism are not the answers. Again,
Patrick Morely writes, with skill and insight:

Money is intoxicating. It is an opiate that addicts as easily and as
completely as the iron grip of alcohol or narcotics. Its power to
change us is close to that of Jesus Christ. Money possesses the
power to rule our lives, not for good and forever, as Christ; but
to lure us, like a moth, too close to the flame until, finally our
wings are set ablaze.
    Money enslaves men—it will work you till you die. And, after
it has conquered your poor soul, its haunting laughter can be
heard howling through the halls of hell. And then it seeks out
another hapless, unsuspecting victim—an ambitious fellow who
wants just a little bigger slice of the good life.[3]

In his book, *When All You Ever Wanted Isn't Enough,* Rabbi Harold Kushner writes:

Our souls are not hungry for fame, comfort, wealth, or power.
Those rewards create almost as many problems as they solve. Our
souls are hungry for meaning, for the sense that we have figured
out how to live so that our lives matter. God is the answer to the
question, "Why should I be a good and honest person when I see
people around me getting away with murder?" God is the answer
not because He will intervene to reward the righteous and pun-
ish the wicked, but because He has made the human soul in
such a way that only a life of goodness and honesty leaves us
feeling spiritually healthy and human.[4]

We are made for God. We are bound up with Jesus. We will
not know the satisfaction of the deepest longings of our soul until
we find it in Him. Trinkets can never replace trust.

Do not lay up for yourselves treasures upon earth, where moth and rust destroy, and where thieves break in and steal. But lay up for yourselves treasures in heaven where neither moth nor rust destroys, and where thieves do not break in or steal; for where your treasure is, there will your heart be also. (Matthew 6:19–21)

> *Heavenly Father, free me from the tyranny of materialism. Save me from the bondage of living for "things." Loose me to serve eternal values with my possessions. Help me to see that all my possessions are merely on loan to me, and I can either use them to invest in heaven or squander them on earth. Let my heart belong to You and not to my wallet. Amen.*

REVIEW

1. The Symptoms of Materialism

Three symptoms of materialism are: being *stingy* in the support of Christian ministries, getting into unmanageable *debt*, and being *unethical* for the sake of financial gain.

2. The Causes of Christian Materialism

Christian *materialism* happens when we believe that *happiness* can be found in *things* rather than in Christ.

3. The Cure for Materialism

Materialsm is *cured* when we choose to believe that our *longings* are met in *Christ*, not in the accumulation of our possessions.

As a memory exercise, write in the missing words in the paragraphs below. Notice that they are the same words as the italicized words in the paragraph above.

1. **The Symptoms of Materialism**

   Three symptoms of materialism are: being _____ in the support of Christian ministries, getting into unmanageable _____, and being _____ for the sake of financial gain.

2. **The Causes of Christian Materialism**

   Christian _____ happens when we believe that _____ can be found in _____ rather than in Christ.

3. **The Cure for Materialism**

   Materialsm is _____ when we choose to believe that our _____ are met in _____, not in the accumulation of our possessions.

RESPONSE

Questions for Group Discussion or Personal Exercises

1. Do you really believe deep down that only in God will your deepest longings be satisfied?

2. What might be serving as a cheap substitute for God in some areas of your life right now?

3. What key decision(s) in the past was made based on a total belief that God's best really was best for you (choosing a spouse, paying off a debt, a career choice, etc.)? Are you facing another decision that takes that same kind of belief, trust, and dependence on God's guidance?

4. What would you say is your family background as it relates to materialism? Did you have an abundance without contentment? Poverty, yet greed? Means with contentment? Lacking, yet satisfied?

SIXTEEN

SPIRITUAL DISCOURAGEMENT

> *Have courage for the great sorrows of life,
> and patience for the small ones. And when
> you have laboriously accomplished your
> daily task, go to sleep in peace. God is
> awake.*
>
> Victor Hugo

C ervantes said, "He who loses wealth loses much; he who loses a friend loses more; but he who loses courage loses everything." It is no small thing to become discouraged. To weary of life is to walk into an emotional "badlands" where desperados of black emotion may ambush you at any turn. When you see the badlands rising on the horizon, pitch your camp, get out your compass, and review your course. There is no valor in offering your back to an assassin.

In his book, *Disappointment with God,* Philip Yancey writes of a young man named Richard who became disappointed with God. "I hate God!" he blurted out. "No, I don't mean that. I don't even believe in God." And for the next three hours, Richard poured out his story, beginning with his parents divorce, going on to his personal frustration with not being able to find God's will, then to the fact that a job opportunity had fallen through. The employer had reneged on a promise to him and hired someone less deserving, leaving Richard with school debts and no source of income. About the same time, Richard's fiancee jilted him. With no warning she broke off contact, refusing to give any reason why. Richard also had a series of physical problems, which only added to his sense of helplessness and depression. As Richard spent hours pouring his heart out to God, nothing happened, and God's silence finally got to him. One night something snapped.

> I picked up my Bible and a couple other Christian books and walked downstairs and out the back door. I shut the door softly behind me, so as not to wake anyone. In the backyard was a brick barbecue grill, and I piled the books on it, sprayed them with lighter fluid, and struck a match. It was a moonless night, and the flames danced high and bright. Bible verses and bits of theology curled, blackened, then broke off in tiny crumbs of ash and glided skyward. My faith was going up with them.
>
> I made another trip upstairs and brought down another armload of books. I did this maybe eight times over the next hour. Commentaries, seminary textbooks, the rough draft of [a book I was writing on] Job—all of them went up in smoke. I might have burned every book I owned if I hadn't been interrupted by an angry fireman in a yellow rain slicker who ran toward me, shouting, "What do you think you're doing?" Someone had phoned in an alarm. I fumbled around for an excuse and finally told him I was just burning trash.
>
> After the fireman squirted some chemicals on my bonfire and shoveled dirt over it, he let me go. I climbed the stairs and sank into bed, smelling of smoke. It was almost dawn then, and at last I had peace. A great weight had lifted. I had been honest with myself. Any pretense was gone, and I no longer felt the pressure to believe what I could never be sure of. I felt converted—but converted *from* God.[1]

This is perhaps as bad as spiritual discouragement ever gets. Richard got so discouraged, he quit. Permanently. And while this is an extreme example, if we are honest, we all get discouraged from time to time, and all of us feel like quitting.

Spiritual discouragement is a danger. It is a wasteland that too many wander into, and it is such a misfortune because it isn't necessary. We don't have to get so spiritually discouraged. There is truth which, if we know, understand, and believe, will help give us the strength we need to carry on.

Discouragement: literally, to lose courage. More generally, it means to lose hope for the future, to lose strength and motivation.

Spiritual Discouragement: to feel that your spiritual life is not what it should be, and your Christian experience is not what it ought to be, but that you have grown weary of trying and failing, and do not have hope that you can do anything about it.

Symptoms of Spiritual Discouragement

There are varying degrees of discouragement, and no one is likely to have all the symptoms, but they are the kinds of things that can happen when someone gets spiritually discouraged.

You quit pursuing the things that should feed you spiritually: reading your Bible and praying, going to church, going to other Christian activities, and pursuing overtly Christian friendships. You quit talking about the Lord with other people. You become angry with God or perhaps just depressed about Him. In general, you feel discouraged about your spiritual life.

Causes of Spiritual Discouragement

There are several causes of spiritual discouragement.

First, one of the most common is Biblical confusion: We don't understand some of the most important things in the Bible about living the Christian life.

For example, we are confused about being filled with the Spirit, or walking in the Spirit, or how to live by faith, or how to gain the strength to overcome sin. These are all such terribly important things to know for a satisfying Christian life, and yet there are so many different interpretations of the Bible on these matters.

The things we most need to know are the ones we understand the least. We feel as though we are walking *up* the *down* escalator. We are working hard but not getting anywhere. We feel defeated. We are spiritually discouraged and don't know what to do about it.

A second cause of spiritual discouragement is unanswered prayer. We see passages in the Bible that say, "Ask and you shall receive." So we ask, and we do not receive. What happened? Well, there are all these other conditions. You have to ask in Jesus' name. You have to ask in God's will. You have to ask in faith, believing.

"Great!" we say. "How do I know what God's will is?" Then, we hear a preacher say, "You must have faith to believe. You can't have any of this namby-pamby, willy-nilly, loose-mush praying. Ask! Then believe! God will give it to you!"

But you see, that's just where we came from. That's what started it all. We tried that, and it didn't work!

Unanswered prayer, for the thinking Christian, can become a profound discouragement, until you learn how to deal with it.

A third cause of spiritual discouragement is frustration over God's refusal to bless the things we do. For example, He leads you to start a church, you think, and in the beginning, everyone is excited about it, feeling a sense of destiny about it. "There. It's started." You dedicate all that you are and all that you have to the mission. You pray about it consistently. A number of you agree on it and feel a God-given consensus about it. You work hard for the next several years, struggling every inch of the way. Finally, you see the handwriting on the wall. It isn't going to survive.

"Lord, what's the answer? Did You or did You not lead us to begin the church? If You didn't, why didn't You let us know somehow in the beginning? We would have listened. Or if You did, why didn't You bless us so that it would prosper? As far as I know, our intentions were only honorable."

Or, "Lord, I thought You led me to start this new business, and now I've lost my shirt. Did You or did You not lead me? I was willing not to start it. Why didn't You let me know? I would have turned around. If You did, why did You allow me to lose my shirt on the deal?"

You can probably supply your own example of a time when you felt certain you were following God's will—at least to the best you were able to discern at the time, and it turned to disaster. Why? It can be very discouraging spiritually.

Finally, perhaps the most acute is anger or disillusionment over the suffering that God allows. Rabbi Harold Kushner, who wrote *Why Bad Things Happen to Good People,* says that anytime he gets involved in a discussion about religion, sooner or later the conversation always turns to: "Why do the righteous suffer?" Dorothy Sayers said that the only question worth discussing is "Why do the righteous suffer?"

How can God be good, and still allow His children to suffer? The problem of pain: "If God is all good and if God is all powerful, then from whence cometh the evil?" Either God must not be all good, in which case He doesn't care about the evil, or else He is not all powerful, and He can't do anything about it.

"God, how could You have let my baby die?" "How could You have let my husband lose his job and our life savings, and his self-esteem?" "How could You let me get into a divorce when I tried so hard to save the marriage?" "How could You, how could You, how could You?"

The problem of pain, the suffering of God's children, the pain in the world, is one of the most acute causes of spiritual discouragement. If we don't understand how to handle it, it can shackle us spiritually.

When it is all said and done, the bottom line is that we don't understand God or we can't reconcile what we see in the world with what we think we know about God. We don't understand why His will and our will don't coincide more often. Why won't things work out? Why won't He bless us? Why can't I be happy? Why won't He relieve the pain? Why won't He correct the wrong? Why won't He take compassion on me and visit me, either with an end to my suffering or with a greater measure of grace? Whether it is in a pointed and painful area, or a dull and confusing area, it is the problem of pain. Why does God allow suffering? Why is He so silent? Why does He not seem to care?

C.S. Lewis wrote these words in the midst of deep grief after his wife's death from cancer:

> Meanwhile, where is God? This is one of the most disquieting symptoms. When you are happy, so happy that you have no sense of needing Him . . . you will be—or so it feels—welcomed with open arms. But go to Him when your need is desperate, when all

other help is vain, and what do you find? A door slammed in your face, and the sound of bolting and double bolting on the inside. After that, silence. You may as well turn away. The longer you wait, the more emphatic the silence will become.[2]

"Why, God? Why?", we cry.

The Search for Solutions

These are some of the things that can cause spiritual discouragement. Few of us are immune from its effect. In our search for solutions, there are several things to cling to.

First, assume that there is still some information you don't have.

As an illustration, years ago in Holland, just after the turn of the century when Corrie Ten Boom was just a child, she was traveling on a train with her father, a watchmaker, and asked him what the word "s-e-x" meant. She had come across the word inadvertently and didn't know what it meant. Her father didn't answer. Later, when the train on which they were traveling stopped, he said, "Corrie, will you carry my bag for me?" His tool repair bag was much too heavy for her to carry. As she tried, she said, "I can't, Father. It's too heavy for me. You'll have to carry it." To which he answered, "Yes, I know. And the answer to the question you asked me is too heavy for you to carry now, and you will have to let me carry it until you are old enough to carry it yourself."

There are many things about God that we are too little to carry. We just don't have all the information, or we don't have the ability to understand.

Our first step in combating spiritual discouragement is to assume that there is yet some information, some understanding, which we don't have.

Second, we need to accept that our ability to comprehend is limited.

Margie and I used to have a very large, black standard poodle. We named her Sugar Bear, because she was half sugar and half bear. We let her coat grow "au naturale," and she looked pretty much like a black Old English Sheepdog. When she was about six months old, we began to try to train her. The first command was *come.* The book said that you were to say *come,* and if she didn't come, you were to go get her and bring her to where you were when you said *come* and that you were to do that in an enclosed space until she learned to come to you everytime. Then you were to graduate to an open space. I don't know if that was the best way, but it did work.

However, at first, Sugar Bear didn't understand what it was all about. She was intimidated by this change in her routine and this limitation on her freedom. She got apprehensive and insecure, and thought that we were unhappy with her. Her eyes clouded over, and she became immobile. She feared the whole world.

We continued to love her, and work with her, and the day came when she learned not only that command, but every other command which we needed for peaceful co-existence.

After she learned what we wanted, and was reassured that we still loved her, everything was okay. But until that time, she was very unhappy. We had tried to explain to her: "This is not going to hurt you. We aren't angry with you. This is for your own good. This will make your life safer, and better, and improve our relationship."

Nothing mattered. She wanted out. Given the option, Sugar Bear would have bailed out of the learning process without a second thought. But we cared for her too much to let her. So we worked with her, and pushed through the apprehension and insecurity, and the result was a dog that was safer, more pleasant to be around, and had a better relationship with us. She was raised to a higher level of canine existence because of us.

Of course, the point is obvious. God works with us. But we cannot understand what He wants and what He is doing. We get apprehensive and insecure. We may even get a little rebellious, as Sugar Bear did from time to time. We just don't have the ability to understand all that God is doing with us. But if we let Him, God will keep working with us, to push through the barrier, and raise us to a higher level of human existence.

Third, we must see things from God's point of view.

God does not want to be your genie in a bottle. He does not want to be your cosmic vending machine. He does not want to be the answer to your equation. He wants a relationship with you. He wants you to know Him and to love Him. He has created the world so that nothing in our Christian life will work very well unless it forces us to deepen our relationship with Him.

Prayer won't reduce to an equation. Understanding life will not reduce to an equation. Finding God's will won't reduce to an equation. If you are not doing what you can to get to know Him—paying attention to your successes and failures, learning how He works, and getting to appreciate Him—it won't work.

To understand what God is up to, we must go back to original creation. God describes in profound understatement what He did, in stages, and said after each stage, said, "It is good." When He finished with all the stages, He said, "It is *very* good." In Job we read, "the morning stars sang together and all the angels shouted for joy." Proverbs continues the sanguine mood: "I was the craftsman at his side. I was filled with delight day after day, rejoicing always in his presence, rejoicing in his whole world and delighting in mankind."

"Oh, that their hearts would be inclined to fear me and keep all my commands always, so that it might go well with them and their children forever!" God cries. "Oh, Jerusalem, Jerusalem," Jesus lamented, "How I have longed to gather you to my self as a hen gathers her chicks under her wings, but you refused me!"

God longs for an encounter with us. He longs for a relationship with us. He longs to know us and have us know Him. He longs to be intimately related to us. He longs for us to love Him, and to believe Him, and believe *in* Him, and follow Him. In response, He promises untold blessings. Typically, like an undisciplined child or untrained dog, we won't follow Him completely enough, long enough to taste the blessings.

We get frustrated, or the pain gets intense, and we begin to resent God. We clench our fists and grind our teeth and squint our eyes in rebellion. Why doesn't God fix our problems?

We have not yet begun to see things from God's point of view. God is not unaware or unaffected by our suffering. When we hurt, God hurts. He feels our pain. He takes in all our pain. In some mysterious way, a God who is complete and lacks nothing, links Himself with our suffering.

I have always felt that Jesus had credibility. He came to earth, and suffered far more than He asks most of us to suffer. When He asks me to suffer, while I may not enjoy it, He has credibility with me. The Bible teaches that Jesus delighted to do the Father's will, but He did not delight to go to the cross. Scripture says that Jesus "endured the cross" (Hebrews 12:2). Luke 22:44 indicates that in the Garden of Gethsamene, Jesus was in emotional agony, and sweat profusely. Hebrews 5:7 says He cried. He asked for the help of friends who deserted him in Mark 14:32. He had to have angelic assistance to continue (Luke 22:43). Again in Mark 14, He said, "My soul is overwhelmed with sorrow to the point of death." If Jesus asks anything of me, I feel a sense of fraternity with Him. Anything He asks me to suffer will be less than He suffered for me.

But I confess to struggling with God. It always seemed unfair to me for God to be up in His celestial glory, untouched by the ravages of sin in the world, telling me to be patient, that it would all be over some day, and I'd get my reward.

How wrong I was. God feels our pain. He takes it into His own heart. When we hurt, God hurts. Not only does He feel pain for us, but all those on earth, and not only all those on earth, but all those who have been on earth, and all those who will be on earth. Those of you who are parents know how much pain you go through watching your children hurt. When they are in physical or emotional pain, your heart breaks with them.

Scripture says, "God was in Christ reconciling the world to Himself" (2 Corinthians 5:19). Where is God when it hurts? He is on the cross, taking to Himself in Christ the pain, agony, and terror of all the suffering of all the world for all time. We are united with Christ. When we suffer, God the Father suffers. When we are in pain, God feels and hears and cares.

No, God does not escape. He has chosen not to escape. Even from heaven, when I hurt, God hurts, and so I no longer cry out, "God, why don't you make it stop hurting?" He is hurting with me. And so there must be a reason which lies beyond me.

I have been struck so many times when a parent takes a child to visit the doctor or dentist, and the child either fears pain or feels pain. The child cries out from the bottom of his soul when the parent hands the child over to the doctor. Yet when it is all over, and the doctor hands the child back to the parent, the child does not recoil from the parent for handing him over to such pain. Rather, sensing that there is some higher good, and sensing that the parent is hurting even as the child hurt, the child grabs the parents neck, buries his face into his shoulder, and at last is comforted.

We must try to see our suffering from God's point of view. He cares. He hurts with us.

Fourth, we must believe that our suffering matters. We see that it matters in a passage such as Hebrews 12:5–9:

> My son, do not regard lightly the discipline of the Lord, nor faint when you are reproved by Him; for those whom the Lord loves He disciplines, and He scourges every son whom He receives. It is for discipline that you endure; God deals with you as with sons; for what son is there whom his father does not discipline? But if you are without discipline, of which all have become partakers, then you are illegitimate children and not sons. Furthermore, we had earthly fathers to discipline us, and we respected them; shall we not much rather be subject to the Father of spirits, and live?

Yet there is a level on which we cannot see or know the reason. A level we cannot understand. And when suffering comes on that level, we must trust, by faith, that it matters.

In *Disappointment with God,* Philip Yancey writes about the "Great Wager." The book of Job is really more than a book on suffering. It is a book on faith. The heart of it is in the Great Wager in chapter 1 in which Satan wagers that if God takes away all blessing from Job, Job will curse God. God allows the wager.

> When people experience pain, questions spill out . . . the very questions that tormented Job. "Why me? What's going on? Does God care? Is there a God?" This one time, in the raw recounting of Job's travail, we, the onlookers . . . not Job . . . are granted a view behind the curtain. What we long for, the prologue to Job provides: a glimpse into how the world is run. As nowhere else in the Bible, the book of Job shows us God's point of view, including the supernatural activity normally hidden from us.
>
> Job has put God on trial, accusing him of unfair acts against an innocent part. Angry, satirical, betrayed, Job wanders as close to blasphemy as he can get—just to the edge. But chapters 1 and 2 prove that, regardless of what Job thinks, God is not on trial in

this book. Job is on trial. The point of the book is not suffering: where is God when it hurts? The prologue dealt with that issue. The point is faith: Where is Job when it hurts? How is he responding?

Yes, there was a wrestling match in Job, but it was not between God and Job, it was between God and Satan, although . . . most significantly . . . God had designated the man Job as His stand-in. The first and last chapters make clear that Job was unknowingly performing in a cosmic showdown before spectators in the unseen world.

Elihus, one of Job's accusers, says, "Job, you must have sinned terribly to have brought this suffering down on your head." Elihu was flat wrong, however. The opening and closing chapters of Job prove that God was greatly affected by the response of one man and that cosmic issues were at stake.

The "Wager" offers a message of great hope to us all, and Yancey goes on to write, "perhaps the most powerful and enduring lesson from Job. In the end, The Wager resolved decisively that the faith of a single human being counts for very much indeed. Job affirms that our response to testing *matters*. The history of mankind . . . and, in fact, my own individual history of faith . . . is enclosed within the great drama of the history of the universe."[3]

The Bible hints that something like the Wager is played out in other believers. The hint is there that the suffering which we go through which makes no sense to us all is perhaps a cosmic drama in which we are not alone, though in our pain we feel very much alone. But at that moment when we feel most alone, most abandoned, perhaps at that very moment the eyes of heaven and hell are focused most sharply on us to witness the triumph of the grace of God. At that point at which we feel most removed from reality and purpose in this world, we are the most involved in reality and purpose in the next world.

Sometimes God gives us, today, a chance to see behind the veil—to get a glimpse of what He is doing and why. Recently, a lady in our church told me a most remarkable story. When the opportunity came up for a school teacher to be able go into space on the space shuttle *Challenger,* she and her husband prayed about it, and decided that her husband would apply to be the one to go. He had all the prerequisites: He was bright, well-educated, an excellent communicator, a popular teacher, and so on. Their excitement built as they envisioned the possibility of his being the first non-astronaut in space. From the wife's point of view, it was not even really the possibility. It was the probability. There was no one more qualified than her husband.

Even while their hopes were at their highest, they were abruptly and cruelly shattered. Due to a technicality which was beyond their control, they would not be able to get the extensive application in on time. In the most favorable scenario, it would be one day late. No, there could be no extension, no late papers, as it were. No, they would not grant an exception. No, he would not be the first teacher into space, not because he was not qualified, but merely because the application would be one day late.

As the lady told me this story, she related that she was crushed, devastated, even angry with God. It was a bone that stuck in her throat. She couldn't get over it.

Then on the day of the launch, alone, she turned on the television to see the launch. As the *Challenger* was launched, and began surging into that brilliant, cloudless blue sky, she said aloud, "That could have been my husband. God, how dare you!" The moment the words passed her lips, the *Challenger* burst into a ball of flame, divided like a huge smoke wishbone, and dropped lifelessly to the ocean below.

There is more to life than we see. There is more going on than we understand. There is more at stake than simply what we want. What we see is not all there is. Our thoughts do not encompass all information. Therefore, we must always hope in God.

Do not be spiritually discouraged. Take strength. Take encouragement. Your life matters. It counts. God knows you. He loves you. He has not abandoned you. You are not alone. When you hurt, He cares. When you are lonely, He cares. When you are confused and fearful, He cares.

> Now to Him who is able to do exceedingly abundantly above all that we ask or think according to the power that works in us, to Him be glory in the church by Christ Jesus to all generations forever and ever. (Ephesians 3:20–21)

Father in Heaven, strengthen me, encourage me, give me hope and faith. Lift me up on Your wings when I am sinking in spiritual discouragement. Help me believe and trust, when life's blows bend me low. May my weakness be Your strength. There is no one else to turn to. There is no one else I wish to turn to. Be sufficient for my need, to the glory of Jesus. Amen.

REVIEW

1. **Symptoms of Spiritual Discouragement**

   Spiritual discouragement may be accompanied by an *abandonment* of the spiritual disciplines (Bible reading, prayer, etc), by a *withdrawal* from Christian friends, and by anger and/or a sense of *distance* from God.

2. **Causes of Spiritual Discouragement**

   Three common causes are Biblical *confusion*, unanswered *prayer*, and disillusionment over *suffering*.

3. **The Search for Solutions**

   We must realize that we do not have all the *information*, we cannot *understand* all the information we have, and we must *trust* the character of God.

As a memory exercise, write in the missing words in the paragraphs below. Notice that they are the same words as the italicized words in the paragraph above.

1. **Symptoms of Spiritual Discouragement**

   Spiritual discouragement may be accompanied by an _____ of the spiritual disciplines (Bible reading, prayer, etc), by a _____ from Christian friends, and by anger and/or a sense of _____ from God.

2. Causes of Spiritual Discouragement

Three common causes are Biblical _____, unanswered _____, and disillusionment over _____.

3. The Search for Solutions

We must realize that we do not have all the _____, we cannot _____ all the information we have, and we must _____ the character of God.

RESPONSE

Questions for Group Discussion or Personal Exercises

1. Are you willing to let go of the struggle with God, with the knowledge that there are some things you will never understand (but God does)?

2. Are you in the midst of a learning experience? Does it seem God is taking you beyond your limits? What are some of your apprehensions?

3. Is it a revelation to you to know God is hurting with you in your pain? Think about that a moment. He can identify with your pain. That is why He sent Jesus. Is there someone you know who needs to hear this message right now?

4. Who on this earth can you talk to concerning your pain and disappointment? Set aside some time this week to talk with and listen to them.

SEVENTEEN

CARELESSNESS

He is no fool who gives up that which he cannot keep in order to gain that which he cannot lose.

Jim Elliot

I recently read a story which illustrates the theme of this chapter. Adapted from Gary Richmond, the incident follows like this:

Bandit was irresistible. No raccoon that ever existed had more natural "cute" than this ninety-day-old bundle of mischief. When my neighbor Julie bought him at the pet store, she was sure they would be lifelong friends. Everywhere she went, he went—usually perched on her shoulder. Bandit's habit of holding Julie's cheeks in his paws and looking into her eyes with sparkling curiosity always melted her and solicited an affectionate kiss and hug. And he grew. Eighteen months passed, and Bandit became a strapping twenty-five-pound adolescent raccoon, still full of the dickens and only slightly less playful. He still loved affection, rode on shoulders, and seemed to be a one-raccoon advertisement that raccoons make great pets.

I mentioned Julie and Bandit to our zoo veterinarian one day and inquired as to why more people didn't keep raccoons as pets. His answer floored me. "They undergo a glandular change at about twenty-four months. After that, they become unpredictable, independent, and often attack their owners."

"Are there any exceptions?" I inquired.

"None that I know of," he said thoughtfully.

"Then Julie is likely to be bitten?"

"Any time now, I should think," the doctor added with conviction.

Since a thirty-pound raccoon can be equal to a one-hundred-pound dog in a scrap, I felt compelled to mention the coming change to Julie. She sat and listened politely as I explained what an eminent world authority had shared with me concerning raccoons and their nature. I'll never forget her answer.

"It will be different for me . . . Bandit is different." And she smiled as she added, "Bandit wouldn't hurt me. He just wouldn't."

Three months later Julie underwent plastic surgery for facial lacerations sustained when her adult raccoon attacked her for no apparent reason. Bandit was released into the wild.[1]

We think it will be different for us. We can hear good advice, and we think, *Oh, yes, that is good advice for others, but I don't need it. It will be different for me.* But it isn't. It isn't different for us. And only too late, sometimes, do we learn.

You *can* lead a horse to water. You just can't *make* him drink. We can be led to water by our parents. We can be led to water by the church. We can be led to water by our friends, or by the Bible, or even fairly directly by the Lord Himself as He convicts us of sin and illumines our minds to Scriptural truth. But *we* must decide whether or not we will drink. We must decide whether we will pay attention to the details, heed the advice, follow the light, exercise the commitment.

For most people, most of the time, the flip side of carelessness is total commitment. Carelessness is a symptom, not a cause. We allow ourselves to get careless, because we are not utterly committed to doing what is right. We're smart enough or we're strong enough to not get caught. It might be good for someone else, but *we* can get by. We can let it slide. But we can't. So how do we gain the commitment to cancel carelessness?

How we act is rooted in what we believe. We don't think it is essential to sweat the details in the Christian life. We don't think we'll get hurt, or that God will care all that much. Or we don't think that what God is asking of us is all that important. But it is. And the principle which, if deeply believed, will motivate us to sweat the details is that everything God asks of us, He does so because He wants to give something good to us.

- In the wilderness He fed you with manna which your fathers did not know, that He might humble you and that He might test you, *to do good for you in the end.* (Deuteronomy 8:16, emphasis added)

- What does the Lord your God require from you, but to fear the Lord your God, to walk in all His ways and love Him, and to serve the Lord your God with all your heart and with all your soul, and to keep the Lord's commandments and His statutes which I am commanding you today *for your own good?* (Deuteronomy 10:12–13, emphasis added)

- So the Lord commanded us to observe all these statutes, to fear the Lord our God *for our good always* and for our survival, as it is today. (Deuteronomy 6:24, emphasis added)

- It was good for me that I was afflicted, that I may learn Thy statutes. (Psalm 119:71)

- And we know that God causes all things to work together for good to those who love God, to those who are called according to His purpose. (Romans 8:28)

Everyone of these passages is saying that what God asks of us, He does so because He wants to give something good to us. If that is true, what does He ask of us . . . and what does He want to give us?

What Does God Ask, and What Does He Give?

As we saw in the beginning of this section of the book, God asks five things of us. First, He asks us to worship Him. Why? Because from the bottom of every human heart, we hear the cry of the soul: Is there a God? Is there anyone there? Do You exist? Do You care? Are You good? Who are You? What do You want from me?

God wants to give us the answer to that cry. He wants to give us a rich and meaningful relationship with the Creator of the universe. He wants us to know Him, to love Him, to be emotionally bonded to Him, and to be secure in having the first great cry of the soul answered.

Second, He asks us to love others. Why? Because from the bottom of every human heart, we hear the cry of the soul: Do I belong? Do others care? Am I secure? Can I fit in? Can I make a difference? Will I matter to others?

God wants to give us the answer to that cry. He wants to give us rich and rewarding relationships with other people, to make life a deeply meaningful experience. He wants us to live in union, fellowship, and harmony with others who will love us and whom we can love, and be wrapped in a robe of security, acceptance, and belonging, and to have the second great cry of the soul answered.

Third, He asks us to esteem ourselves properly. Why? Because from of the bottom of every human heart, we hear the cry of the soul: Who am I? Where did I come from? Why am I here? Where am I going? Do I have worth? Am I significant? Am I secure?

God wants to give us the answer to that cry. He wants us to understand that we have inherent and infinite worth. In Jesus, we can enjoy the fullness of God's love and be part of God's great plan of the ages. He wants us to enjoy having been created in His image and to take deep and rich meaning in who we are.

Fourth, He asks us to be a steward of our resources. Why? Because from the bottom of every human heart, we hear the cry of the soul: Is this all there is? Is life a matter of getting up in the morning, going to work, coming home, and getting up and going to work again? Is life a matter of collecting as many toys as we can, and then we die? Is there not more to life than houses and cars and vacations? Is this all there is?

God wants to give us the answer to that cry. He wants to free us from the tyranny of living for material possessions, because they don't satisfy. He wants us to be free from the malicious deception of climbing the ladder of success only to find it is leaning against the wrong wall. He wants us to escape the bondage of putting all our energies into "things" and, then when we get to the end of life, see that was not where meaning in life comes from.

Finally, He asks us to live a life of ministry to others. Why? Because from the bottom of every human heart, we hear the cry of the soul: What is the meaning of life? What does it all mean? I get, and get, and get, but it doesn't satisfy. Life is a merry-go-round.

What do I do when all I ever wanted isn't enough? How do I sense purpose? Where do I get meaning?

God wants to give us the answer to that cry. He wants us to live our life for that which matters. He wants to give us a satisfying sense of purpose in life. He wants us to invest ourselves in those things which enrich us and satisfy us and reward us, rather than pursue the dark corridors of selfishness, hoping at the end to find meaning, but being disappointed at every turn.

Everything He asks of us is because He wants to give something good to us.

Where do we usually break down? Where we usually break down is in thinking that there are other ways of getting meaning in life than those five ways. We may agree that those are five options, but we can conceive of other ways—most notable, by becoming as rich and famous as possible. Most of us feel that we could be happy if we could just have a little more money, or if people around us would shape up, or we could get more recognition. God says it isn't so.

"The shortest distance between Me and a life of meaning is total obedience to Christ." If we believe that, we strive for total obedience. If we don't believe that, we don't strive for total obedience.

We think that a life of meaning is Christ plus certain people, plus certain possessions, plus certain circumstances. And people, possessions, and circumstances *can* make life easier for the moment, but never at the expense of obedience to Christ. The Christian cannot be disobedient to Christ and have a deeply satisfying life at the same time. If we come to the point where we deeply believe that, then obedience is not a matter of gritted teeth. It becomes a matter of transformed perspective.

The Step of Commitment

Many people fear committing their lives totally to Christ because they feel as though they would be squandering the only life they have. There are two fallacies with that: (1) this is not the only life we have, and (2) if we live in obedience to Christ, we cannot squander it, because of the promise of heavenly reward. It is as

Nate Saint wrote: "He is no fool who gives up that which he cannot keep, in order to gain that which he cannot lose."

The Holy Spirit will bring each of us to a point in our lives
where we must either totally commit ourselves to Him or turn our
back on Him in disobedience. I think this is a one-time event
which we may need to re-confirm, but there is a first time.

The Walk of Discipline

This brings us to some practical matters. Let's say you are at the
point where you believe deeply that everything God asks of you,
He does so because He wants to give something good to you, and
that the shortest distance between you and a life of rich meaning
is total obedience to Christ. Let's say that you have made the commitment, as far as you understand and as much as you are able, to
live in complete obedience to Christ. Now what? Now that you
have made the overall decision, there are a countless hoard of little decisions streaming past you, like lemmings rushing to the sea.
What are some of the decisions you need to make, and how
should you make them?

Eliminate the Negative

One thing we must do is eliminate the negative. What weeds are
growing in the garden of your life that need to be pulled out by
the roots? There are five different kinds of weeds that commonly
grow in the Christian's garden.

1. The media. We live in an age of media bombardment. An
   age in which we are surrounded, soaked, and saturated by
   media exposure. We have been slowly boiled in worldly
   water, but the water warmed so slowly, we didn't notice it
   and jump out. Have you gotten careless in what you watch
   on television, and what you allow your children to watch?
   How about the music you listen to, and the music you
   allow your children to listen to? How about movies you attend? What about literature you read? David said, "I will set
   no unwholesome thing before my eyes" (Psalms 101:3).
   Philippians 4:8 says: "Whatever things are true, whatever

things are noble, whatever things are just, whatever things are pure, whatever things are lovely, whatever things are of good report, if there is any virtue and if there is anything praiseworthy, let your mind dwell on these things." Think back over your television habit, your movie attendance, and your music practices. How does your use of the media stack up to just this one verse? Have you gotten careless with the media?

2. Attitudes. How about your attitudes? Have you gotten careless about your attitudes? Are you pleasant to be around? Or have you let yourself get grouchy, or complaining, or negative, or sarcastic, or whining, or judgmental, or angry? Have you let your attitudes slip?

3. Ethics. How about your ethics at work, or in business, or doing your taxes, or dealing with others at stores or utility companies? Do you stand out in bold relief from the world because of your honesty and commitment to ethical behavior? Or have you gotten careless, allowed yourself to fudge or conveniently overlook something?

4. Relationships. How about your relationships? How are things at home? How are things at work? What about your neighbors, or church, or people in stores. Are you honoring Christ in your relationships? Or have you allowed yourself to get careless?

5. Morals. What about moral areas? Are you keeping morally pure? How about your thought life? Any hidden sins? Have you allowed yourself to get morally careless?

If so, these are places to begin. Weed out the negatives—those things which ought not to be in the life of a Christian. Call upon God for strength, and grace, flee youthful lusts, discard unethical behavior, discard bad attitudes. Purge your lives. Cleanse your homes. Pull the hull of the ship of your life out of the water and let the Holy Spirit use the Word of God to scrape the barnacles off before they sink your ship.

Accentuate the Positive

Another thing we must do is accentuate the positive. There is more to overcoming carelessness than merely eliminating the negative. There is also a need to establish the positive. What are the flowers we need to plant in our garden?

1. We need to place a priority on the spiritual disciplines: Bible reading, prayer, worship (personal and corporate), Bible study, journaling, reading, whatever you can do to foster spiritual growth.

2. Cultivate relationships with those who encourage you spiritually. We become like those we spend much time with.

3. Evaluate everything you do by whether or not it encourages you toward Christ or encourages you away from Christ. Would Jesus do this?

Much of the rest of this book is aimed at helping us plant and nurture the flowers in our spiritual garden, so we won't go into much detail now. But I hope you get the point. Some things have to go, and other things have to come.

In other countries, becoming a Christian is a life and death issue. If our lives were on the line for what we believe, more of us would take a stand for Christ and become as committed to following Him as we should. I believe that when the gauntlet was thrown down, many of us would decide that Christ really is important to us, and that if we must either embrace Him completely, or deny Him, we would embrace Him and pay the price.

However, today in the United States, there is no such gauntlet thrown down. We can go to church, include religion in our lives, and follow Christ carelessly. We pay no price for dabbling with the Divine.

But there is a spiritual gauntlet. Satan has thrown it down. Our society is being ravaged by godlessness. The church is being decimated by carnality. Our personal lives are sapped of purpose, vitality, and joy. We can either content ourselves with floating downstream, or we can pick up the gauntlet, and declare, by the Grace of God, "I will not float downstream. I will not be manipulated by a malevolent spiritual monster. I will not resign my life to careless-ness. I'm in the battle. I'll join the fray. Take me to the front lines. Lead on!"

How about you? Will you take up the gauntlet?

Do you not know that those who run in a race all run, but only one receives the prize? Run in such a way that you may win. And everyone who competes in the games exercises self-control in all things. They then do it to receive a perishable wreath, but we an imperishable. Therefore I run in such a way, as not without aim; I box in such a way, as not beating the air; but I buffet my body and make it my slave, lest possibly, after I have preached to oth-ers, I myself should be disqualified. (1 Corinthians 9:24–27)

Dear Heavenly Father, count on me! I'm in the battle! It will not satisfy me to sit on the sidelines of the spiritual war. The stakes are too great for myself, for those I love, and for the world at large. Take me and use me however You see fit. All I ask is, please, do not lead me where your grace will not sustain me. Trusting You, I say, lead on! I will follow in Jesus' name. Amen.

REVIEW

1. What Does God Ask, and What Does He Give?

God asks total *obedience* to Him, and He offers the *fulfillment* of the deepest *longings* of my soul.

2. The Step of Commitment

There must come a *point* in each person's life in which he *gives* himself totally to living for the *Lord*.

3. **The Walk of Discipline**

In living the *disciplined* life, we must eliminate the *negative* things from our lives and nurture the *positive* things.

As a memory exercise, write in the missing words in the paragraphs below. Notice that they are the same words as the italicized words in the paragraph above.

1. **What Does God Ask, and What Does He Give?**

God asks total _____ to Him, and He offers the _____ of the deepest _____ of my soul.

2. **The Step of Commitment**

There must come a _____ in each person's life in which he _____ himself totally to living for the _____.

3. **The Walk of Discipline**

In living the _____ life, we must eliminate the _____ things from our lives and nurture the _____ things.

RESPONSE

Questions for Group Discussion or Personal Exercises

1. Do you agree that carelessness is usually just a symptom of a lack of commitment? Why or why not?

2. If you have never committed your whole to Jesus' lordship, take a moment and do it now!

3. If you have been trying to live a committed life of discipleship, what have you found that "derails" you? What causes you to drift off into carelessness?

4. Read Hebrews 12:5–11. See what God is committed to doing to turn the wayward Christian back to Him. Have you experienced God's discipline in the recent past?

EIGHTEEN

TOYING WITH SIN

There is no man so good, who, were he to submit all his thoughts and actions to the laws, would not deserve hanging ten times in his life.

Montaigne

I heard one time the story of an animal trainer in a circus who performed a feat with a boa constrictor. While the snake was still young and fairly small, he trained it to crawl out of a cage, slither across the floor toward him, and wind himself up around the trainer's body until it looked him in the face. After a number of years, when the trainer was confident he had trained the snake—and the constrictor had grown large enough to give the act some excitement—he introduced it on the circus tour.

It was a stunning act which left the audience breathless. He performed it successfully for a number of years, during which time, the snake grew larger and larger, making the act only more exciting. Then one day before a large crowd, the snake crawled from his cage, wound himself up around the animal trainer, and for some unknown reason, crushed the life out of him.

When the trainer started out, there was no question; he had control of the snake. But then one day, and no one knows when for sure, the snake gained control of the trainer. And the trainer paid with his life.

That is what sin is like. We toy with it while it is little. We feed it. We play with it. All the while we think we have control over it. And perhaps we do at first. But eventually the beast grows, and before we realize it, it gains control over us. In the end, if it isn't caught in time, it crushes the spiritual life out of us.

We don't like to admit it, but toying with sin is something that virtually all of us have done at some time, and perhaps are in the middle of right now. You might wonder how the last spiritual snare, "Carelessness," differs from this one, "Toying with sin." They are both dangerous. And often the difference is only a matter of degree.

"Carelessness" stumbles into a sensual TV program and gets caught watching it. "Toying with sin" turns the TV on looking for one. "Carelessness" stumbles into an inappropriate relationship at work. "Toying with sin" goes looking for one at night. "Carelessness" stumbles into a dishonest business practice, because everyone else is doing it. "Toying with sin" decides that he doesn't have enough money to live on and goes to work looking for ways to put illicit money in his pocket.

Temptation is the fire that boils to the surface the scum of the human heart. Things that we thought were lying there, idle, comatose, or perhaps we didn't know were there at all, or we thought we had gotten rid of altogether, come floating like flotsam to the top when the heat of temptation brings life to a boil. To master sin in our lives, we must understand temptation.

When we are tempted to toy with sin, the object of our desire causes remarkable changes in us, like Dr. Jekyl turning into Mr. Hyde. The eyes narrow until all you can see is . . . *that*. The mind concentrates until all you can think about is . . . *that*. The heart focuses until all you desire is . . . *that*. Up until that time, you can be reasoned with. You can think. You can evaluate. But after that time, reason is lost. A paralyzing, suffocating blindness sets in, and you *will* have your way!

Deitrich Bonhoeffer wrote, in his book *The Cost of Discipleship*: "When you are tempted to sin, you do not say, 'I hate God and God hates me.' Rather, you simply forget about God. And you do what you want."

It is a terrible snare—a ravaging, savaging snare which destroys us, sometimes quickly and sometimes slowly. We have seen it with television evangelists, we have seen it with congressmen, we have seen it with pastors, we have seen it with friends and loved ones, and unless we are careful, we will see it in ourselves.

Why Do We Toy with Sin?

In looking at temptation, we need to address three questions. First, why do we toy with sin? I think one reason is that we are dissatisfied with the life we have in Christ, and we try to find satisfaction outside of Christ.

Dissatisfaction with Life

We do not have the joy, the peace, the sense of meaning in our Christian experience that we long for. Others seem to have it, but we don't. Our eyes start roaming the horizon. We see other things that promise what we want. Indeed, the grass does look greener on the other side. Maybe God will help those who help themselves. We jump the fence and start grazing.

Adam and Eve are a good example of that. Satan said, "Has God done the best for you?" Doubt was created that God was looking out for Eve's best interests—that God cared, that God knew, and that God was doing all that was necessary. Eve says, "Yeah, maybe you're right." Then her eyes drifted over to the tree of the knowledge of good and evil. She saw, she desired, she took.

That is what we do. We have a fundamental doubt that God is looking out for our best interest, that He cares, that He knows, and that He is doing all that is necessary to give us a meaningful and satisfying life. With that as a background, something comes along; we see it, we desire it, and we take it.

Misperception of Our Worth

We have such a shallow vision of who we are. We think we are nobodies in the kingdom of God. He hasn't used us greatly in the past, and He won't use us greatly in the future. So it really doesn't matter all that much.

You are so wrong! You are not a nobody! You are a somebody! It does matter! God wants to use you!

What is the greatest thing you can conceive of God accomplishing through you? I don't mean an unrealistic thing, like replacing Billy Graham, but things that would mean a great deal to you, and you would enjoy. There is a very good chance that is the kind of thing God wants to do with you. The fact that it came to your mind might be an indication that you are gifted in that area, and God is preparing you for the time when He would use you for that.

You underestimate yourself. You think you are not losing anything by toying with sin. But you are. You are forfeiting the things that you would really love to do if you could just have the chance. You don't realize that God is in the process of getting you ready.

Bondage to Sin

A third possible reason for toying with sin is that you are addicted or in bondage to a sin. We believe that Christ is the answer for the deepest longings of our heart, but we are in a bondage that we cannot break. This is a special category, and one that lies outside the scope of this book. Nevertheless, there are some general guidelines that are worth mentioning. Bondage to sin presents some great challenges to the Christian. But bondage to anything—food, alcohol, drugs, sex, television, pornography—seems to require heroic personal effort in response to God's work in the life.

Anything that works very frequently is usually closely related to the twelve steps of Alcoholics Anonymous. I have paraphrased the twelve steps below, and included in following parentheses some information I think is helpful for the Christian, so that we are not merely trying to "pull ourselves up by our own bootstraps."

1. Admit that you are powerless over the sin.

2. Believe that God can restore you.

3. Turn your life over to Him. (For salvation, if that has not yet been done, John 3:16—or for total dedication, if that has not been done, Romans 12:1–2.)

4. Make a searching and fearless inventory of yourself. (Ask the Holy Spirit to reveal the sin in your life.)

5. Admit to God, yourself, and another human being the exact nature of your wrong. (Confess your sin, ask for His help in overcoming it, and accept restoration to His fellowship, 1 John 1:5–2:2—and place yourself in a spiritual accountability relationship with another mature Christian, Galatians 6:1–5.)

6. Be entirely ready to have God remove the defect of character.

7. Humbly ask God to remove your shortcoming.

8. Make a list of all persons you have wronged and become willing to make amends to them all.

9. Make amends wherever possible, unless to do so would injure them or others.

10. Continue to take personal inventory, and when wrong, promptly admit it.

11. Seek, through prayer and meditation, to improve your conscious contact with God, praying for knowledge of His will and power to carry it out. (Be sure you are involved in the Christian disciplines of prayer, reading your Bible, studying it with other Christians, attending a church where you worship God meaningfully, and develop relationships with other Christians who can encourage you in your battle.)

12. Carry this message to others and practice these principles in all your affairs.

Consequences of Toying with Sin

Men are usually hit the hardest in the area of moral and ethical purity. Men seem to tend toward compromise in these areas more readily than women—not that some women don't and not that all men do. Purity of thought life is often the battle ground. Men are visual. The visual appeals to them. The visual tempts them. Immoral women know that, and advertisers know that. We live in a society in which there are no holds barred, visually. From cars to beer to computers, visual temptation is the standard medium to appeal to men. It's like an alcoholic having to swim in liquor. There is no shame. There is no discretion. There is no sense of morality.

Christian men must be made of iron, and that iron must be laid at the foot of the cross if they are to escape being ravaged by the sensual, immoral, shameless visual society in which we live. If they aren't, there are three steps toward their destruction:

1. *Contamination.* They start looking once, twice, or too long. The looks turn into thoughts. The thoughts turn into desires that cannot be fulfilled within God's will. They get contaminated.

2. *Stagnation.* They start getting dissatisfied with what God has given them. They start wanting more than the will of God will give them. They keep up the facade, while fulfilling fantasies on the inside. They look for ways to fulfill the increased desire that the first illicit look created.

3. *Devastation.* They get hooked on pornography, or they become open to a relationship outside God's will. They begin following, either openly or secretly, a lifestyle that feeds the inner desires. Finally, they fall into immorality, and their life is destroyed. Chalk up another one.

The same is true with ethical behavior and honesty with words and money. In an effort to get ahead, or catch up to break even, they fudge on words or on numbers. It becomes a habit. The habit becomes a character. The character becomes a destiny. They loose their reputation and credibility at best. At worst, they lose their job or their kids (who become like them), or wind up in jail.

Women have their own set of temptations. Often, they become open to illicit relationships. Men tend to look to their accomplishments to give their lives meaning. Women tend to look to relationships to give their lives meaning. With men, a new illicit relationship is another conquest. With women, it is central to a new life which they are longing for. If they do not keep their temptations under control, three things can happen:

1. *Contamination.* They become emotionally involved with a man who will not lead them closer to Christ. They like it, and they do not turn away from it. The purity of their devotion to Christ is contaminated.

2. *Stagnation.* They begin to excuse it. They find ways to justify it.

3. *Devastation.* They get involved in a relationship that takes them away from Christ.

I cannot tell you how many women I have seen start dating someone, get emotionally involved, lose their perspective, their ability to evaluate, get married, and *regret it almost overnight.* It is as though some fever comes upon them, and they cannot be reasoned with. And as soon as the honeymoon is over, the fever breaks; they wake up from their delirium and ask, "What in the world have I done?" Certainly, that problem is not limited to women, but it is an acute problem.

The same is true of women who get a divorce and marry someone else, only to discover that they have simply exchanged problems.

Teenagers and young singles are particularly vulnerable to the pursuit of pleasure. Peer pressure becomes the dominating influence in their lives, and they begin to act like everyone else. Like lemmings, they follow everyone else and rush off the cliffs. Teenagers will follow almost any absurdity or any immorality if other teenagers are doing it—with no thought for the consequences.

Finally, everyone is susceptible to the siren song of society—be rich, be good looking, be successful. We hear it with every television commercial, see it in every magazine, and listen to it in every song. And when we feel we aren't making the progress that satisfies us in these areas, we go beyond the will of God for them.

We aren't as rich as we want to be, so we get head over heels in debt. We aren't as good looking as we want to be, so we become sensual and dress in ways that dishonor God and ourselves. We aren't as successful as we want to be, so we put on as though we were, and perhaps even become dishonest about it.

James sums up the consequences as succinctly and as well as anyone:

> Let no one say when he is tempted, "I am being tempted by God." For God cannot be tempted by evil, and He Himself does not tempt anyone. But each one is tempted when he is carried away and enticed by his own lust. Then when lust has conceived, it gives birth to sin; and when sin is accomplished, it brings forth death. (James 1:13–15)

The consequences of toying with sin are that you step off onto a slippery slide, and there is no place to get off. It is dangerous, and when played out, it will destroy your life every time.

How Can We Escape the Destruction of Sin?

First, we must choose to live by faith. We must choose to believe that the Bible is true and that the deepest longings of our soul can only be met in Christ. If we don't believe that, we will have trouble acting properly.

As a practical step, you must build your faith by reflecting on the truth of Scripture. You must strengthen your ability to see and believe deeply that Christ and only Christ can bring you the satisfaction and longing of your soul. Nothing but Christ can satisfy you completely enough and long enough to fulfill the deepest longings of your soul. Anything else will satisfy for a while. But then it's not enough. You need more. It is like cocaine. It promises you immediate gratification, but in the end, it slits your throat.

Second, get tough with the spiritual disciplines such as prayer, Bible reading, worship, fellowship with other Christians, and so on. Often this is the problem. You fail at getting tough with these, and so you do not have the basic nourishment for spiritual growth. If you struggle with these, get help from others who are mature in these areas. They will give you the assistance you need.

In his book *Strengthening Your Grip*, Chuck Swindoll tells the story of the value of having gotten tough with the discipline of Scripture memory:

When I was in the Marines, I spent nearly a year and a half in the Orient. Some of the time I was stationed in Japan, most of the time on the island of Okinawa. Eight thousand lonely miles away from my wife and family. Lots of free time . . . plenty of opportunities to drift into sexual escapades. Brightly lit bars, with absolutely gorgeous (externally, that is) females of any nationality you pleased, were open seven nights a week, 365 days a year. The sensual temptation was fierce.

I was in my mid-twenties. I was a Christian. I was also one hundred percent human. It didn't take me long to realize that unless I learned how to force my body to behave, I'd be no different from any other Marine on liberty. Without getting into all the details, I developed ways to stay busy. I occupied my time with creative involvements. When walking along the streets, I walked fast. I refused to linger and allow my body to respond to the glaring come-on signals. My eyes looked straight ahead . . . and sometimes I literally ran to my destination. I disciplined my mind through intensive reading, plus a scripture memory program. And I began most days praying for God's strength to get me through. The battle was terribly difficult, but the commitment to sexual purity paid rich dividends, believe me.

It worked, and it will work for you too. Now, before you think I'm the monk type, let me declare to you nothing could be further from the truth. I simply refused to let my body dictate my convictions.[1]

Third, catch sin early. Benjamin Franklin wisely said, "It is easier to deny the first impulse than to satisfy all that follow." The first time you are attracted to a woman, ask yourself on the spot: Am I willing to destroy my wife, my children, my reputation, and my financial well being for the sake of this woman? If the answer is *no*, then run from the temptation and see the end from the beginning. It is predictable. Catch sin early.

The first time you are tempted to be dishonest in business dealings or with your taxes, ask yourself if you are willing to go to jail. If the answer is no, then turn from the temptation and see the end from the beginning. It is predictable. Catch sin early.

I have a friend who was on a strict diet. He was traveling, and the only thing on the hotel menu he could eat was the "Slim Jim," a half pound of ground round with cottage cheese and a tomato slice. When it came, it had a peach half on top of the cottage cheese. The peach half was forbidden.

He ate the meat and cottage cheese and was still hungry. The uneaten peach half beckoned to him. "Well, I've already paid for it, and it is only a minor infraction," he rationalized. He ate it. He was smitten with guilt. He was still hungry. "Well, I've ruined perfection, so a little more won't hurt." He ordered a hamburger. He thought he would only eat the bottom half of the bun. It wouldn't be a major violation.

Several minutes later, a *cheese*burger arrived. The cheese was melted over everything. No use trying to separate anything from anything. He ate it all.

The cheeseburger automatically came with french fries. He hadn't realized that. "If I've eaten the cheeseburger, a few fries aren't going to matter." He ate the fries.

He sat there with guilt washing over him like ocean waves at high tide. "How could I have done it? How could I have been so weak? How could I have failed so miserably?" Finally the failure loomed so large that nothing else seemed to matter. He ordered and ate a large helping of apple pie a la mode!

Every little sin is like the top of the slide at the city park. Step off, and there is no place to stop. It is essential to catch sin early, before it gets out of hand.

Fourth, be ready for temptation before it comes. Understand ahead of time that temptation will come to you in several predictable areas. Morality, ethics, success—decide ahead of time how you will respond to them.

Fifth, cleanse your environment and relationships. What is in your home that is not honoring to God? Get it out. Burn it, trash it, cancel it, sell it, get it out. Who among your friends pulls you away from Christ? "Bad company corrupts good morals." Sever the relationship if it pulls you away from Him.

Sixth, learn when to hold 'em and when to fold 'em. Learn when to fight and when to flee. The Bible says, stand firm in your faith, resist the devil, and he will flee from you. This is the area of trials and satanic attack from which you cannot escape.

The Bible also says, "flee youthful lusts." These are temptations which you can get away from. Flee.

For the life of us, we cannot get this right. We usually get it backwards. We try to stand in the face of temptation, and we try to flee trials. We must turn it around.

Finally, know what God expects from you and accept God's forgiveness for failures. God is sympathetic with our weakness. He is patient with our sincere weaknesses. He deals harshly with our rebellion, but He is patient with our honest weaknesses. Psalm 103:8–13 says, "He knows our weaknesses, and is mindful that we are but dust."

Basketball players are made in the summer, not in the winter. Winter is when basketball season is, but that is not when basketball players are made. That is when it is revealed what they became in the summer. If you want to achieve your potential in the winter, summers must be spent lifting weights, running, doing calisthenics and stretching exercises. That is when you must do dribbling exercises, ball handling exercises, working on your reflexes, and shooting, shooting, shooting the ball. Endless foul shots.

Then, in the winter, that is when we play. That is when we scrimmage with our teammates, and then the games begin, and that is the test of what we became in the summer.

Most people who play basketball do not pay the price in the summer to be at their best in the winter. Their sights are not high enough. They are satisfied with mediocrity. Or they lack vision. Or they do not know how important the summers are.

Many times, basketball players get discouraged with dribbling, and weights, and running, and foul shots. They think, "This isn't basketball." Oh, but it is. And those who are most faithful in the off-season and preseason maximize their potential as a player.

The same is true in the Christian life. God has to train us, He has to get us in shape, He has to teach us the game, He has to help us "become" before He puts us into the game. The trouble is, many of us won't do it. We won't pay the price in the summer to be our best in the winter.

Is it that you lack vision for what God would like to do through you? God wants to do great things through you. He wants to fulfill some of your greatest dreams. Believe that God will do great things with you if you remain under His training regimen until He says you are ready.

Is it that you lack faith that He actually wants to do it? Look at the examples of Joseph, David, and Paul. It was years and years before their dreams came true.

Francis Schaeffer spoke at Dallas Seminary when I was a student there. In an informal question and answer session after a lecture someone asked him how he accounted for the fact that no one had heard of him, and suddenly, he burst on the evangelical scene with dramatic force. His answer: "I stayed home and did my homework for 20 years."

Temptation and toying with sin can be likened to fishing. When you go fishing, you are trying to tempt the fish to take the bait. You take something the fish really likes, and you hide in it a hook. Then, the fish thinks it is getting the worm, and he does. But he gets something else he didn't bargain for . . . the hook.

What are you tempted to go outside the will of God to get?

- More money? There's a hook in it!

- A husband? or a wife? There's a hook in it!

- A girlfriend or boyfriend? There's a hook in it!

- More fun? There's a hook in it!

- More respect? There's a hook in it!

- A house? There's a hook in it!

- A car? There's a hook in it!

- A job? There's a hook in it!

There may be nothing whatsoever wrong with these things if the will of God is giving it to you. But if you must go outside the will of God to get it, there is a hook in it.

Don't take the bait. Believe that God will satisfy you in the end.

> Do not be deceived, God is not mocked; for whatever a man sows, this he will also reap. For the one who sows to his own flesh shall from the flesh reap corruption, but the one who sows to the Spirit shall from the Spirit reap eternal life. And let us not lose heart in doing good, for in due time we shall reap if we do not grow weary. (Galatians 6:7–9)

Father in Heaven, give me presence of mind to always be aware of "hooks" in the things that beckon to me from this world. Give me strength to resist. Give me clarity of thought in the midst of temptation to bring to mind that which I already know. Save me from the heartbreak of foolish sin. Lead me not into temptation, but deliver me from the evil one, for Yours is the kingdom and the power and the glory forever. Amen.

REVIEW

1. **Why Do We Toy with Sin?**

   We toy with sin because we think it will *satisfy,* or we think it won't *hurt,* or we are *addicted* to it.

2. **Consequences of Toying with Sin?**

   Our spiritual life experiences *contamination, stagnation,* and finally, *devastation.*

3. **How Can We Escape the Destruction of Sin?**

   We must choose to live by *faith,* we must get tough with the spiritual *disciplines,* and we must catch sin *early.*

As a memory exercise, write in the missing words in the paragraphs below. Notice that they are the same words as the italicized words in the paragraph above.

1. **Why Do We Toy with Sin?**

   We toy with sin because we think it will _____, or we think it won't _____, or we are _____ to it.

2. **Consequences of Toying With Sin?**

   Our spiritual life experiences _____, _____, and finally, _____.

3. How Can We Escape the Destruction of Sin?

We must choose to live by _____, we must get tough with the spiritual _____, and we must catch sin _____.

RESPONSE

Questions for Group Discussion or Personal Exercises

1. Have you ever seen someone else go through the contamination, stagnation, and destruction process? Why could they not break the process?

2. Are you toying with sin right now? Where are you in the process? Stop right now and determine what you must do to break the process. Commit your plan to the Lord and ask for His guidance and strength.

3. Are you addicted to some sinful habit? Is there a support group or individual whom you think the Lord might use to help you break the habit?

4. Do you feel God is taking you through "summer training" right now?

5. Can you relate an experience in your life when you got a "hook" along with the bait, as you went outside the will of God to find satisfaction?

NINETEEN

SPIRITUAL EXHAUSTION

Fatigue makes cowards of us all.

Vince Lombardi

We each have an inner reservoir of spiritual and emotional energy. If that reservoir is depleted at a rate that is faster than it is replenished, then sooner or later we will eventually collapse, emotionally and spiritually, like a Florida sinkhole. Sometimes this is called burnout. Sometimes it is called Baby Boomer Syndrome. It is always called "The Pits." Gordon MacDonald writes in his book *Ordering Your Private World*:

> Recently, the residents of a Florida apartment building awoke to a terrifying sight outside their windows. The ground beneath the street in front of their building had literally collapsed, creating a massive depression that Floridians call a sinkhole. Tumbling into the ever-deepening pit were automobiles, pavement, sidewalks, and lawn furniture. The building itself would obviously be the next to go.
>
> Sinkholes occur, scientists say, when underground streams drain away during seasons of drought, causing the ground at the surface to lose its underlying support. Suddenly everything simply caves in, leaving people with a frightening suspicion that nothing—even the earth beneath their feet—is trustworthy.
>
> There are many people whose lives are like one of Florida's sinkholes. It is likely that at one time or another many of us have

213

perceived ourselves to be on the verge of a sinkhole-like cave in. In the feelings of numbing fatigue, a taste of apparent failure, or the bitter experience of disillusionment about goals or purposes, we may have sensed something within us about to give way. We feel we are just a moment from a collapse that will threaten to sweep our entire world into a bottomless pit. Sometimes there seems to be little that can be done to prevent such a collapse. What is wrong?

If we think about it for very long, we may discover the existence of an inner space—our private world—about which we were formerly ignorant. I hope it will become apparent that if neglected this private world will not sustain the weight of events and pressures that press upon it.[1]

Some of us have experienced that collapse, and, like Humpty-Dumpty, are trying to figure out how to put the pieces back together again. Others of us fear we are collapsing at this moment. Many of us are aware of a severe leak in the dike, and while we may not be fearful of imminent collapse, we do not look forward to living like this the rest of our lives.

What do we do about it? Why is it so common today? What are some of the symptoms? And what can we do to avoid it? What can we do if it has already happened?

Why Is Spiritual Exhaustion So Common?

Time magazine ran an issue in which the cover story was on "time." Looking back it called life in the 80s a rat race: "a lifestyle which is wearing everybody out, wrecking families, and destroying marriages."

Life was not supposed to turn out this way, and the prognosticators are surprised and disappointed. In 1965, during a testimony before a U.S. Senate subcommittee, social planners predicted that in 20 years, by 1985, people would be working only 22 hours a week. But we can see that they were completely wrong. Actually, the opposite has happened. Many people now work 50 hours a week, while some work 60 hours a week or more. Professionals, self-employed, and especially women who combine careers with homemaking, labor 80 hours a week or more.[2]

The final paragraph of the article concluded that, in order to correct the situation which is slowly destroying our society, it will require more than simplistic innovations. Little adjustments and timely hints for living are not going to be enough.

> If we are going to restore a climate in our nation where the family is going to be reinforced instead of ripped apart, and, if we are going to create an environment where children and adults are going to enjoy life rather than constantly complain that they are either worn out, depressed or lonely, this will demand major changes. In fact, in the author's own words, this will demand dramatic changes in both attitude and economics.[3]

These are not preachers heralding this message. They are secular observers. Our society is in serious condition. We have abandoned Biblical principles so quickly and so dramatically that we have nothing to hold the fiber of our society together.

Spiritual exhaustion is so common because we live in a time-pressed society where exhaustion is common. This is social mud, and by rubbing up against it, Christians get muddy, just like everyone else does.

A second reason why spiritual exhaustion is a serious problem for Christians is because of media bombardment, primarily television, music, movies, and magazines. The media are out of control and pander to the lowest common denominator of moral, ethical, educational, and social acceptance. The media are concerned with one thing: money. And it is willing to pillage American society to get it. If it were doing it by force, it would be by far the gravest injustice in the history of mankind. However, it is not doing it by force. It finds, in Americans, a willing partner. If that were not astonishing enough, the church, largely, is also willing.

The offerings of the media are like sugar to the diet. There is no nutritional value, and feeding on it excessively causes malnutrition and exhaustion. By feeding on media with no spiritual nutrition, we expend mental and emotional energies without getting anything in return. Television, music, movies, and magazines are dangerous to one's spiritual health if not scrutinized carefully. Like picking raspberries among the thorns, fruit can be found, but you must be careful, or you will get scratched.

The hyperactive pursuit of pleasure on the lowest common denominator has gutted us of our sense of dignity and worth, stripped us of our sense of purpose, decimated our capacity to care about truly worthy things, and has left us lying face down on the sidewalk of life, frazzled in the pursuit of things that do not satisfy.

I am aware of the arguments about whether the media reflects society or influences society. It seems clear to me that it does both. It reflects the disintegration in society, and in doing so, speeds the disintegration of society. Because of the media, what took hundreds of years to happen in the decline of Rome is happening in one generation in America.

A third reason Christians are affected by the time pressures is because, like all people, we are driven inherently by a desire for peace and prosperity. To get them we must control people, possessions, and circumstances. But controlling people, possessions, and circumstances is like a one-armed man trying to stuff an unwilling cat into a burlap sack. We can't control those things completely enough, or long enough, to bring us the sense of satisfaction that we long for. So, we redouble our efforts. The more unsatisfied we feel, the harder we strive for these things, until like a disoriented swimmer in the middle of the Atlantic Ocean, with no hope for rescue, we slip below the surface.

Finally, we are affected by time pressure because it is a tool of spiritual warfare. We get deceived into thinking that a hurried life is where meaning comes from. Remember, Satan is a deceiver and a destroyer. Those are two names of Satan: the "Deceiver" and the "Destroyer" (Revelation 9:11). He deceives in order to destroy. He deceives us into buying the world's value system, and with it, he destroys our spiritual health.

What Are the Symptoms?

Physical exhaustion is one symptom. All you want to do is rest, to get away from the demands on you. You try to find ways of escape. You may stop performing certain responsibilities. You may start watching too much television. You may get too involved in hobbies or sleep too much.

A second symptom is that you stop caring about things you ought to care about. A sort of emotional numbness sets in, and you don't care about the lost; you don't care about the starving masses; you don't care about the disadvantaged, because you are in your own sort of survival game.

Third, you have a short fuse, and your emotional weakness can be brought out at the drop of a hat. If it's anger, or fear, or depression, or whatever your emotional weakness is, you may be fine one minute and buried by your weakness the next.

Those are all personal symptoms. There are also family symptoms. Tim Kimmel, in his book, *Little House on the Freeway,* writes of seven marks of a hurried home:

1. A family which cannot relax. It is not that they don't want to. It's that they cannot.

2. A family which cannot enjoy quiet. A TV or radio or something has to be going all the time.

3. A family which never feels satisfied. They are always waiting for something to happen so they will be happy.

4. A family which has no absolutes. The parents never stand for anything, so their children fall for everything.

5. A family which constantly serves other people, because they are insecure and need to convince themselves that they have value. The result is that they live overcommitted lives.

6. The family where things are quiet on the surface, but storms are brewing below the surface.

7. The family where everyone is overachieving with accomplishments, so they never have time for each other.[4]

What Can Be Done About It?

There are practical things which can be done to help bring our lives into control and reduce the frazzle factor. These by themselves will not be sufficient, but they will help and will pave the way for taking the second step which we will look at in a moment.

First, cut back on your schedule and get more physical rest. Stop watching the evening news. Go to bed instead. Reduce your commitment to evening activities. Stay at home more often. Make Sunday a day of rest. If circumstances allow it, take a nap each afternoon for 20 minutes. If not, perhaps some other time. There is therapy in sleep.

Next, get organized. This is a tough one, because this is one of the things you don't want to do. It may take you a while to get squared away on it, but ultimately it takes less energy to be organized than disorganized.

Third, if a certain activity replenishes you, work it into your schedule—playing the piano, listening to soothing music, reading a good book, painting, cross-stitching, mowing the yard, exercising, such as walking or jogging, or doing something with your hands. If it replenishes you, work it into your schedule.

In addition, get help from others. Align yourself with other people who encourage and strengthen you—Sunday school class, bird-watchers, fellow workers.

Also, learn to say *no*. You say it by placing the tip of your tongue on the ridge of your mouth right behind your front teeth, then verbalizing the vowel "O" through your nose. NNnnoooo.

Finally, cultivate the inner life. Gordon MacDonald suggests four ways in *Ordering Your Private World*. Let us elaborate on his four ideas:

1. Solitude and Inner Silence: Wayne Oates writes in his book *Nurturing Silence in a Noisy Heart*, "Silence is not native to my world. Silence, more than likely, is a stranger to your world, too. If you and I ever have silence in our noisy hearts, we are going to have to grow it. You can nurture silence in your noisy heart if you value it, cherish it, and are eager to have it."

Am I crazy? Is this preacher out of touch with reality? No. We live in an extreme age, and it will take extreme measures for many of us to thrive . . . if not to survive.

2. *Listening to God:* This is not a matter of waiting for God to speak audibly to you in the middle of the night. Rather, it is a mind of receptivity for the Holy Spirit to work in your heart, to illumine truth to you from the Scripture, and to place God's burdens and directions on your heart.

MacDonald suggests journaling. Journaling is very individual. Each person probably does it slightly different. For many, it is like keeping a diary of your spiritual life and inner thoughts. By regularly getting alone with God and writing down your thoughts, you place yourself in a position to be silent before the Lord and let Him work in your life. Bill Hybels, in his book, *Too Busy Not to Pray,* also extols the virtues of journaling. I find myself able to get in touch with the Lord more effectively through journaling than any other discipline I have tried.

3. *Reflection and Meditation:* Often this will come about while journaling, but it need not be limited to journaling. Reflection and meditation are lost activities and are one reason why the world is so shallow. It takes time to think significant thoughts. Insight into life does not come out of thin air. It comes from reflection and meditation.

4. *Prayer and Worship:* One of the greatest challenges to the Christian is to find significant ways to worship. There is a beehive of activity in the "daily devotional" scene. Books and magazines abound to help pull you out of bed in the morning and give you some time with the Lord. Since worship is so personal, no one can answer what you should do. But you should do something to foster a personal quest for satisfying ways to worship the Lord. By the way, don't forget a hymnal. You can buy one at any Christian bookstore (don't take one home from church Sunday!), and it can be a wonderful aid to personal worship. If you can get away with singing, then sing! (Remember, all you have to do is make a joyful noise. That is within the realm of all our abilities.) If you can't get away with singing out loud, then sing in your mind, or take it in the car with you as you drive to work (don't mind the stares from people who think you are talking to yourself). Remember that

Jesus Himself sang a few hymns while worshipping with His disciples the night He was betrayed. It is a great way to worship.[5]

In addition to these practical measures for coping with the frazzle factor, there are two very important internal requirements.

How do you have inner rest in the midst of outer turmoil? To gain peace in a troubled world and calm in a hurried life, while all about you life is spinning out of control, you must choose to rest. Rest is a choice. Jesus said, "Come unto me, all you who are weary and heavy laden, and I will give you rest. Take my yoke upon you and learn from me, for I am gentle and humble at heart, and you will find rest for your souls" (Matthew 11:28).

When we find ourselves not resting, when we find ourselves weary and heavy laden, it is usually because we are carrying a burden that Jesus never intended for us to carry. If it is His yoke, we will find rest. If it is not His yoke, it will be heavy and burdensome. This is a very difficult thing to learn. It is an art that is only mastered by constant attention over time, nurtured by constant reaffirmation of truth.

Resting is believing that everything God said is true and acting accordingly. Resting is believing that the important things in life are the things God says are important and acting accordingly. Resting is believing the promises of God and acting accordingly. We must, as the writer of Hebrews mentions, "Labor to enter into God's rest" (Hebrews 4:11).

Next, we must develop a counter-culture mentality. I am not suggesting that we wear beards, plain clothes, and drive horses and buggies. That misses the point. I am suggesting that we develop the mindset that "I am no longer one of them." I am no longer a red-blooded American first. I am Christian first.

The United States used to be so Christianized that you did not have to make a choice about whether you were a Christian first or an American first. The two could easily be synonymous. However, because the two are diverging so rapidly and so dramatically, there are times when we must choose between the two.

Patrick Morely, in his book *The Man in the Mirror*, gives this example:

> I am sure you have seen a daring circus performer riding two horses at the same time. He has one foot firmly planted on the

back of each horse. He can do this because they are so close together. If the two horses begin to move apart from each other, though, the performer must pick one or the other to ride. So it is with our spiritual pilgrimage.[6]

We are now at the point, and I say it reluctantly and with great sadness, that we must begin to choose whether first to be American or whether first to be Christian. And I say, we must choose first to be Christian. The great dilemma facing the church today is that most of us are choosing first to be American without realizing how often it is causing us to be sub-Christian in our attitudes and behavior.

Let me be very clear. I am not saying we ought to lessen our love for our country, or our concern and labor to improve it. I love America just as much as anyone, and pray for her and do what I can to improve her. But America is in a moral crisis today. Her greatest need is not political in nature. It is moral. And by calling people to morality, I am doing much for her welfare. John Adams once said that American government was suitable only for a moral people. Let morality disappear, and we lose our ability to govern ourselves. We are seeing the truth of that statement unfold before our very eyes.

As a church, we must understand what is happening to us. The horse of Christianity and the horse of American culture, which we used to be able to ride together, are now diverging, and we must decide which one we are going to ride. It may be American to act this way and do those things. But is it Christian? Until we distinguish between the two, and have the strength to choose to be Christian above being American when we are forced to choose, our Christian life will flounder, and the church in America will flounder.

Next, we must take life as it comes. We must accept circumstances as the will of God brings them to us. We must rest in the reality that this life is not all there is. One beer company used to have a commercial that said, "You only go around once in life, so grab all the gusto you can." It isn't true. This life is not all there is. If you miss out on something you wanted in this life, it is no tragedy, because whatever you want in the next life, you will have.

This world is not our home. We are just passing through. We are strangers—sojourners. This is, as C. S. Lewis said, a shadow land. Reality is in the next world.

Again, Gordon MacDonald writes as he concludes *Ordering Your Private World*:

> As Thomas Kelly says, "We are trying to be several selves at once, without all our selves being organized by a single, mastering Life within us." Life is meant to be lived from a Center, a divine Center. Each one of us can live such a life of amazing power and peace and serenity, of integration and confidence and simplified multiplicity, on one condition—that is if we really want to.
>
> And that is the condition with which we must finally deal. Do we really want order within our private worlds? Again, do we want it?
>
> That center is God, Jesus, the Holy Spirit. There, He is more than what is contained in some doctrinal statement about Him. He is more than the mushy words of some contemporary song. At the center, He commands attention as the risen Lord of life; and we are compelled to follow after Him and draw from the strength of His character and compassion.
>
> When we have turned within, to live life from the center out . . . from the inside out, the public world can be managed and properly touched. Relationships with family and friends, with business associates, neighbors and even enemies take on a new and healthier perspective. It becomes possible to forgive, to serve, to not seek vengeance, to be generous.
>
> Our work will be affected by exercise at the center. Work will be given new meaning and a higher standard of excellence. Integrity and honesty will become important items of pursuit. Fear will be lost, and compassion will be gained. We are less apt to be seduced by the false promises and seductions of those out to capture the soul.
>
> All of this and much more goes into motion when the private world is ordered first . . . before the Christian walks in the public world.[7]

To handle the crush of the world, to avoid the frazzle factor, to keep from being spiritually exhausted, we must cultivate an inner life, tuned to an eternal perspective, where our spirit can be strengthened, where our inner reserves are replenished at a rate equal to their depletion. This is where we can avert spiritual exhaustion.

> Those who wait for the Lord will gain new strength; they will mount up with wings like eagles, they will run and not get tired, they will walk and not become weary. (Isaiah 40:31)

Heavenly Father, May I be filled with the knowledge of Your will in all wisdom and spiritual understanding; that I may walk worthy of You, fully pleasing You, being fruitful in every good work and increasing in the knowledge of You; strengthened with all might, according to Your glorious power, for all patience and longsuffering with joy; giving thanks to the Father who has qualified me to partake of the inheritance of the saints in the light. I pray in Jesus' name, Amen. (Colossians 1:9–12)

REVIEW

1. Why Is Spiritual Exhaustion So Common?

We live in a *society* which fosters a breakneck *pace* in life and promotes impossible *dreams*.

2. What Are the Symptoms?

Three common symptoms are physical *exhaustion,* a lack of *caring,* and a short emotional *fuse.*

3. What Can Be Done About It?

There are three things that can aid spiritual exhaustion significantly: control your *schedule,* do things that *replenish* you, and cultivate your inner *spiritual* life.

As a memory exercise, write in the missing words in the paragraphs below. Notice that they are the same words as the italicized words in the paragraph above.

1. **Why Is Spiritual Exhaustion So Common?**

   We live in a _____ which fosters a breakneck _____ in life and promotes impossible _____.

2. **What Are the Symptoms?**

   Three common symptoms are physical _____, a lack of _____, and a short emotional _____.

3. **What Can Be Done About It?**

   Three things can aid spiritual exhaustion significantly: control your _____, do things that _____ you, and cultivate your inner _____ life.

RESPONSE

Questions for Group Discussion or Personal Exercises

1. Is the "frazzle factor" part of your current experience? Which of the symptoms do you find in yourself (exhaustion, stopped caring, short fuse)?

2. Which has the greater tendency to lead you to spiritual exhaustion, the external factors or the internal factors?

3. What have you found to be helpful to bring you genuine rest (a quiet place, reading, yard work, music, etc.)?

SECTION FIVE

SPIRITUAL WARFARE

*When we enter the Christian life,
we enter not a playground
but a battlefield. Life is not a waltz.
It's a war. In addition to the snares
we might inadvertently step into
on our journey, we must be constantly
on guard against spiritual attack.*

TWENTY

SPIRITUAL WARFARE

*Humanity falls into two equal and opposite
errors concerning the devil. Either they take
him altogether too seriously or they do not
take him seriously enough.*

C.S. Lewis

Warfare isn't merely a matter of putting people on two sides of a line drawn in the sand and "having at it." There is also the diplomacy, the espionage, the negotiations, and maneuvering behind the scenes. So it is with spiritual warfare. It isn't all blood and guts. Part of it is a chess match behind the lines.

The newspapers reported a fellow waiting at the Portland airport for the arrival of the Portland Trailblazers, a professional basketball team. They had just defeated the Los Angeles Lakers, and he wanted to capitalize on the upbeat mood of the fans by trying to scalp a couple of good tickets to the next game. He was asking the outrageous price of $150 each!

He approached a well-dressed man and offered the tickets to him. The gentleman fixed a frozen stare on him and replied, "Do you realize I'm a plain-clothes policeman?"

The scalper turned to jelly. He began to babble. He begged for mercy. He talked about a large family back home, how they would

227

starve if anything happened to him, and how this was the first time he had ever done this sort of thing and would never do it again.

The other man said, "Just hand over the tickets, and we'll call it even. Now get out of here before I change my mind. And I had better never catch you down here again!"

We think, *what a tangled web we weave, when first we practice to deceive!* But wait. That's not all. The well-dressed gentleman was not a plain-clothes policeman at all. He was just a quick-thinking pirate who used his resourcefulness to scalp the scalper.

That's war! That's the chess match. Just as men pit wits against other men, so there is a pitting of wits against each other in the spiritual war. There is also behind-the-scenes maneuvering which is part of spiritual warfare. That's the kind of trickery that we will fall prey to if we try to do battle on our own. It isn't only a matter of slugging it out in the trenches. We are perhaps safest when we know we are in spiritual combat. We are perhaps most vulnerable when we don't realize we are in spiritual combat. Satan is as slick as a melting ice cube and just as cold. The plain-clothes pirate is an amateur compared to him. Spiritual warfare does involve blood and guts combat on the front line. But it also involves spiritual sleight-of-hand behind the lines. Hang on to your sword, but hang on to your wallet, too. We must be ready for both.

Since we live in a nuts and bolts world, it is sometimes hard for us to focus in on spiritual warfare. Think of it this way. There are hundreds of people in the room with you right this moment! You do not see them, nor do you hear them, but they are there, riding along on television and radio signals. We are in an ocean of radio signals and television signals. The evening news, public television, dramas and comedies are swirling around us like mosquitoes on a fishing trip; only they are invisible. We are utterly unaware of them until we turn on the television.

Is it difficult, then, for us to accept that it may be so with another dimension? Is it difficult to imagine that there may be angels and demons in the room with us, even though we are not aware of it? Just as our five senses are not designed by God to pick up radio and air waves, so they are not designed by God to pick up the presence of angels and demons. But just as the radio signals are there, so may the angels and demons be.

There is a spirit world around us which we are not aware of. In Daniel, chapter 10, we read of the angel Michael coming to Daniel in answer to his prayer, and admitting that he would have been there sooner, but he was detained by the prince of Persia, an evil angel sent to interfere with his mission. None of this warfare was visible to man, however.

We read of the angel announcing the coming of Jesus to Mary, and later of many angels announcing His birth to shepherds. One minute the angels were visible, and the next they were invisible (Luke 2:8–20). In the Gospels, we read of people being possessed by invisible demons (Matthew 9:32–33). In Hebrews 13:2, we read of people entertaining angels without realizing it. In Revelation, the spiritual warfare comes out in the open, and we see the forces of light and the forces of darkness locked in mortal combat throughout the book. Spiritual warfare is a reality!

If we do not prepare for spiritual war, the next casualty may be us. Peter writes: "Be sober, be on the alert. Your adversary the devil walks about like a roaring lion, seeking someone to devour" (1 Peter 5:8). Paul writes that Satan "disguises himself as an angel of light" (2 Corinthians 11:14). Jesus asserted that Satan was "a liar, and the father of lies" (John 8:44).

Revelation 9:11–12 gives us insight into Satan's strategies. He is a deceiver and a destroyer. He deceives in order to destroy. This, of course, is in keeping with his appearing as an angel of light, and his being a liar and the father of lies.

Satan can take poison and make it taste like candy. He is the master illusionist. He takes what is good and makes it look bad. He takes what is wrong and makes it look right. He takes what is true and makes it look false. He takes what is ugly and makes it look beautiful. He makes it easy for us to rationalize it.

There are two vital areas which are part of his "front line" offense. First, he wants to get us to sin by increasing the reward or by lowering our resistance. After this, he wants to bury us with guilt.

Getting Us to Sin

Satan deceives us in several ways into sinning. He convinces us to say to ourselves that "it isn't so bad . . . it won't hurt." He convinces us that no one will find out, and that God will forgive anyway. He convinces us that what he is tempting us will actually satisfy us. He saps our spiritual convictions, so that we don't care. He gets us overtired and frazzled so that we don't care. We just want immediate relief, and we are willing to do whatever will give us immediate relief. He twists our thinking so that we don't know what is right anymore.

These and other strategies are honed to a fine art. He has been plying his craftsmanship for centuries. Those of us who have only been around for a measly twenty to eighty years are no match for him by ourselves.

Temptation

The wares he has for sale appeal to three things: the desires of the flesh, the desires of the eyes, and the pride of life (1 John 2:16). A desire, of course, is not wrong. But when it begins to control you, it becomes a lust, and then it becomes wrong. A desire may be your servant, spurring you on to good things. A lust is your master, enslaving you to bad things.

The desires of the flesh include physical things—food, sleep, sex, activity, and so on. These, in and of themselves, are wholesome and God-given. When they begin to control us, they become a lust and a major avenue for Satan's destructive work. Gluttony, alcohol and drug abuse, and sexual immorality become ends in themselves, enslaving us and destroying us.

The desires of the eyes include a desire for beautiful things. When this desire begins to control you, it is a lust. Whether it is cars, or houses, or clothes, or jewelry, or "collections of things," or even things which might seem insignificant to others, if the desire controls you, it is lust, and can destroy your walk with God. Of course, there is nothing wrong with beauty or enjoying beauty. God is a God of beauty. Nevertheless, uncontrolled, it can destroy one's Christian experience, and even worse.

The pride of life includes power, ambition, and doing things that bring recognition. Again, there is nothing wrong with desiring great things, but if the desire conflicts with walking closely with God, it becomes a lust which can enslave us. We are all tempted in these areas. It is not wrong to be tempted. Jesus Himself was tempted. But it is wrong to succumb to the temptation.

Jesus is our best model for how to fight this temptation. Luke chapter 4 shows us not to try to fight temptation merely in our own strength. When Jesus was tempted, He met each temptation with Scripture. Satan said, "Command this stone to become bread." Jesus said no because "it is written, man shall not live by bread alone, but by every word that proceeds out of the mouth of God." Satan said, "Throw yourself down from this tower." Jesus said no because "it is written, you shall not put the Lord your God to the test." Satan, upon showing Him all the kingdoms of the world, said, "It shall all be yours." Jesus said no, because "it is written, you shall worship the Lord your God, and serve Him only."

If Jesus used Scripture to fight off temptation, how much more must we? If we are not learning Scripture, we leave ourselves vulnerable to Satan's deceit and will find ourselves nostril deep in the quicksand of life.

Spiritual combat can come in two forms: temptation and spiritual opposition. When we are tempted to sin, we are to flee ("flee youthful lusts," 2 Timothy 2:22). When we are confronted with spiritual opposition, we are to fight ("resist the devil and he will flee from you," James 4:7).

Most of us have a genius for reversing the two. When we sense that we may be involved in spiritual opposition in our life and ministry, we want to flee. And when we are presented with temptation to sin, we usually want to stand and fight.

Erosion

To get us to sin, Satan must either increase the incentive or reduce the resistance. So, the first powerful stratagem Satan has to get us to sin is temptation: offering us powerful incentives to overcome our resistance. The second stratagem he uses is to weaken our resistance.

In this area, he has hit on the most powerful tool in the history of mankind—modern media. The media (television, music, movies, and literature) have been used as a tool to neutralize the lives of many Christians. Satan stocks the shelves of our mind with sand and sawdust and gravel and poison. When we go shopping, we need wisdom and strength and integrity and purity. But the shelves are full of the other. We can't get what we want.

Satan plants the same seeds in the mind of the Christian as the non-Christian. We find ourselves wanting the same things non-Christians want, thinking the same things non-Christians think, doing the same things non-Christians do, laughing at the same things non-Christians laugh at. The values of Christ are relegated to philosophical remnants in the back of the mind.

The accumulation of material things becomes center stage for the neutralized Christian. Homes, cars, clothes, vacations, conveniences, gadgets, schools, extracurricular activities—the trappings of American society—all become focal points for them. It is not that they want these things instead of Christ. It is that they want these things in addition to Christ.

They still want to go to church, but the church needs to meet the same standards as the rest of their lives. The church must have the preaching of Billy Graham, the music of the Mormon Tabernacle Choir, the program offerings of a junior college, and the facilities of a country club.

As a result, many churches, which operate with a commitment to excellence, find their pews filled with people on Sunday morning, but find these people unwilling to involve themselves in things that call for commitment and sacrifice. The Christian church is being neutralized. It is being turned into a country club. Its affairs are primarily internal, with little effect on the world.

This is an area of spiritual warfare, and we are hapless victims of someone who is brighter and more powerful than we are. We are being manipulated by a superior mind into a form of behavior which, if we thought clearly about the issues, we would choose to avoid.

Guilt and Forgiveness

The first great tactic which Satan uses in his spiritual warfare is to get us to sin. The second is to nullify in our minds the work which Christ did on the cross for us.

Sin separates us from God. Before we accept Christ, it separates us from Him eternally. After we accept Christ, it separates us from Him in fellowship. If Satan can keep a Christian mired in guilt, it keeps the Christian from the joy of Christ and eliminates him as an effective force in leading others to Christ. Satan is constantly accusing Christians of their sin, and convincing them that they have no business continuing their charade of Christian living.

"You lousy phoney!" he screams in the daytime. "You worthless human defect," he whispers at night.

"You're right. You're right. Who am I? What do I think I am doing?" we agree. And then he has us right where he wants us.

It is true, as we grow in Christ, we keep coming across things we ought to stop doing, as well as things we ought to start doing. In both cases, the Christian is usually a little weak in the early days, particularly if he comes to Christ as a later teenager or adult. Being a little weak, there are sometimes sins which he commits repeatedly or omits repeatedly.

Of course, God does not want us to sin, but He knows that we will. Everyone, no matter how old, how educated, how talented, how experienced when he comes to Christ, he comes as a spiritual baby. All babies exhibit inferior behavior for an adult. But they grow, and in time, are able to conduct themselves as a mature adult. The same thing is true spiritually. All spiritual babies exhibit inferior behavior for an adult. But they grow, and in time, are able to conduct themselves as a spiritually mature adult.

However, the scenario in the Christian life often goes something like this: The young Christian sins. He feels remorseful. He asks forgiveness from the Lord and asks for strength not to sin again. Then he sins again—the same things. He feels doubly remorseful. He goes back to the Lord and says he did it again, but he is sorry and will not do it again. Please forgive him. Then he does it again. He comes back to the Lord and admits that he did it again, but please forgive him, for he *will not* do it again. Then he goes out and does it again. He comes back to the Lord and says, "Lord, I've done it again. But I *promise* I will not do it again. Please forgive me." Then he goes out and sins again.

Now he is defeated. He has gone to the Lord so many times, and the last time he promised he wouldn't do it again. He is now convinced that his name brings a noxious odor to the nostrils of God. He is embarrassed to go to God again.

Have you ever felt this way? Satan then continues his strategy. He begins to hurl epithets at you. However, he does it in the first person, so you think you are talking to yourself. "You bum. You dizzy failure. You odious slice of humanity. You pitiful excuse for a Christian. Who do you think you are, anyway? You should have known from the beginning that you couldn't make it as a moral success. You *are* a failure, so you were a fool to even try. The Christian life might work for others, but it won't work for you. You are inherently flawed. If you were a fish, the church would throw you back. If you were a car, the manufacturer would have to recall you. Give it up. Stop trying to fake it. Come back into the old life where you belong!" And you believe him. You go down in flames.

Now what is the answer to such a scenario? Surely God doesn't want you to sin. He doesn't take sin lightly. God cares that you are sinning. But you seem powerless to overcome it immediately. How can you come to Him when you are so aware of your sin?

There are several facets to the answer to this question. Part of the answer depends on the kind of sin you are dealing with. If it is general sin of immaturity, you must accept that you will take time to grow out of it. For example, a nasty temper, or bad driving habits, or failure to act lovingly toward people, or neglect of a regular time in Scripture and prayer are things which we must work toward, and be patient with God as He gives you the spiritual growth to put these things behind you.

We are afraid to teach this, because we fear others will abuse it and go out and sin like crazy. However, when someone truly understands the love of God, that our relationship with Him depends not on our ability to cleanse ourselves but on His grace, the result is not going out and sinning like crazy. Rather, the result is just the opposite: a dropping down to the knees and crying out to God in gratitude and thanksgiving that, in spite of all your shortcomings, He does not desert you. A profound gratitude and increased desire to be holy is the result.

Peter did us a tremendous favor by demonstrating that we could not sin so often, nor so badly that God would not forgive us. First, he came to Jesus, and said, "Lord, how many times should I forgive my brother who sins against me? Seven times?" Peter probably thought he was going the extra mile in saying seven. Two or three seems plenty! Jesus' answer to him was, "Not seven times, but seventy times seven." Jesus was not saying "490 times." Rather, He was saying, "However many times it happens." If God expects us to forgive others that many times, then He will forgive us that many times. By asking this question, Peter demonstrated that we cannot sin so many times but what God is willing to forgive us.

Second, Peter demonstrated that we cannot sin so badly that God is not willing to forgive us. The worst sin I can imagine is cursing God and denying that you even knew Him. And that is exactly what Peter did. As Jesus was enduring the kangaroo courts and mock trials, Peter was turning to jelly. A little girl came along and said, "I know you. You are a follower of Jesus." Peter swore and denied he ever knew the Lord. Yet, just days later, Peter was sitting on the shores of the sea of Galilee, eating breakfast with the risen Lord, in perfect fellowship and harmony with Him. And Peter's days of most significant ministry came after the denial (not that denial makes you stronger, but that such an awful sin does not make you unusable in the future).

So Peter demonstrated that you cannot sin so often, nor can you sin so badly, but what God will forgive you. Many of us have Peter's blood flowing in our veins. We are impetuous, inconsistent, fickle, and undisciplined. God doesn't want us to be that way. He will work with us to grow us out of those characteristics. Nevertheless, we are His children, and He will love us through those things. Never fear to come to Christ for forgiveness. As often as you come, that's how often He will forgive you.

Central to accepting these marvelous truths is understanding what Christ did for us on the cross and how we gain acceptance with God in the first place.

The Victory

The secret to withstanding Satan's accusations is not merely what we do, it is what Christ did on the cross. If we truly understand it, we can stand against Satan's accusations. If we don't, we might not be able to.

As John White wrote in his book, *The Fight:*

> The Father does not welcome you because you have been trying hard, because you have made a thorough going confession, or because you have been making spiritual strides recently. He does not welcome you because you have something you can be proud about. He welcomes you because His Son died for you.
>
> Therefore, when you find the grey cloud descending, whether it be as you pray, as you work, as you testify or whatever, when you find the ring of assurance going from your words because of a vague sense of guilt, look up to God and say, "Thank you, my Father, for the blood of your Son. Thank you, even now, that you accept me gladly, lovingly in spite of all I am and have done—because of His death. Father and God, I come."[1]

Resist the efforts of Satan to accuse you, to bury you with guilt, to make you feel worthless and unqualified to come to Christ again. It is part of his warfare strategy to make you ineffective as a witness and unhappy as a disciple. Be on guard against his wiles, recognize them, and stand firm against him.

Does God ignore our immaturities? No. Just as a young child may be spanked for disobedience to his parent, so a young Christian may get spanked for disobedience to God. As a young child is chastened and disciplined to curb undesirable behavior and encourage desirable behavior, so the Lord chastens and disciplines His children to encourage desirable behavior (Hebrews 12:4–13). But none of it changes the acceptance which God has of us as His children. Never would it keep Him from accepting a sincere request to be forgiven of sin and restored to fellowship.

God is patient with weakness and immaturity. He is stern and decisive with rebellion. Weakness says, "I want to, and I am trying, but I fail." To this God says, "Come to me, my child, for strength and forgiveness, and restoration to fellowship." Rebellion says, "I don't even want to, and I am not going to even try." To this God says, "Be prepared to taste the consequences of your actions."

In Corinthians 11, Paul says of some of the Corinthian believers who abused the Lord's Supper, that some of them were weak and sick, and some of them had even died. Nevertheless, they were His children.

These two areas—"getting us to sin" and "guilt"—are not all there is to spiritual warfare. Rather, they are examples of spiritual warfare. The point, then, is to alert us to the reality of spiritual warfare, and to prepare us to fight well. In the next chapter, we will look at the weapons of war.

> Finally, be strong in the Lord and in the strength of His might. . . . For our struggle is not against flesh and blood, but against the rulers, against the powers, against the world forces of this darkness, against the spiritual forces of wickedness in the heavenly places. (Ephesians 6:10, 12)

Heavenly Father, help me to be aware of spiritual warfare, and help me not to be so foolish as to think that I am capable in myself of standing against the evil army. Protect me, guide me, keep me dependent upon You. May I abide in Christ, always, and be victorious in Him. I pray in His name. Amen.

REVIEW

1. Getting Us to Sin

Satan tempts us with the lust of the *flesh*, the lust of the *eyes*, and the pride of *life*.

2. Guilt and Forgiveness

We cannot sin so *badly,* nor so *often,* that God is not willing to *forgive* us when we repent.

3. The Victory

It is because of what *Christ* has accomplished for us on the *cross* that God is able to offer us *forgiveness.*

As a memory exercise, write in the missing words in the paragraphs below. Notice that they are the same words as the italicized words in the paragraph above.

1. Getting Us to Sin

Satan tempts us with the lust of the _____, the lust of the _____, and the pride of _____.

2. Guilt and Forgiveness

We cannot sin so _____, nor so _____ that God is not willing to _____ us when we repent.

3. The Victory

It is because of what _____ has accomplished for us on the _____ that God is able to offer us _____.

RESPONSE

Questions for Group Discussion or Personal Exercises

1. Do you have a tendency to give Satan too much credit or not take him seriously enough?

2. Where is Satan's temptation defeating you right now? Be honest!

3. Are you embarrassed to go back to God for forgiveness "yet another time?" Remember, you can't out-sin the grace of God.

TWENTY-ONE

SPIRITUAL ARMOR

But still our ancient foe,
Doth seek to work us woe;
His craft and power are great,
And armed with cruel hate,
On earth is not his equal.

Martin Luther

I magine you are a Roman soldier. You have enlisted in the Roman army, and this is your first day on the job. The Roman army was the finest in the world, and it was no small thing that you were selected to go to officer's candidate school. It was the Roman equivalent of the "Top Gun" school in our modern Air Force—"Top Sword," perhaps. You go to bed early the night before, eager to begin your first day. Your rooster goes off at 5:30 a.m. Rise and shine! Time to get dressed and present yourself for inspection.

After a quick shower, you put on your tunic, and then walk over to your foot locker where your battle gear is stored. First, you put on a thick leather belt that holds your tunic in place and will later hold your sword. Second, you put on your breastplate, a beautiful gold metal cast of a human torso. It makes you look better than you really do. Third, you strap on your leather shoes which are designed not only to protect your feet from cobblestone roads, but also have small spikes in them to give you traction under the worst conditions.

Fourth, you pick up your shield, a large piece of wood shaped like a crest, which is covered by decorative metal. Fifth, you put on your helmet which is a metal cast of your head, with two protective bars coming down past your temples to protect your cheeks. It has a red plume sticking up like a rooster's comb out of the metal. Finally, you pick up your sword which is sheathed to your leather belt. You are ready for inspection, and you are ready for war, for this is the gear of the soldiers of the greatest army in the world.

The Apostle Paul had many opportunities to study the armor of the Roman soldier. As a prisoner of Rome for many years, he had first-hand knowledge of the armor that protected the Roman soldiers in physical combat. While writing the book of Ephesians, Paul included instructions on how the Christian could protect himself in the spiritual combat. To give a visual image to help us remember, he likened the spiritual soldier's protection to the Roman soldier's armor.

You can imagine Paul pacing up and down in front of lines and lines of soldiers as he gives them their battle instructions. "You're in the army now! Christ's army. You will be doing battle the rest of your life. The forces you will be fighting are not forces you can see. They are spiritual forces, and they can only be defeated with spiritual weapons. So listen up! Here are your weapons of war and here is how you are to use them!"

The Need for Spiritual Armor

It all seems like strange talk to us. We are not used to thinking about invisible foes and celestial combat. We live in a nuts-and-bolts world. It's hard to get used to.

In his book *Spiritual Warfare*, Ray Stedman writes:

> What would you answer if you were asked "what is the thing that gives you the most difficulty in life; of what does the struggle of life consist?" Many would say that it is other human beings. There are the Communists, for instance who are always causing difficulty. They can never let anything rest in the world but are forever stirring up some kind of trouble somewhere. And then there are the Republicans or, if you are on the other side, the Democrats. They never let anything rest either but are always

making difficulties. In their bullheaded obstinacy they are continually refusing to "see the light."

And let us not forget the Internal Revenue Service. Certainly they are devils, if there ever were any. And the country tax department! And don't leave out your wife—and her family! Or your husband and his family. Then, how about our ancestors? . . . Our heredity is at fault. It is because we are Scotch or Irish or Italian—our family has always been this way; we have always had a hot temper. And so it goes.

But the Apostle Paul says that you cannot explain life adequately on that level. You must look further and deeper than that. The battle is not against flesh and blood. Rather, it is against the whole human race that certain principalities and powers, world rulers of darkness, wicked spirits in high places are set. There is your problem, Paul says. Those are the enemies we are up against. And it is not just Christians who are opposed by these, but every man, everywhere. The world race is opposed by the principalities and powers. There is Paul's explanation of the struggle of life.[1]

In the New Century Version Paul states flatly: "Our fight is not against people on earth. We are fighting against the rulers and authorities and the powers of this world's darkness. We are fighting against the spiritual powers of evil in the heavenly world."

If we are not careful, we will be duped into thinking we are battling people and circumstances in a "cause and effect" context, when all the time, things are being orchestrated by a mastermind behind the scenes. The evil mastermind is more intelligent and more powerful than we are. If we try to pretend he is not there, or if we try to do battle with him in our own intelligence or strength, we are doomed to failure.

That is why Paul urges us to put on the armor of God and *then* do battle. Paul says, "take up the full armor of God, . . . and *having done everything* to stand firm" (emphasis added). If we don't take up the armor, we can't stand firm.

We see, then, that the six pieces of spiritual armor refer to six spiritual truths which we must know, understand, and embrace if we are to be successful in the spiritual war. Christ "in us" is our defense, but by studying the spiritual armor, we can gain more specific and practical understanding of how to do spiritual battle.

The first three pieces of armor are fixed to the body. The belt is tied around the waist. The shoes are laced to the feet, up the ankle and calf, and secured just below the knee. The breastplate is secured to the torso. The second three pieces, the shield, the helmet, and the sword, are pieces which are taken up and put down. There does not seem to be any obvious significance to this fact, but it does cause a division of the pieces of armor into two segments, as well as a mental picture, which can make it easier to remember all six pieces.

Pieces of Armor Fixed to the Body

The Belt of Truth

The officers of the Roman army wore short *skirts* much like Scottish *kilts*. Over these shorter *skirts* they wore a longer, decorative tunic that hung down to the ankle. When going into battle, they tucked the long tunic up under the wide, heavy, leather belt which held the skirt and tunic at the waist. This got the long material out of their way so they wouldn't trip or get their sword caught up in the cloth. Also, their sword and other gear hung on the belt. The belt was a foundational piece of equipment.

The belt of truth, then, symbolizes having accepted absolute truth as revealed in the Bible and in Jesus, and being committed to following that truth with integrity. We might define it as: "You have placed yourself in an unhindered state of readiness for spiritual combat by accepting the reality of absolute truth."

If we didn't accept absolute truth in the Bible, we would do many things backwards. For example, the first shall be last, the great must be servants, to find one's life he must lose it, to give is better than to receive. Therefore, we must see truth as God sees it, or else we have no hope of winning the battle.

So, when you find yourself discouraged and tempted, how does the belt of truth help you specifically? You must remind yourself that you have accepted God's truth and decided to live your life based on His truth, and that truth is unchanging, the same yesterday, today, and forever. The things that are tempting you or discouraging you are not true. Oh, there may be some truth in them, but half-truth is a lie. Say, "I reject that tempting thought or that discouraging thought. I reject it as being false, and I commit myself to believing only what is true and acting accordingly."

A summary statement which will help us keep in mind the truth of the belt of truth is: I accept the truth of Scripture and commit myself to following it with integrity.

The Breastplate of Righteousness

The second piece of armor is the breastplate of righteousness. The breastplate, as we said, was a metal cast of the torso of a man, and was worn over the torso to protect the vital organs.

Theologians debate as to whether the spiritual meaning of the breastplate of righteousness in the Christian life refers to "imputed righteousness" or "imparted righteousness." Imputed righteousness means the righteousness that was given to us when we received Christ personally as our Savior. At that time Christ's righteousness was *imputed* to us. To *impute* means to give to, or to attribute to, or to place in one's account. For example, if I had the ability and inclination, I could take $100,000 and put it in your bank account. All I would need is your account number, and I could give the money to a teller and request that the $100,000 be deposited to your account. The bank, then, could contact you and tell you that $100,000 had been imputed to your account.

That is what Christ did for us. He deposited His righteousness to our account. We now possess His righteousness, because he placed it in our account. He imputed it to us.

Imparted righteousness means a quality of righteous living that comes when God works in our heart to "will and to do His good pleasure" (Philippians 2:13). When, by His work, we respond to His call to holy living, and begin to turn from sin and live lives which copy God's character and example, we are enjoying the imparted righteousness.

These are the two potential definitions of what it means to put on the breastplate of righteousness. It might mean imputed righteousness, and it might mean imparted righteousness. Theologians are divided as to which one it is. One argument says that it can't be imputed righteousness, because if Christ's righteousness is something that is placed on our account at the moment of salvation, there would be no need for Paul to instruct us to "take it up." It would already be in place. On the other hand, others say that it can't be imparted righteousness, because we aren't righteous enough in ourselves, apart from Christ's righteousness, to stand against the devil. Only Christ's strength and righteousness is sufficient for that.

My opinion is that they are both right. Here is how, I think, we can hold to both imputed and imparted righteousness being involved.

It is clear that if we toy with sin, or knowingly and willingly tolerate the presence of sin in our lives, we open ourselves up to influence from the "dark side." If we are sinning, and we know it, and we don't care, we are set up for Satanic deception and entanglement (see John 5:14). The worse the sin, the worse the trouble we open ourselves up for. For that reason, imparted righteousness is important. We must strive according to the grace of God that works in us to live lifestyles of righteousness. Philippians 2:12–13 reads, "Work out your salvation with fear and trembling, for it is God who is at work in you both to will and to work for His good pleasure." We must be concerned about living out the will of God. Romans 6:13 reads, "Do not go on presenting the members of your body to sin as instruments of unrighteousness; but present yourselves to God as those alive from the dead, and your members as instruments of righteousness to God." We must be concerned about living lives that do not willingly and habitually harbor known sin (see 1 Peter 1:15-16). This is surely part of what it means to put on the breastplate of righteousness.

On the other hand, the imputed righteousness of Christ, in my opinion, also comes into play. Here is how. No matter how desirous we are of living righteous lives, we will sin. First John 1:8 says, "If we say we have no sin, we deceive ourselves . . ." But, we read in 1 John 2:1–2 ". . . if anyone sins, we have an Advocate with the Father, Jesus Christ the righteous; and He Himself is the propitiation [satisfaction] for our sins; and not for ours only, but also for those of the whole world." When we sin, as we will, Jesus Christ is our advocate before the Father, and He, Himself, is the satisfaction before God for our sins. Therefore, "if we confess our sins, He is faithful and righteous to forgive us of our sins, and to cleanse us from all unrighteousness" (1 John 1:9).

If we forget that Christ is the one who makes us acceptable to God, we may fall into a "works" oriented basis for trying to find favor with God. It cannot be done. Isaiah says that all of our righteousness is as filthy rags to God. It is Christ and Christ alone who makes us righteous and fit to stand before God. It is by grace that we are saved, through faith (see Ephesians 2:8–10). So we dare not begin to think that by being good, we earn acceptance with God.

Another danger of not taking into account the imputed righteousness of God is that we can get discouraged and give up. We try to live holy lives, and we stumble. If we do not understand that God knows and understands that, we may begin to feel that our inconsistency makes God sorry that He ever saved us. We begin to feel that our name brings a noxious odor to the nostrils of God. We begin to feel like, "what's the use?" And we give up.

Again, Ray Stedman writes skillfully:

> Christians, through one circumstance or another, often lack assurance; they feel unworthy of God. They feel they are a failure in the Christian life and that God, therefore, is certain to reject them, that He is no longer interested in them. Christians are so aware of their failures and shortcomings. Growth has been so slow. The first joy of faith has faded, and they feel God is angry with them or that He is distant. There is a constant sense of guilt. Their conscience is always stabbing them, making them unhappy and miserable. They feel God blames them. This is simply a satanic attack, a means of opposing the destroying what God intends to do.
>
> How do you answer an attack like this? You are to remember that you have put on the breastplate of righteousness. In other words, you do not stand on your own merits. You never did. You never had anything worthwhile in yourself to offer to God. You gave all that up when you came to Christ. You quit trying to be good enough to please God. You came on His merits. You came on the ground of His imputed righteousness—that which He gives to you. You began your Christian life like that, and there is no change now. You are still on that basis.[2]

That is what Paul meant in Romans 8:1 when he wrote, "There is therefore now no condemnation for those who are in Christ

Jesus." No condemnation. That does not mean that God doesn't care if we sin. He does. It doesn't mean that He doesn't care whether we grow spiritually. He does. But it means that no matter how well we do spiritually, we are going to sin. John states it flatly: "If we say that we have no sin, we are deceiving ourselves, and the truth is not in us" (1 John 1:8). But, if anyone sins, he has an Advocate with the Father, Jesus Christ the righteous, and He Himself is the one who takes away our sins (1 John 2:1). If we confess our sins, He is faithful, and righteous, and will forgive us of our sins and cleanse us from all unrighteousness (1 John 1:9).

Therefore, it is on the basis of Christ's work in our behalf that we are acceptable to God. Therefore, there may be sin that we need to confess. But the point is, God accepts us in Christ, and in Him, we are covered, protected, with the breastplate of righteousness. We must remind ourselves of that during spiritual warfare. To remind ourselves of this is also involved in putting on the breastplate of righteousness.

If we were to summarize what we are saying that it means to put on the breastplate of righteousness, we might say: By God's grace, I dedicate myself to living as much like Christ as I know how, counting on Christ's righteousness to make me acceptable to God, and rejecting Satan's accusations against me when I fail.

The Shoes of the Preparation of the Gospel of Peace

The third piece of armor is the shoes of the preparation of the gospel of peace. Paul explains, "having shod your feet with the preparation of the gospel of peace." The NIV translates it, "with your feet fitted with the readiness that comes from the gospel of peace." The shoes of the Roman soldier were leather and were strapped to the legs with leather thongs. Often, the combat boots had short spikes to give sure footing in combat. A soldier with both feet in mid-air was a vulnerable soldier.

It is uncertain exactly what this means, and Bible commentaries differ on the meaning. However, it seems safe to conjecture that when we received Christ, we gained peace with God. We were no longer at odds with Him, alienated from Him, and subject to His wrath. We no longer fear death and condemnation. We have assurance of His presence and provision in the midst of life's diffi-culties. When we review His promises to us, and *count on them*, they can give us a sense of calm and well-being.

Let me illustrate this. I do not like to fly. On the other hand, I love to ride motorcycles. However, I do not ride motorcycles. But on the other hand, I do fly. It all seems backwards, doesn't it? The reason I don't ride motorcycles is that, in spite of the fact that I enjoy them immensely, they are dangerous. I can look at the statis-tics and see that it is not a good idea. On the other hand, though I do not like to fly, I do, because I look at the statistics and see that flying is relatively safe.

When I am at 35,000 feet and hit turbulence, my stomach al-ways ties up in knots, my knuckles turn white, and I clench my jaw. My breathing becomes erratic, and my eyes glaze over. I begin con-fessing every sin I have ever committed. Instead of calmly saying, "Lord, into Thy hands I commend my spirit," I start making irra-tional promises, like, "Oh, Lord, if you get me out of this, I prom-ise I will never get on an airplane again."

Then, I begin reviewing the truth. Airplanes almost never go down. I cannot ever remember a plane dropping out of the sky at 35,000 feet. They sometimes crash upon take off and landing (times at which I am never afraid), but they never drop out of the sky at 35,000 feet (the time when I am most afraid). As I review these truths, peace and sanity are restored.

In the same way, knowing that we have peace with God gives us a readiness to do battle, spiritually. We know that God will protect us and enable us to do whatever He calls us to. We know that in the end, we will live forever with Him. We know that the victory is already won, though the battle is still raging. We know that He loves us and will never stop loving us. Nothing can happen that will ever make Him reject us. Knowing these things gives us peace and inner calm. Knowing we have peace with God gives us the peace of God. And that gives us a readiness for warfare. We are ready, willing, and able to go into spiritual battle for Him.

The Bible says, "If God be for us, who can be against us?" With that kind of backing, we can have peace in the midst of battle. "In all these things we are more than conquerors through Him who loved us. For I am convinced that neither death, nor life, nor angels, nor principalities, nor things present, nor things to come, nor power, nor height, nor depth, nor any other created thing, shall be able to separate us from the love of God, which is in Christ Jesus our Lord" (Romans 8:31, 37–39). So when we hit the turbulence of spiritual battle, we remind ourselves of truth, and peace can be restored.

Putting on the shoes of the gospel of peace, then, might mean: I believe the promises of God, and count on them to be true for me, and then, I can have His peace in life.

With these three pieces of armor already in place, the only thing to say is "pick up the other three pieces and *charge!*"

The Pieces of the Armor Not Fixed to the Body

The Shield of Faith

The fourth piece of armor is the shield of faith. The shield for the Roman soldier was a large piece of wood, perhaps two-and-a-half feet by four-and-a-half feet. It was covered with metal or leather, and was held by leather straps. As the soldiers stood beside each other behind their shields, they formed a wall of protection between them and the enemy. When arrows, or spears, or swords reigned down on them, the blows were deflected without harm.

Flaming arrows were wrapped with pieces of cloth near the tip and soaked in tar or pitch. They not only pierced, but they also burned. They were usually fatal. Also, they could be used to start on fire tents, or buildings, or wagons, or anything else which would burn. The shields would either deflect them, or would extinguish them.

The "faith" in this context must not be confused with the body of faith in the Bible which we believe as Christians. Rather, it refers to the practice of exercising faith in life's situations. It means "believing what God has said and acting accordingly." When Satan comes along and attacks us with something false, we can catch the thought in mid-air and say, "No! I do not accept that. It is counter to what God has said, and I will not believe it, nor will I act upon it. I will believe what God has said and act upon it."

Satan says, "Psssst . . . hey! How about this little piece of sin? Interested?"

And you say, "Well . . . I don't know. It does look awfully nice. Lord? What do you think?"

And the Lord says, "Stolen bread *is* sweet, but while it is in your mouth, it turns to gravel. And remember, I am not mocked; whatever you sow, you will also reap."

At this point, to follow the impulse to sin is to fail to use the shield of faith. To turn from sin in obedience to God, because you believe what He says, is to use the shield of faith.

So Satan hurls at you a fiery dart, and you deflect it with the shield of faith. He says, "You'd be happier with another spouse." You say, "No! By faith, I believe I must commit myself to making this marriage a testimony of the grace of God."

He says, "You'd be happier if you made more money, even if you had to cheat a little to get it. No one would ever know." And you say, "No! By faith, I believe that money gotten dishonestly will not make me happy. If I cannot be happy without money, I will not be happy with it."

He says, "Tell your boss to go jump in the lake." And you say, "No! By faith, I accept that the anger of man does not achieve the righteousness of God."

He says, "Hang on to your money. Don't give any of it away. It's your only security." You say, "No! God is my security. I'll give to Him as He asks and trust Him to be my security."

He says, "God doesn't love you. Look at all the things He has done to you." You say, "All things work together for good."

He says "Why don't you bail out of the church? It's full of hypocrites." You say, "I'm part of the body of Christ, and my task is to help the church be more righteous."

And so it goes. The fiery dart comes, and you deflect it. Another dart comes, and you deflect it. Satan prompts you to sin, and the Holy Spirit prompts you to righteousness. You must choose, by faith, to do what God says. When you do, you are using the shield of faith to extinguish the fiery darts of the evil one.

Taking up the shield of faith, then, might mean: Whenever I feel like doubting, or sinning, or quitting, I will reject those thoughts and feelings, because I deeply believe that God's truth and will are best.

The Helmet of Salvation

The fifth piece of armor is the helmet of salvation. The helmet for the Roman soldier was a metal headpiece designed to protect the head from blows.

The helmet of salvation does not refer to personal salvation in Christ. This is addressed to people who were already Christians. Rather, it refers to a future aspect of salvation. There are three dimensions to salvation found in the Scripture:

1. "Salvation past" occurs the moment we receive Jesus as our personal Savior. That saves us from the penalty of sin.

2. "Salvation present" is our present personal spiritual growth as we grow more and more away from the dominating power of sin in our everyday life.

3. "Salvation future" is when we will receive new bodies unaffected by sin and will stand before the Lord completed, perfected, and untouched by sin.

It is the hope of our *future* salvation that gives us an eternal perspective in this life and keeps us on course. In 1 Thessalonians 5:8, Paul calls this same piece of armor "the helmet" which is "the hope of salvation." In Romans 8:22–24, Paul refers to our future salvation: "Having the first fruits of the Spirit, even we ourselves groan within ourselves, waiting eagerly for our adoption as sons, the redemption of our body." Peter speaks of this hope when he writes, "God . . . has caused us to be born again to a living hope through the resurrection of Jesus Christ from the dead, to obtain an inheritance which is imperishable and undefiled and will not fade away, reserved in heaven for you, who are protected by the power of God through faith for a salvation ready to be revealed in the last time (1 Peter 1:3–5)." This hope helps us keep an eternal perspective on present trials. As Paul wrote,

> Momentary, light affliction is producing for us an eternal weight of glory far beyond all comparison, while we look not at the things which are seen, but at the things which are not seen; for

the things which are seen are temporal, but the things which are not seen are eternal. (2 Corinthians 4:17–18)

Therefore, we must not grow weary in doing good, knowing that in due season, we will reap, if we do not faint. (Galatians 6:9)

As part of the spiritual warfare, we must keep an eternal perspective on all present circumstances, and "fix our hope completely on the grace that is to be brought to us at the revelation of Jesus Christ" (1 Peter 1:13). That is the helmet of salvation.

Taking up the helmet of salvation, then, might be described as: I fix my hopes and affections, not in this world, but in Christ and the next world.

The Sword of the Spirit, the Word of God

Now we come to the final piece of equipment for the spiritual warfare, the sword of the Spirit which is the Word of God. This is not referring to the entirety of the Word of God, or the Bible. If that had been meant, Paul would have used the Greek word *logos*. Rather, it applies to a specific passage or verse from the Word of God, and the word which is used is *hrema*. It implies using a specific truth from the Word of God for a specific situation in life.

It was modeled so well by Jesus in His temptation account in Luke 4. The devil came to Jesus just after His baptism and attempted to derail Him by promising to give Him all the same things which God the Father was going to give Him. However, Satan's offer violated God's timetable and God's method. Satan tempted Jesus three times. Each time Jesus rebuffed Satan's attempt with a quote from Scripture.

Satan said, "May I tempt you with this?" Jesus said, "No, because it is written . . . ," and He quoted Scripture. Satan came back, "Well, then, may I tempt you with that?" Jesus said, "No, because it is written . . . ," and He quoted another Scripture. Finally, Satan said, "Okay, how about the other thing?" Jesus said, "No, because it is also written . . . ," and He quoted a final scripture and then said, "So begone!"

This is a beautiful example of how the Scriptures are used as the sword of the Spirit. Specific truths from the Word to match specific situations in life. When you know the Bible well enough to apply it to life's situations, it becomes as a sword—able to defend against the attacks of the enemy, as well as to be an offensive weapon to put the enemy to flight.

One reason we struggle in life is that we do not know the Bible well enough to use it skillfully. We continuously get into trouble, which the Bible might have kept us out of had we known it better. We have to get serious about studying the Scriptures! Until we learn the Bible well enough, we must look to godly teachers and counselors who already know the Word well. They can help keep us from stumbling into problems. But ultimately, we must know them ourselves. We can't always have a scholar at our elbows.

Taking up the sword of the Spirit might mean, then: I will master the Word so well that I will be able to use it to strengthen and guide me in life's specific circumstances.

Conclusion

These are the pieces of armor. They are metaphors, or word pictures, for everyone:

1. Belt. I accept the truth of Scripture and commit myself to following it with integrity.

2. Breastplate. I dedicate myself to living as much like Christ as I know how, counting on Christ's righteousness to make me acceptable to God and rejecting Satan's accusations against me when I fail.

3. Shoes. I believe the promises of God and count on them to be true for me, and then, I can have His peace in life.

4. Shield. Whenever I feel like doubting, or sinning, or quitting, I will reject those thoughts and feelings, because I deeply believe that God's truth and will are best.

5. Helmet. I fix my hopes and affections, not in this world, but in Christ and the next world.

6. Sword. I will master the Word so well that I will be able to use it to strengthen and guide me in life's specific circumstances.

Be of sober spirit, be on the alert. Your adversary, the devil, prowls about like a roaring lion, seeking someone to devour. . . . Therefore, take up the full armor of God, that you may be able to resist in the evil day, and having done everything, to stand firm. (1 Peter 5:8, Ephesians 6:13)

> *Father in Heaven, in Christ may I stand firm against the adversary. With Your armor on, may I resist him. May I be sober and vigilant, knowing that he will come, sometimes like an angel of light and other times like a roaring lion, but each time his goal is to deceive me and to destroy me. I accept the call to vigilance and to arms. But, oh, Lord, be my protector and my strength. Amen.*

REVIEW

1. The Need for Spiritual Armor

Since our life *battles* are not physical but *spiritual*, we need spiritual *weapons*.

2. The Pieces of Armor Fixed to the Body

Because of the work of Christ in our lives, we already have in place the belt of *truth*, the breastplate of *righteousness*, and the shoes of the gospel of *peace*.

3. The Pieces of Armor Not Fixed to the Body

Since we must be active in the warfare, we must daily put on the shield of *faith*, the helmet of the future *hope* of salvation, and the sword of the Spirit, which is the *Word* of God.

As a memory exercise, write in the missing words in the paragraphs below. Notice that they are the same words as the italicized words in the paragraph above.

1. **The Need for Spiritual Armor**

   Since our life _____ are not physical but _____, we need spiritual _____.

2. **The Pieces of Armor Fixed to the Body**

   Because of the work of Christ in our lives, we already have in place the belt of _____, the breastplate of _____, and the shoes of the gospel of _____.

3. **The Pieces of Armor Not Fixed to the Body**

   Since we must be active in the warfare, we must daily put on the shield of _____, the helmet of the future _____ of salvation, and the sword of the Spirit, which is the _____ of God.

RESPONSE

Questions for Group Discussion or Personal Exercises

1. What truths of Scripture do you find yourself needing to reaffirm, to be spiritually stronger? For example—God is always with you. He can't love you any more than He does right now. You can't earn God's acceptance through works. Satan is a created being, not an evil co-equal, etc.

2. Which of the pieces of armor already in place have you been relying on the most (truth, righteousness, peace)? Which one have you been relying on the least?

3. Which of the pieces of armor which you are supposed to "take up" (shield of faith, helmet of salvation, sword of the Spirit) have been "resting on the floor," waiting to be used in your life?

TWENTY-TWO

THE BATTLE
FOR THE MIND

*He that cannot command his thoughts will
soon lose command of his actions.*

Woodrow Wilson

James Dobson laments that the trouble with life is that just about
the time your face clears up, your mind begins to go. Someone
said that as you get older, there are two predictable things that
begin to happen to your mind. The first is that you become forget-
ful. And second is . . . uhm . . . and I can't remember the second
one. The mind is, indeed, a delicate thing, and no two are alike.

Someone reportedly asked Albert Einstein how many feet were
in a mile. He said he didn't know. "How is it that you, an eminent
scientist, would not know how many feet were in a mile," the ques-
tioner asked? To which Einstein replied, "Why should I clutter up
my mind memorizing trivial facts which I could easily look up?"

Compare that with the staggering memory demonstrated by
the great conductor, Artur Toscanini. Just before a concert, a clari-
netist came up to Toscanini and said that he would be unable to
play since the E-natural key on his instrument was broken. Toscanini thought deeply for a moment and then announced, "It's all
right; you don't have to play an E-natural tonight."[1]

It is hard for most of us to identify with that level of intelligence and memory. Most of us identify more closely with Joseph Jefferson, a renowned actor during the Civil War. One time he was coming down the elevator of a building in New York, and when the elevator stopped on a floor, a man got on who was familiar to Jefferson. He greeted Jefferson very warmly and commented that it had been some time since they had seen each other. Jefferson tells a friend the story: "He was very gracious and friendly, but I couldn't place him for the life of me. I asked him as a sort of feeler how he happened to be in New York, and he answered, with a touch of surprise that he had lived there for several years. Finally, I told him in an apologetic way that I couldn't recall his name. He looked at me for a moment, and then he said very quietly that his name was U.S. Grant."

"What did you do, Joe?" his friend asked.

"Do?" he replied, with a self-deprecating smile. "Why, I got out at the next floor for fear I'd ask him if he had ever been in the war."[2]

The Mind Is the Gateway to Our Lives

We joke about our mind, and properly so if we are to keep our perspective. But there also is a serious side to the mind. The mind is the gateway for all we are, all we have been, and all we will be. Our habits, our attitudes, our values, and our actions will all stem from what we do with our mind. The old proverb says, "You are what you eat." It is saying that whatever you eat will eventually be metabolized and become part of your physical body. If you eat well, you will be healthy. If you do not eat well, you will be sick.

The same is true of your mind. Whatever you think about will eventually form your beliefs, attitudes, values, and habits. These, in turn, determine the outcome of your life. "You are what you think." And "you think about that which you let into the mind." The Bible says, "As a man thinks in his heart, so is he" (Proverbs 23:7). "Watch over your heart with all diligence, for from it flows the springs of life" (Proverbs 4:23).

We know also that spiritual warfare is waged in the mind. That is, when the evil one wants to tempt you, and deceive you, he works through the mind. In Romans 7:23, we read, "I see a different law in my members of my body, waging war against the law of *my mind* . . . " (emphasis added).

Peter calls us to do battle by guarding the mind: "Gird your minds for action, keep sober in spirit, fix your hope completely on the grace to be brought to you at the revelation of Jesus Christ" (1 Peter 1:13).

Paul wrote in Philippians that what we think about determines the amount of peace we have in life:

> Whatever is true, whatever is honorable, whatever is right, whatever is pure, whatever is lovely, whatever is of good repute, if there is any excellence and if anything worthy of praise, let your mind dwell on these things. The things you have learned and received and heard and seen in me, practice these things; and the God of peace shall be with you (4:8–9).

And finally, Paul said in Romans 12:1–2, that the key to having a happy life was to have our mind transformed:

> I urge you therefore, brethren, by the mercies of God, to present your bodies a living and holy sacrifice, acceptable to God, which is your spiritual service of worship. And do not be conformed to this world, but be transformed by the renewing of your mind, that you may prove what the will of God is, that which is good and acceptable and perfect.

Once again, if we work this passage backwards, we see that the final outcome is that our lives become living demonstrations of the fact that God's will is good, perfect, and acceptable.

In order to be such a living demonstration, we must not be conformed to this world. In order not to be conformed to this world, we must have our minds transformed. In order to have our minds transformed, we must present our bodies as a living sacrifice.

All these passages combine to provide a powerful thesis that the mind is instrumental to all that we hope to be. We must guard carefully what we put into the mind, and we must regulate with considerable precision what we allow the mind to think about.

We Must Guard Our Minds

Therefore, two things must become top priority in our lives. First is that the Scriptures must be learned with great dedication. Jesus said, "You shall know the truth, and the truth shall set you free" (John 8:32). If we do not know the truth, conversely, we will be in bondage to bad decisions, poor judgment, foolish actions, bad habits, crippling attitudes, and detrimental values. I cannot tell you how many times people have come with heart-rending problems, which, had they known and followed the Scriptures, could have been avoided altogether. They are tragically unnecessary problems.

The second inescapable conclusion to which we are led is that we must guard carefully that which we allow into the mind that neutralizes or militates against the truth of the Scripture. This is an urgent problem in modern society because of the pervasiveness of the media. Television, radio, movies, and literature are everywhere, and everywhere they promulgate a philosophy which neutralizes or militates against the Scripture.

I must speak carefully and softly here, because otherwise I may be rejected as a blind counter-culturist. I hope I am not that. But it is of little question that television, in particular, has become the single most powerful force in the history of mankind. And largely, the influence has been detrimental. The degree of social, moral, educational, and cultural disintegration that took four hundred years to occur in the Roman Empire has occurred in forty years in America, largely because of television.

The standards of television, music, movies, and literature, in the main, are somewhere between sub-Christian and anti-Christian. The message of television is sexual freedom, individual freedom, and violence. The message of most modern literature follows. The message of movies is the same as television but much more extreme. Television has followed behind the movies by a decade or so but has gone the same route. The message of rock and roll music is largely sex, drugs, and rebellion. The message of country and western music is largely sexual escapades, infidelity, and drunkenness. The message of elevator music is little better, though usually not as aggressive or clear.

Now, this is not to say that there aren't good songs in each of these musical categories. A number of years ago, a country and western singer, John Conlee, recorded a song entitled "In My Eyes," which told the story of a husband who was reassuring his wife that, even though she was getting older, she was only getting more beautiful to him. It was really a very touching song. I came across it one day after listening to Paul Harvey on that station. But it is one song in one hundred, or perhaps one thousand. The same could be said of the other musical media.

In the same vein, there is much good in television, and there are good movies that come along. And certainly, there are good books being written. So it is not accurate to wave a hand at the whole mess and say "it's all bad!" It isn't all bad. However, it is so predominantly bad that we cannot listen, watch, or read indiscriminately and not pay a fearful price.

The programming in television and movies that is not overtly harmful can have a distorting effect on people's perception of life in that God utterly is left out. This is a subtle but real problem. When we watch people solve problems and pursue happiness without ever looking to God or the Scriptures for guidance and enlightenment, then it tends to program us to solve problems and pursue happiness without looking to God or the Scriptures. We find ourselves living life the only way we know how—the same way the people on the television do. This traps us in a lifestyle that is sub-Biblical and keeps us from reaching the heights of enjoyment in life which we might normally experience in Christ.

This is a partial explanation for an unusual phenomenon today in which we have a generation of Christians who embrace the truth on a philosophical level, but whose lives contradict that truth. They hold to one level of truth, but they have only seen a lesser level modeled in real life, and the modeling has the greater impact.

On a related theme, harmless television viewing can begin to erode the spiritual life if done excessively, not so much because of a negative effect directly, in so much as that it keeps you from doing better things. Sports programming is a common culprit in this category. Everyone needs diversion and relaxation, and I certainly have nothing against using television for such. However, if taken to excess, it begins to have an overall harmful effect.

The point is not that if we watch something, or listen to something, or read something that violates Biblical standards that it makes God mad and He is going to get us for it. That misses the point of this chapter. The point is we cannot move away from God without moving closer to pain. We cannot move away from good without moving closer to bad. We cannot move away from helpful without moving closer to harmful. Every time we violate God's standards, we harm ourselves. That is one of the reasons God hates sin. It hurts His children.

God has made us, and He knows what will work and what will not work in our lives. It is the same as the automobile manufacturer who makes the car, and so it knows what is best for the car— what will work and what will not work. We read the owner's manual and we say, "How narrow minded. Indeed. Only premium gasoline. I could save a lot of money by buying inferior gasoline." And so you could. But later on, you will have to pay that price and ten times more to have the engine repaired.

It is not a matter of legalism. It is a matter of adhering to the inevitable principles of life. Obey God's standards and benefit; disobey them and pay a price.

Now, it is probably no more harmful to watch one television program, or listen to one rock and roll song, or one country and western song, than it is to eat one Twinkie. But if you start eating ten Twinkies a day, you begin to pay a terrible price. Live on Twinkies, and your life would be threatened.

So we each have a decision to make. We must protect our minds. We must guard our minds. We must watch over and nurture our minds. What we allow into our minds has a determinative impact on our lives. It determines our attitudes, our values, and our habits. It determines who we become. And if we hope to become like Christ, we cannot allow our minds to feed on things which neutralize or militate against that goal.

Breaking the Hold of Besetting Sin

One of the fiercest battles of the mind rages on the front of *besetting sin*. By besetting sin, we are talking about some attitude or habit that we fall prey to consistently. It may be anger in traffic, or impure thoughts, or overeating, or aggression at work, or yelling at the kids, or sarcasm, or insensitivity toward your spouse, or too much television.

When the Holy Spirit convicts us of sin in one of these areas, and places in our heart a desire to be free from it, there is a mental process of reviewing Biblical truth which, when embraced, strengthens the individual against these sins and helps to break their power.

Remember Who You Are

We must deeply believe who we have become in Christ. We are no longer a child of the world. We are a child of God—born again, re-created spiritually to be holy and righteous. The pull to sin does not come from within this renewed spiritual being which we have become. It comes from outside, from the flesh which is as yet unredeemed. When we feel these pulls to sin, we recognize them as imposters. We say, "No! That is not me! That is the world, the flesh, or the devil, but it is not me, and I choose not to accept it as me!" And we catch the temptation in mid-air.

Recognize Your Deep Longings

We must come to deeply believe that we have deep personal longings for love and meaning, for security and significance. These are perhaps the two driving natural forces in our lives. Everything we are motivated to do is influenced by a desire to be secure in a loving relationship that is comprehensive and unending, to feel significance as a person, and to have a sense of purpose and meaning in life. It is not wrong to have these longings. They are given by God. However, we instinctively sense that we must try to gain our security and our significance through our own resources or accomplishments. There is a sense of incompleteness and dissatisfaction with our life. As a result, we are tempted to go outside the will of God to bolster our self-esteem.

Recall That Christ Alone Can Meet Your Deepest Needs

We must come to deeply believe that those deepest longings cannot be met sufficiently outside of Christ. When we deeply believe that the fundamental longings of our soul cannot be met fully except in Christ, it becomes counterproductive for us to entertain sin. It only interferes with what we long for—a sense of security in a love relationship, a sense of significance personally, and a sense of meaning and purpose with what we do with our lives.

When we deeply believe this, we understand that sin takes us in the opposite direction of why we sinned in the first place—because we thought it would give us a more satisfying life. If we deeply believe this, we gain new strength not to sin.

Resist the Temptation, Knowing It Is a Lie

Having affirmed that truth, we must break with anything that feeds the old desires, and we consciously focus on removing the besetting sin from our actions, habits, or attitudes. The break with that sin may not be made immediately. But new strength can be gained, and the battle can eventually be won.

In saying what I have about breaking the power of besetting sin, I'm talking about sins of habit and attitude. There is another matter—addiction. This must be dealt with differently. There are a number of things you can be addicted to: alcohol, drugs, cigarettes, sex, pornography, eating. These sins often have their root in unhappy childhoods and are often tied to some kind of abuse (physical, sexual, emotional, chemical/alcohol) in the background. If addiction to one of these or other activities is part of your experience, or if you have one or more of the kinds of abuse in your background, your sin must be dealt with somewhat more specifically. Such is not the scope of this book, however. Organizations such as Alcoholics Anonymous, various hospitals and treatment centers, and Christian counselors can be very effective in dealing with addictions. If you think you may have an addiction, it may be necessary to seek help from one of these organizations specifically set up to handle these special needs.

For though we walk in the flesh, we do not war according to the flesh, for the weapons of our warfare are not of the flesh, but divinely powerful for the destruction of fortresses. We are destroying speculations and every lofty thing raised up against the knowledge of God, and we are taking every thought captive to the obedience to Christ. (2 Corinthians 10:3–5)

> *Dear Father in Heaven, I agree with the need to protect my mind. Convict me of sin when I do not guard my mind adequately. By Your grace, I will destroy ungodly speculations and every lofty thing raised up against the knowledge of You, and I will take every thought captive to the obedience of Christ. Catch me when I stray. Hold me to Yourself, in Jesus power and name. Amen.*

REVIEW

1. The Mind Is the Gateway to Our Lives

The mind is the gateway to all that we *are*, all we have *been*, and all we will *be*.

2. We Must Guard Our Minds

We must *fill* our minds with the truth and must *screen* out that which *neutralizes* the truth.

3. Breaking the Hold of Besetting Sin

To break the hold of sin, we must remember who we are, *recognize* temptation, *recall* that only Christ can fill our longings, and *resist* temptation.

As a memory exercise, write in the missing words in the paragraphs below. Notice that they are the same words as the italicized words in the paragraph above.

1. **The Mind Is the Gateway to Our Lives**

   The mind is the gateway to all that we _____, all we have _____, and all we will _____.

2. **We Must Guard Our Minds**

   We must _____ our minds with the truth, and must _____ out that which _____ the truth.

3. **Breaking the Hold of Besetting Sin**

   To break the hold of sin, we must remember who we are, _____ temptation, _____ that only Christ can fill our longings, and _____ temptation.

RESPONSE

Questions for Group Discussion or Personal Exercises

1. Can you remember a piece of advice that was given you in the past which you repeated to yourself so many times that it has become a part of you?

2. Have you overcome a particular battle of your mind (cursing, pornography habit, mental revenge, worry, etc.)? Share this with someone as encouragement to them that God can indeed change our thoughts.

3. Memorize 2 Corinthians 10:5 and Philippians 4:8 this week and next.

SPIRITUAL DISCIPLINES

*Thomas Jefferson once wrote
that the price of liberty is
eternal vigilance.
In the same manner, the price
of spiritual liberty is eternal vigilance.
Living the Christian life is
like paddling upstream. If you stop
making forward motion,
you automatically
begin traveling backward.*

TWENTY-THREE

PRAYER

> *We cannot all argue, but we can all pray;*
> *we cannot all be leaders, but we can all be*
> *pleaders; we cannot all be mighty in rheto-*
> *ric, but we can all be prevalent in prayer. I*
> *would sooner see you eloquent with God*
> *than with men.*
>
> Charles Haddon Spurgeon

Many of us are uneasy about prayer. To one degree or another, we feel unworthy, and we feel inadequate. We're not sure if we are qualified to pray, and we're not sure if we know how to pray. We identify with Abraham Lincoln, who told the following story on himself many times:

> Two Quaker ladies were discussing the relative merits and prospects of Abraham Lincoln and Jefferson Davis during the War Between the States. "I think Jefferson will succeed because he is a praying man," said one. "But so is Abraham a praying man," said the other. "Yes," rejoined the first lady, "but the Lord will think that Abraham is joking."[1]

Many of us have the nagging suspicion that when we pray, the Lord thinks we are joking.

On the other hand, we all feel pulled to pray. We instinctively thank the Lord for good things. We call on Him in times of trouble. We see the inherent virtue in prayer, and we wish that we were better at it. St. Augustine said, "There is a god-shaped vacuum in every man that only Christ can fill."[2] We were created by God for fellowship with Him, and without it we feel a sense of void. God is calling us. Nothing else will satisfy. We want to draw near to God, and have Him draw near to us (see James 4:8).

Most of us don't pray as much as we feel we should, not because we are unwilling, but because we are uncertain how to pray and don't understand why our prayers aren't answered more consistently. It is frustrating to keep doing something that you are not sure is working.

It is helpful to divide a discussion of prayer into two categories: that which we do know and understand and that which we don't know and understand.

What We Understand About Prayer

There are four main things we understand about prayer.

1. God Wants Us to Pray.

God wants us to pray, not in the same way that the IRS wants us to file our income tax—with hands on hips, one eyebrow raised, and ready to box our ears if we don't. But rather, in the same way that a loving parent wants to hear his child's requests—with an earnest desire to answer if he should (see 1 Thessalonians 5:17).

2. God Will Answer Prayers.

He will not answer all prayers, as we will see later, but some prayers. His offer to us to pray is a valid one, though not without its qualifications (see Matthew 7:7–11).

3. Some Things Interfere with Our Prayers.

There are some predictable things that will interfere with our prayers. For example, willingly tolerating personal sin (see Psalm 66:18), bad motives (see James 4:3), treating one's wife badly (see

1 Peter 3:7), skepticism about God's faithfulness (see James 1:6–7), or rejection of God's Word (see Proverbs 28:9).

4. We Are to Pray According to Jesus' Instructions.

Jesus mentioned several things about prayer.

Privately: In Matthew 6:5–6, Jesus said, "When you pray, you are not to be as the hypocrites; for they love to stand and pray in the synagogues and on the street corners, in order to be seen by men. Truly I say to you, they have their reward in full. But you, when you pray, go into your inner room, and when you have shut your door, pray to your Father who is in secret, and your Father who sees in secret will repay you."

This isn't saying that it is wrong to pray in public at a public service. But in your personal prayer, it is wrong to pray just so that people will hear you and think you are spiritual. You are to get alone with God and pray to Him privately.

Sincerely: Jesus went on to say, "When you are praying, do not use meaningless repetition, as the Gentiles do, for they suppose that they will be heard for their many words."

This doesn't mean that it is wrong to pray for the same thing repeatedly. Jesus gave an example in Luke 18 of an insistent woman before a judge. The judge granted her petition because of her insistence. This suggests that we can ask God for things on an ongoing basis. But we are to do it with our mind in gear, with sincere mental participation in the prayer.

In Mongolia, the peasants write prayers on pieces of paper and put the paper under little windmills with the belief that each time the blade of the windmill turns, it offers the prayer to God once. In a brisk wind, the same prayer could be offered 50,000 times in a day. This isn't what God has in mind.

Orderly: Jesus gave us a *pattern* to use as a model in our personal prayer.

Worship: "Our Father who art in heaven, hallowed be Thy name."

This phrase tells us several things. First, it reminds us that we are a child of God (our Father), and we have as much right to come before Him in prayer as the children of the Queen of England have to come before her, their mother. Yes, He is God, and we must recognize and honor Him as God. But at the same time we must never forget that we are His children. Next, it tells us that we should worship and praise God for who He is and what He has done for us (hallowed be Thy name).

Yield: "Thy kingdom come, Thy will be done on earth as it is in heaven."

It means we make Him the boss of our life. We set Him on the throne of the kingdom of our personal life. It means we yield to Him in all matters relating to our marriage, vocation, finances, family, relationships, talents, and time.

Request: "Give us this day our daily bread."

We recognize our dependence on God for physical provision and ask Him to provide for us according to His will.

Confess: "Forgive us our debts as we forgive our debtors."

We confess our sins, accept restoration to His fellowship, and live in a forgiving attitude toward others.

Flee: "Lead us not into temptation, but deliver us from the evil one."

We flee from temptation and flee to God for His strength and protection from temptation and the evil one.

Acknowledge: "For Thine is the kingdom and the power and the glory forever. Amen."

Acknowledge that God is supreme in what He wants to do, and in His ability to do it. Implicit in this acknowledgment is a thankful spirit for His blessings.

The Lord's Prayer was not intended to be an incantation or magical formula. I don't think it is wrong to use the Lord's prayer in public or private worship. But it is not to be repeated mindlessly. Rather, each of these areas (worship, submit, request, confess, flee, acknowledge) are to be elaborated upon in a spontaneous and personal way as we pray to Him.

What We Do Not Understand About Prayer

With a minimum of effort, prayer can become stupefyingly complex. This is not a book on prayer, so we must resist the pull to get in over our heads. But it is safe to say that most of the questions about prayer can be traced, one way or another, to the question: "Why doesn't God answer my prayers more often?"

We ask this, not only because we want all our prayers answered, but also because of passages in the Bible which seem to say that He will. However, the complete picture on prayer is a very complex one, and no single passage in the Bible can be taken without understanding how it fits with all the other passages.

As an example, Peter writes in his first epistle (2:13–17) that we are to obey the government and those in authority over us. Period. No qualifications. Yet that same Peter says in Acts 5:29, when chastened by religious leaders and commanded not to preach the gospel anymore, "We must obey God rather than man." Are these two verses contradictory? No. Rather, they are complimentary. Drawing from both verses, we could draw the single principle that we are to obey government and those in authority up to the point of disobeying God. When we come to that point, we must obey God rather than man.

Using that as an illustration of integrated Bible teaching, we see that no single passage on prayer can be taken at face value without being integrated with all the other passages on prayer. When we do this, we see a more orderly picture of prayer emerging, and it helps answer some of our concerns about unanswered prayer.

Levels of Prayer

There seem to be several levels of restriction on receiving answers to prayer. One verse says, simply, that we should ask, and we will receive (Matthew 7:7). Period. No qualifications. With this single verse taken in isolation, we would assume that there would be no request denied us.

However, there are other verses that add qualifications on our asking. For example, in James 1:5–7, we see that we must "ask in faith, without any doubting. . . ." In John 14:13, we must ask in

Jesus' name. In John 15:7, the qualification is that we must "abide in Him, and His word must abide in us," and *then* we can "ask what we will, and it will be given to us."

Why didn't the writers of the Bible list all the possible qualifications in one place? Perhaps because we do not always need to meet all the qualifications. For example, a brand new Christian cries out to God for an answer to prayer. He hasn't had time to abide in Christ and have Christ's Word abide in him. He hardly knows what it even means to "have faith." In his "new-birth" condition, he does not know all the qualifications. But he cries out to God, out of all that he does know and understand. He simply asks. And God simply answers. "Ask and you will receive" is fulfilled. But later on in his spiritual life, God holds him accountable to know more of the Scripture, and now, may require some of the qualifications to be met before answering a given prayer.

The following chart is not exhaustive, but it is perhaps representative of how the Christian might analyze his prayers before God.

Level 1	No qualifications Ask and you shall receive
Level 2	Specific qualifications In faith, without doubting Without unconfessed sin In God's will Without selfish motives In Jesus' name
Level 3	General qualification Abide in Me/My Word in you
Level 4	Final qualification Thy will be done

First, he is given the open invitation to simply ask. If he does not receive an answer, he may check himself on level 2. Is he asking in faith? Does he have any unconfessed sin which could be hindering the answer? Does the request conflict with anything in the Bible (which would assure him that it is not in God's will)? Is he asking with proper motives?

If he gains no insight, or does not receive an answer on that level, he then may check his overall spiritual maturity. Is he abiding in Christ and allowing Christ's Word to abide in him? Perhaps God is delaying the answer to prayer because He wants to drive the Christian to a deeper level of walk with Him.

If he gains no insight or receives no answer on this level, he goes to level 4, in which he simply prays, "Thy will be done." This is, of course, the prayer which Jesus prayed in the Garden of Gethsemane when He asked that the Father would take this cup (being crucified) from Him . . . but then said, "Nevertheless, not My will but Thine be done."

In reality, prayer is not this compartmentalized. We ought to make a simultaneous mental check of all these things we are praying. However, having them written out this way helps us see if we have overlooked something. By going back through each of these qualifications, the Holy Spirit may help us see something which we didn't see before.

Delays

Sometimes God delays His answers to our prayers. For a while, we thought He wasn't going to answer, and then He did. Why does He delay answers to prayer? There may be several reasons:

1. It may be because the timing is not right. He may answer it, but later.

2. Another reason for delay is to clarify the request. When the answer comes, God wants us to be able to recognize it. Often we don't even recognize an answer because we did not crystallize the request in our minds.

3. A third reason why God might delay the answer is to create a sense of expectation and to call attention to the fact that it was He who answered, and it was not just good luck, or natural consequences.

4. A fourth reason He might delay an answer to prayer is to deepen our understanding of Him and His Word.

5. A fifth reason is to draw us into a deeper relationship with Him.

When things come easily, they are taken lightly. God does not want prayer to be taken lightly. Therefore, answers do not come easily. When we fear our prayer is not being answered, and we can find no personal reason why, it may be that the answer is being delayed for one or more of these reasons.

Focus on Relationship

The relationship between an earthly child and his earthly parent gives insight into the relationship between the child of God and his heavenly Father. When the earthly child is young, uneducated, and immature, he asks for things which are preposterous and even dangerous. He wants to have only candy for lunch, and wants to drive the car and run the vacuum—things he clearly cannot or should not do. The loving and perceptive parent would surely not grant all the requests of a two-year-old.

As the child grows older, the requests he makes become less ridiculous and impossible. His whole life becomes more in line with the parent's will. Yet even in the childhood and teenage years, the parents cannot grant all requests. There are still foolish requests, and even more, there are selfish and manipulative requests. ("Can I go to the library tonight?" Not because he wants to study, but because he can meet a girlfriend there.)

As the child grows into enlightened adulthood, there are very few requests that are made that are not granted. Why? Because they are asked with a knowledge and understanding that is consistent with the parents' will.

The adult child understands (especially if he has children of his own) that his parents did not refuse childhood requests because they didn't love the child, but rather because they did love him. The denial was rooted in greater knowledge and wisdom.

God is not a Cosmic Service which will be rendered according to your will if you just learn how to ask properly. Rather God is a heavenly Father. If we envision Him as one who loves us and wants the best for us, and who answers or doesn't answer based on what His superior will is, then we can avoid a sense of failure when our prayers aren't answered. We must interpret all unanswered prayers in light of the fact that God is good, He loves us, He wants the best for us, and He is, in fact, our heavenly Father.

When a request is not granted, rather than to eye the Heavenly Vending Machine suspiciously and say, "What in the world is wrong with this thing?" and be tempted to give it a good swift kick, we can say, as we would of a loving parent, "Well, I guess that request is not what is best for me at this time, and since I want what is best for me, I will accept the denial."

The bottom line in prayer is that God wants a relationship with us. That is His ultimate desire. So He refuses any approach that will allow us to simply go through an equation to get what we want. Equations won't work. The only thing that will work is personally drawing closer to Him.

That is why no one fully understands prayer in a way that can be communicated to others as a "system." There is a very personal and intimate dimension about prayer. There is no "system." It is you and God alone in a room, looking for what is best for you and learning to trust and follow Him. Only by getting to know Him better will prayer begin to make sense.

So pray! Risk praying poorly. Pray the best you know how. Don't let that which you don't understand about praying keep you from praying. And do not let that which you don't understand about prayer destroy that which you do understand. *Pray!* God will lead you into fuller understanding over time.

Notes About Prayer

There are several other thoughts that we need to keep in mind as we pray.

- You can pray to God because Christ has made you acceptable to Him. Hebrews 10:19–22 says: "So, brothers, we are completely free to enter the Most Holy Place [a metaphor for worshipping and praying directly to God]. We can do this without fear because of the blood of Jesus' death. We can enter through a new way that Jesus opened for us. It is a living way. And we have a great priest over God's house. So let us come near to God with a sincere heart and a sure faith. We have been cleansed and made free from guilt."

- Because God knows everything, you can be completely and utterly honest, totally transparent before Him, and know that you will be accepted, understood, and helped.

- When we hurt, God hurts. Therefore, we cannot accuse Him of not caring and being distant, when our prayers for relief are not answered.

- To pray effectively, ultimately, we must know the Scriptures well, because to know God's will, we must know His Word and be obedient to it.

- Gratitude should be our attitude in prayer for all that God does for us.

- Learning to pray well takes time. When God wants to make a squash, He can do it in six weeks. When He wants to make a great oak, it takes decades.

I've often been amazed by dogs and how they absolutely love to do that for which they were bred. Bird dogs love to hunt birds. Put them in the truck and start driving toward the fields, and they will begin to whine and quiver with uncontrolled excitement. Sled dogs in Alaska "live" to pull sleds. They bark and howl in runaway anticipation as they are hitched to the sled. When the whip cracks, and they hear their master shout "Mush!" their ecstasy is undisguised. Their cheeks grin in wide, foolish pleasure, and their tongues loll out the corners of their mouths in unembarrassed joy as they strain forward into their harnesses.

When these dogs do what they are created to do, they are the most full of joy. So it is with man.

I am not suggesting that you ought to be quivering and whining in anticipation of your prayer time, but I am saying that there is a quiet, deep joy and satisfaction when fellowshipping with God that nothing else can duplicate, and the longing for it is something that nothing else will satisfy.

Ask, and it shall be given to you; seek, and you shall find; knock, and it shall be opened to you. For everyone who asks receives, and he who seeks finds, and to him who knocks it shall be opened. Or what man is there among you, when his son shall ask him for a loaf, will give him a stone? Or if he shall ask for a fish, he will not give him a snake, will he? If you then, being evil, know how to give good gifts to your children, how much more shall your Father who is in heaven give what is good to those who ask Him! (Matthew 7:7–12)

> *Father in Heaven, teach me to pray. Help me fellowship with You. Bring me beyond the barriers of self-discipline and ignorance. Lift me above the level of my natural inclinations, and let me commune with You. Help me to respond to that which I understand, and help me trust in that which I don't understand. Don't let what I do not understand destroy that which I do. Teach me to pray, I ask in my Savior's name. Amen.*

REVIEW

1. What We Understand About Prayer

We understand that God *wants* us to pray and will *answer* according to His *will.*

2. What We Do Not Understand About Prayer

When God doesn't answer our prayer, we must *search* the Scripture to see if our *understanding* of prayer needs to *mature.*

3. Focus on Relationship

In the end, prayer does not reduce to an equation or an automatic *system*; instead, it *depends* on an ever-deepening *relationship* with God.

As a memory exercise, write in the missing words in the paragraphs below. Notice that they are the same words as the italicized words in the paragraph above.

1. **What We Understand About Prayer**

   We understand that God _____ us to pray and will _____ according to His _____.

2. **What We Do Not Understand About Prayer**

   When God doesn't answer our prayer, we must _____ the Scripture to see if our _____ of prayer needs to _____.

3. **Focus on Relationship**

   In the end, prayer does not reduce to an equation or an automatic _____; instead, it _____ on an ever-deepening _____ with God.

RESPONSE

Questions for Group Discussion or Personal Exercises

1. Do you think God takes *your* prayers seriously? Why or why not?

2. What is one prayer request you have been repeating for over six months? Go through the four levels of qualifications to see if God reveals any insights as to why He may not have responded yet.

3. Scripture says to come to God as a child. Have you been a bit demanding of God (vending-machine mentality)? Why not thank God right now for His *un*answered prayers (if it is true that He has your best interests in mind)?

TWENTY-FOUR

WORSHIP

> *Religion, of which the rewards are distant, and which is animated only by faith and hope, will glide by degrees out of the mind unless it be invigorated and reimpressed by external ordinances, by stated calls to worship, and the salutary influence of example.*
>
> Samuel Johnson

In her excellent little book, *Up with Worship*, Anne Ortlund writes:

When I was little we used to play church. We'd get the chairs into rows, fight over who'd be preacher, vigorously lead the hymn singing, and generally have a great carnal time.

The aggressive kids naturally wanted to be up front, directing or preaching. The quieter ones were content to sit and be entertained by the up-fronters.

Occasionally we'd get mesmerized by a true sensationalistic crowd-swayer—like the girl who said, "Boo, I'm the Holy Ghost!" But in general, if the up-fronters were pretty good they could hold their audience quiet a while. If they weren't so good, eventually the kids would drift off to play something else—like jump rope or jacks.

Now that generation has grown up, but most of them haven't changed too much. Every Sunday they still play church. They line up in rows for the entertainment. If it's pretty good, their church may grow. If it's not too hot, eventually they'll drift of to play something else.[1]

What is worship, and how do we do it? It is easy for us to get confused and substitute other things for worship. Many years ago, Thomas K. Beecher once preached for his brother, Henry Ward Beecher, at the Plymouth Church in Brooklyn, New York. Henry was a very famous preacher, and many people had come to hear him. When Thomas stood up to preach, some people began to move toward the doors. Realizing that they were disappointed because he was substituting for his brother, Thomas raised his hand for silence and announced, "All those who came here this morning to worship Henry Ward Beecher may leave now. All who came to worship the Lord may remain."[2]

It happens to us, doesn't it? We go to church, not because God is there (I realize He is everywhere), but because a certain preacher is there, or a certain choir or vocalist is there. There is nothing wrong with enjoying good preaching and music, but those are only aids to worship. God still is why we worship. We have to be sure we are getting it right.

Corporate Worship

Worship is not an emotion. Rather, it is an offering to God. We offer to God our praise, our prayers, and our public declaration of the greatness of His person and His work. Sometimes worship will stir us emotionally, and sometimes it will not. But in a worship service, primarily we give something to God, and secondarily we receive something for ourselves.

Again, in *Up with Worship*, Anne Ortlund writes concerning corporate worship:

> So the people all come together in rows in the church, and they face forward. So what?
>
> Well, it's the same physical setup as a stage play, and everybody knows about those. You plunk down in a seat. At H-hour the lights go up, the actors start performing, a prompter offstage whispers cues—and the spectators lean back and evaluate how they do.
>
> But church? NO, NO, NO, NO, NO, NO, NO!

> The church is unique. Whether the people in the congrega-
> tion ever discover it or not, they are the actors. The up-front
> people are the prompters, whispering cues as needed—and God
> is the Audience, looking on to see how they do. (Kierkegaard
> said it first. I didn't. But that analogy has really helped me.
> Maybe it will you.)
>
> Many poor churches don't even know who's supposed to be
> doing it! What lousy, lousy plays they put on! The actors sit
> around lethargically while the prompters practically exhaust
> themselves trying to do all their lines for them so the play will
> still give a lively appearance.[3]

The Christian, in order to worship God as He wants to be worshipped, must have a sense of participation, and that God is, meta-
phorically, "out in the audience" while the worshipper sings his
praise, declares his allegiance, and proclaims the inestimable value
of who God is, and what He has done.

So go and mentally participate in what is said, sung, and
prayed, and *mean it,* and as you do, you will worship.

It is true that some forms of worship are more meaningful for
some than for others, and there is nothing wrong with seeking out
the church which is most meaningful to you. Some people prefer
an informal family-style atmosphere for worship. I used to attend a
church in which all the children were in the service. The noise
level was equivalent to a 747 taking off. There were two levels of
humanity. The top level was adults. They were sitting on chairs.
The bottom level was children under age six. They were on the
floor. It reminded you of earthworms in the bottom of a can. People would rise up in the middle of the sermon and wander to the
back of the room to refill their coffee cup. We met in a school. A
building wasn't important. We, the people, were the church. I enjoyed it at the time. I thought we were freed up.

Now, I prefer a little more structure, as do many people. Some
place a high priority on outward things to cultivate a sense of reverence, such as an attractive auditorium, stained glass, and a skillfully played organ.

Both are right. Neither are wrong. It is a matter of preference.
You might find that you like one approach during one chapter of
your life, and then find yourself evolving to prefer another approach. That is perfectly acceptable.

You may struggle finding a church that has a worship service that you like. If you cannot find one, you must settle for limited objectives in corporate worship. No church will be perfect. The service does not have to be emotionally moving in order for you to worship. If you mentally participate in what is said, sung and prayed, and *mean it*, you will worship. There is no one else in a worship service who can keep you from worshipping.

Also, if you choose your church because you feel that it has the strongest overall ministry (worship, edification, and evangelism) but it is weak on worship, then find other times and places when you can worship. During Christmas and Easter, churches might have special services that you could attend which would give you additional opportunities for satisfying corporate worship. Also, from time to time, there might be things on television. Around the holidays, public television often has wonderful services which can lead a person to worship. You might even conduct some special services in your home, if there are others whom you know who would enjoy having a special home service.

The point is, you take control over your life in the pursuit of God. Don't see yourself as a victim of the ability of others to perform for you. Assume responsibility for your own spiritual health. Join others who are like-minded. If there is something missing in your life, don't be passive. Don't wait for others to solve the problem for you. Take the initiative yourself and find ways of satisfying the longing for worship on a level that is meaningful to you.

There are several things you might look for as you evaluate which services are right for you.

First, look for a sense of worship in the others in the service— those leading and those participating. Look for a sense that what they are doing is real, that *they* mean it. If the others in the service are in tune with the Lord, it should be apparent; and if they aren't, it should also be apparent. Of course, this has nothing to do with the building, or pews, or anything else that is physical. I have worshipped in lovely buildings, and I have been paralyzed in lovely buildings. I have worshipped in humble buildings, and I have been paralyzed in humble buildings. What matters is what is in the hearts of the others in the building. God wants people who worship Him in spirit and in truth, not in pretense or habit.

Second, the Scriptures must be honored. It must be clear that the Bible is respected and relied upon for guidance, direction, wisdom, and information. The Bible must be taught in the pulpit.

W. A. Criswell, pastor of First Baptist Church in Dallas, Texas, tells the story of when he was in seminary. He and a friend of his visited a church one Sunday morning, and the preacher was preaching from Shakespeare. After the service was over, Criswell and his friend went up to the minister and said, "Sir, we think that in a church, a minister ought to preach from the Bible."

The minister replied, "Oh, I preach from the Bible. In fact, I preached from it last year, but I finished it, and so this year I am preaching from Shakespeare!"

Third, the people must be friendly and have a sense of inner spiritual life. If people are cold and aloof, and uninvolved in each others' lives, then it is clear that either they haven't heard the Scriptures taught, or they have heard them but haven't responded. The Bible cannot be respected and upheld on the one hand, and have an auditorium full of cold hearts on the other.

Fourth, there should be a good education program for children, youth, and adults, and there should be an effort to lead all the people to spiritual maturity.

Fifth, spiritual maturity always manifests itself, eventually, in reaching out to non-Christians and to disadvantaged people. If a church is not reaching out to the non-Christian world, and is not helping the disadvantaged, then the edification ministry of that church is not yet mature.

Personal Worship

Someone once said that when it comes to living the Christian life, too many Christians are like half empty glasses trying to spill over. Our glass is half full of truth but half empty of life. We have the right kind of stuff for a vibrant life, but not enough of it. The truth hasn't made that infinite eighteen-inch journey from the head to the heart. We know truth, but we have trouble living it.

One reason is that we spend inadequate time alone with the truth and with God. We spend too little time reflecting on truth, praying to God, meditating on life. Someone asked Thomas Edison how he came up with the idea about the light bulb. Edison replied, "By thinking about it all the time." Edison also agreed that genius was 10 percent inspiration and 90 percent perspiration. Who knows what inventions we might come up with if we thought about something all the time.

On the other hand, who knows what kind of spiritual insights and wisdom we might have if we thought about it all the time. Our wonder at our struggle in the Christian life should be no greater than our wonder at our inability to come up with inventions. We don't think about it enough.

The only way to get the glass full enough to spill over is to spend more time thinking about it, more time praying, more time meditating upon the Scripture, and more time with God, asking Him to open our minds to His truth.

Ask yourself, if you spent a proportionate amount of time practicing basketball as you do working at being a better Christian, would you be on the starting five? Would you even be on the team? If you spent as much time practicing the piano as you do working at being a better Christian, would you be able to conduct a decent recital? If you spent as much time painting as you spend working at being a better Christian, would you be able to do more than draw stick figures?

These questions are not designed to make you feel guilty. They are merely designed to point out an inescapable truth. Doing anything well takes time. If we invest no time in athletics, or music, or art, or the Christian life, we will be less than mediocre.

When we talk about personal worship, it is not a hollow exercise. We are not going through some perfunctory motion. This is at the heart of our quality of life. We must pay the price of self-investment to know God, and if we don't, we won't.

The Pursuit of God

Nevertheless, without significant investment of ourselves in the pursuit of God, we will remain spiritual midgets. So what should we do? This is a challenge. While each person has to find an approach that is right for him, there are some inescapable elements.

First, we should read the Bible. It is our guide for life—our divine owner's manual, if you will. It is such a huge book that it is very difficult to keep familiar with all of it. The only way to do so is to have a habit of just "free-reading" the Bible. Many people follow a program which will guide them to read the Bible through in year. That is not a minor undertaking. It takes the average person usually about twenty minutes to thirty minutes a day to read through the Bible in year. If you are a fast reader, you would cut that time in half, at least. Others read a chapter a day. That is a manageable pace for anyone.

I have practiced for many years the habit of reading at least five minutes a day before I go to sleep at night. I find that I am never too tired to read at least five minutes. I have had to read standing up to keep from falling asleep, but I am personally committed to not missing. If I don't do something regularly, I have trouble doing it at all. Others might have success with more flexibility, but I have found that, unless I make it an inviolable part of my daily schedule, I eventually lose my grip on it altogether.

Second, we must study the Bible. By reading the Bible, we gain a breadth of knowledge. By studying it, we gain a depth of knowledge. There are many books available which can guide you in studying the Bible. However, for most people, the best way for someone to study the Bible is in a home Bible study or Sunday school class where a group of people study the same passage together. There is accountability and greater learning in this pattern, as well as of fellowship, prayer, and just plain fun.

Third, we must pray. Following the pattern of the Lord's prayer in Matthew 6:9–13 is an excellent way to begin. Or, the common acrostic, *ACTS* is helpful—*A* stands for adoration, a time of worship and of praise to God for who He is and what He has done for us; *C* stands for confession of any sins the Lord makes known to us and ask Him for restoration to fellowship; *T* stands for thanksgiving, to thank Him and cultivate a spirit of gratitude for His blessings in our lives; and *S* stands for supplication, praying for our own needs and the needs of others. A prayer list is helpful to guide us, and also to create a record of answered prayers, which can be very encouraging.

Fourth, we should investigate things which help us bond emotionally to God. Someone has suggested that relationships are strengthened when two people share a pleasant experience. I have seen this happen, for example, at a men's retreat. Two people do not know each other before the retreat. Then, they happen to play on the same basketball team. They find out that they are both pretty good shots. They win a few games. They come back friends.

What happened? Did anything about them change? No. They were the same people before as they were after, but they weren't friends before. What created the friendship? A shared pleasant experience.

Counselors will use this truth when counseling husbands and wives who want to improve their relationship. If they will share pleasant experiences, it will strengthen the marriage relationship.

So it is with God. If we share pleasant experiences with Him, it will strengthen our relationship with Him. Many of us feel distant from God. It is because we have shared few pleasant experiences with Him.

So how can the Christian share a pleasant experience with God? You are the only one who can answer that, because the answer is different for each person. If long walks out in "nature" help foster our sense of emotional bonding to God, then that is an activity which should become a priority. Listening to music is very helpful for some. Get alone and listen to music which is meaningful to you. Some people write poetry to God. Others keep a diary to God. Reading certain kinds of books can be helpful. Experiment and talk with others. Find ways to cultivate your sense of emotional participation with the Lord. Find pleasant experiences which you can share with God.

There are certainly more things that can be done to foster personal worship. The goal for now is not to be exhaustive in personal worship possibilities, but simply to make the point that these cannot be ignored without short-circuiting your relationship with the Lord and stunting your satisfaction in life.

This is one of the greatest challenges Christians face. Most Christians have a long and glorious record of failure at developing a consistent habit of personal worship. However, no one is defeated until he gives up. Start again whenever you fail.

> Oh give thanks to the Lord, call upon His name;
> Make known His deeds among the peoples.
> Sing to Him, sing praises to Him;
> Speak of all His wonders.
> Glory in His holy name;
> Let the heart of those who seek the Lord
>   be glad.
> Seek the Lord and His strength;
> Seek His face continually.
>   (Psalm 105:1–4)

Father in Heaven, I pray, may You may be with me, may You not leave me or forsake me, that You may incline my heart to Yourself, to walk in all Your ways and to keep Your commandments and Your statues and Your ordinances. May my heart be totally devoted to You, my Lord and my God, to walk in Your statutes and to keep Your commandments. Amen. (1Kings 8:57, 58, 61)

REVIEW

1. Corporate Worship

In true *worship* the *congregation* are the players, and God is the *audience.*

2. Personal Worship

Personal worship requires a sincere *investment* of our *time* and *energies.*

3. The Pursuit of God

Included in the pursuit of God, we must be *faithful* in the spiritual disciplines, we must seek out common pleasant *experiences* with God, and we must never *quit.*

As a memory exercise, write in the missing words in the paragraphs below. Notice that they are the same words as the italicized words in the paragraph above.

1. Corporate Worship

In true _____ the _____ are the players, and God is the _____.

2. Personal Worship

Personal worship requires a sincere _____ of our _____ and _____.

3. The Pursuit of God

Included in the pursuit of God, we must be _____ in the spiritual disciplines, we must seek out common pleasant _____ with God, and we must never _____.

RESPONSE

Questions for Group Discussion or Personal Exercises

1. Do you view yourself as an active participant in your worship? Why or why not?

2. What have you found to be most helpful in prompting personal worship? Least helpful?

3. What common pleasant experiences have you had with God that caused you to feel closest to Him?

BALANCING LIFE'S COMPETING PRIORITIES

> *No man has a right to lead such a life of*
> *contemplation as to forget in his own ease*
> *the service due to his neighbor; nor has any*
> *man a right to be so immersed in active life*
> *as to neglect the contemplation of God.*
>
> St. Augustine

I n his booklet, *No Little People,* Francis Schaeffer writes:

As a Christian considers the possibility of being the Christian glorified, often his reaction is, "I am so limited. Surely it does not
matter whether I am walking as a creature glorified or not." Or,
to put it in another way, "It is wonderful to be a Christian, but I
am such a small person, so limited in talents—or energy or psy-
chological strength or knowledge—that what I do is not really
important." The Bible, however, has quite a different emphasis:
with God there are no little people.[1]

Schaeffer uses the rod of Moses as an example. Moses said,
"Who am I, that I should lead the people of Israel?" God directed
Moses attention to the simplest thing imaginable—the staff in his
own hand, a shepherd's rod, a stick of wood somewhere between
three- and six-feet long. However, upon God's command, he threw
it down, and it became a snake. Moses fled from it in terror. Then

God commanded Moses to pick it up again. In obedience and submission to God, Moses picked up the serpent, and it became a rod again, but now it surged with divine power. No longer was it referred to as the rod of Moses. Now it was referred to as the rod of God.

The ten plagues of Egypt, the crossing of the Red Sea, the bringing forth of water from a rock, all were performed with the rod of God. Schaeffer again:

> Consider the mighty ways in which God used a dead stick of wood. [The phrase] "God so used a stick of wood" can be a banner cry for each of us. Though we are limited and weak in talent, physical energy, and psychological strength, we are not less than a stick of wood. But as the rod of Moses had to become the rod of God, so that which is "me" must become the "me" of God. Then I can become useful in God's hands. The Scripture emphasizes that much can come from little if the little is truly consecrated to God. There are no little people and no big people in the true spiritual sense. The people who receive praise from the Lord Jesus will not in every case be the people who hold leadership in this life. There will be many persons who were sticks of wood that stayed close to God and were quiet before Him, and were used in power by Him in a place which looks small to men.[2]

Each Christian is to be a rod of God in the place of God for him. We must remember throughout our lives that in God's sight there are no little people and no little places.

No Little Tasks

Following this line of thought, we would have to say, also, that there are no little tasks. There are no big tasks, and there are no little tasks. There is only faithfulness to what God asks of us. That is all there is—faithfulness to God. We may be faithful in things that look big to men, or we may be faithful to things that look little to men. But to God, there is only faithfulness to what He asks each of us to do. That is why Billy Graham may receive no larger heavenly reward than someone whose ministry is to pray for missionaries in a way totally unknown to others.

In the same way, if God asks us to work in a factory eight hours a day, then we can be faithful to Him in that. And our reward will be just as great as the person who was faithful to God in studying and teaching the Bible for that same eight-hour time period. No little people, no little places, no little tasks.

Spiritual Versus Secular

If you were to rank the following uses of time, how would you rank them? Reading the Bible, running the kids around, praying, worshipping the Lord, going to work, going to church, doing household chores (fixing the car, mowing the lawn, etc.), teaching Sunday school.

If you are a typical person, you would noodle over them, and finally rank them something like this:

- worshipping the Lord
- praying
- reading the Bible
- going to church
- teaching Sunday school
- going to work
- doing chores (fix car, mow lawn, etc.)
- running the kids around

It seems spiritual to rank things like this. The problem is that we spend more time doing things on the lower part of the list than we do on the higher part of the list. Perhaps we should start spending forty hours a week praying and worshipping the Lord, and an hour a day working. It sounds like a good way to starve to death. Do I accept that God isn't happy with my time allocation, and just hope He doesn't bring it up in church next Sunday? Or must I (perish the thought) quit my job and become a missionary or pastor? What do I do with the time flip-flop?

To begin, we must alter our perspective about the "secular" activities. Everything, if it is done for God, is a sacred activity, whether it is changing a diaper or plowing a field, or working an on assembly line, or playing ball with the kids, or putting together a corporate merger, or doing someone's taxes, or giving someone an insulin injection. All of life belongs to God, and all of life is meaningful to Him.

Work is noble to God. God is a worker (see Genesis 1:1–2). Man was created to be a co-worker with God (see Genesis 1:27–28). The nature of work is inherently and intrinsically good (see Ephesians 4:28). Jesus was a carpenter, and His life was totally pleasing to God (see Mark 6:3). We can serve God while we work (see Colossians 3:22–24).

Life should not be seen as stair steps, with mundane things on the bottom rung and God on the top rung. Rather, life should be seen as a wheel, with God at the center and the rest of life as balanced spokes going out from the center.

Aiming for Balance

There are five major areas of life that need to be kept in balance: personal life, family life, work, church, and society. We have obligations in each of these areas, and each of them must be kept in balance with the others. There are many commands and principles for each one of these areas. They cannot be relegated to a hierarchical system. They must be kept in balance with each other, and integrated into our relationship with the Lord.

In our personal life, we are to:

- care for our bodies

- nurture our minds

- cultivate our talents

- grow spiritually

In our families we are to:

- love and respect our spouse

- nurture our children in the Lord

- provide for our family materially

- promote a positive environment in the home

In our work, we are to:

- do everything as unto the Lord (excellence)
- serve others (customers and co-workers)
- manifest Christ in our ethics
- honor our employers

In our church, we are to:

- help those in need
- fellowship with other Christians
- use our spiritual gift
- support the ministry financially

In our society, we are to:

- honor law and government
- contribute to the moral fiber of society
- protect creation
- advance Biblical principles in society

It is just as wrong to spend so much time preparing a Sunday school lesson that we neglect our children as it is to spend so much time at work that we neglect our children. On the other hand, it is just as right to honor God in our work as it is to honor Him by worshipping Him personally each day. We all know of "preacher's brats" who have flipped-out spiritual lives because their fathers were so busy with the church that they didn't have time for their kids.

When any one part of our life gets so consuming that we cannot fulfill our proper obligations in the other parts, we are out of balance. Like a broken fan, our life begins to wobble, and we have to bring things into balance.

The part of life that consumes most of us is work. For most people, work is in the secular market place. For some women, it is work in the home. But for all people, the principles are the same, and they must be able to find meaning in what they are doing. If they can't, their life will have a void at the center. We simply cannot spend forty to sixty hours a week doing something that has no meaning for us and expect that we can have a fulfilled life.

All Is Important to God

From where, then, does the meaning come? It comes first from recognizing that anything God has called us to is important to God. And if God has called us to work at secular vocations, then that secular vocation is important to Him.

When God created the world, He intended for man to oversee the creation. In a sense, He intended for man to rule the creation under Him. Therefore, all aspects of society and culture become important to God. Being a medical doctor is important because, in God's plan, we need people to take care of us medically. Being a mechanic is important because, in God's plan, we need mechanics to keep our cars running. Selling computers is important because, in God's plan, computers are central to today's life. Paving streets is important because, in God's plan, we must have paved streets.

Certainly, there are things that are not in God's plan—things that are unethical and immoral. But if something is ethical and moral, and makes a valid contribution to life, it is important to God. It is part of God's overall design for man. All of us must fit together into a larger whole in the outworking of God's plan for man.

Specifically for homemakers, rearing children and keeping a home is important to God, because the home is the center of all society. As the home goes, so will go a nation. As the poet says, "The hand that rocks the cradle rules the world." Rearing children to contribute to society and live for the Lord is one of the noblest things a person could do.

Today, we are faced with two kinds of uneasiness about this. One, there are women at home who are having difficulty finding meaning in being a homemaker. They have the aprons which read: "I went to college for this?" They need to be assured that college or no college, it is difficult to imagine a more important undertaking than rearing the next generation. The world may not think it is important, but God and perceptive people do.

The other uneasiness is the growing number of women who are in the work place, but who wish they could be homemakers. More and more women are finding that the grass is no greener on the other side of the fence, but circumstances force them to continue working outside the home.

We can't answer the question of working mothers here. The point is this: if you are doing what God wants you to do, whether it is in the home or outside the home, it matters, it is important, it makes a contribution and is worthy of your time.

We Can Invest Meaning in What We Do

We can invest what we do with meaning, because we do what we do as unto the Lord. We serve the Lord in what we do. We can repair engines to the glory of God. We can write contracts to the glory of God. We can cook omelettes to the glory of God. We can mow lawns to the glory of God. We can teach school to the glory of God. We can raise children to the glory of God.

How do we do these things to the glory of God? First, mentally commit the activity to God. Your words might go something like: "Lord, I realize that my job makes a contribution to man's welfare on earth, and is, therefore, significant to you. Therefore, I do it as unto you. I offer my labor to you as an act of worship and dedication."

Second, we must then do the job as well as we can. Probably many of us know of people who can do our job better than we do. That doesn't matter. We all have limitations of time, talents, and resources. We do not have to do our job as well as possible. We have to do it as well as we can, in light of our limitations in time, talent, and resources. If we have six kids, we might not keep our house as neat as if we had only one child. We are limited in our time. We serve the Lord, not a fixed external standard. We can all feel good about knowing that we did as well as we could do with our combination of abilities and limitations.

Third, we can reflect the character of God in all that we do. We can be ethical and honest in all our dealings. We can be fair. We can uphold the dignity of other people we deal with. We can be kind and loving. We can serve them. We can do our job with the same ethical and moral sense that Jesus would if He had our job.

Fourth, we can use our workplace or our home to witness for Christ. Certainly, there is no virtue in being obnoxious about our faith. But if people see that there is something different about our life, they will listen to our message.

When we work with these things in mind, our labor takes on significance and gives us meaning.

Keeping the Balance

Balance is the key, and balance usually flows from the use of our discretionary time. We all must sleep. We all must work. We all must eat, and drive, and brush our teeth, and get our hair cut. When we take out the obligatory hours from our weekly schedule, what we have left is our discretionary time. How we use the discretionary time usually determines whether or not our life is in balance.

This is a little dangerous, of course, because a man with small sons may say he has to work eighty hours every week, and therefore he has no discretionary time. That won't fly, however. God would never ask a man to do a job that forces him to sacrifice his family.

Nevertheless, as a general rule, this method of establishing your amount of discretionary time may be helpful in analyzing your use of time. How you use this time will determine whether or not your life is brought into balance. You must spend time with the Lord, but He also wants you to spend time with your spouse and children. You should exercise for your health, but you should also make a contribution to your society. Only you can determine how much time must be allocated in each area. Balance for someone else might not be balance for you.

When one area of our life is being neglected because we are over balanced in another, we must make difficult choices to cut back in the overbalanced area. This requires sacrifice. It may involve lowering our standard of living. It may mean foregoing a raise, which would bring money and prestige with it. We must pay the necessary price if we long for God's full blessing in our life. We cannot ignore God's truth on the one hand, and then go to

Him asking for His complete blessing in our life on the other. The spiritual life doesn't work that way.

God's richest blessing and the deepest fulfillment in life are offered to those who, in full faith, trust God in everything and demonstrate that trust by being faithful to all He asks of us—obedient from the heart in all things.

> The Lord is compassionate and gracious,
> Slow to anger and abounding in lovingkindness.
> He will not always strive with us;
> Nor will He keep His anger forever.
> He has not dealt with us according to our sins,
> Nor rewarded us according to our iniquities.
> For as high as the heavens are above the earth,
> So great is His lovingkindness toward those
>   who fear Him. . . .
> For He Himself knows our frame;
> He is mindful that we are but dust.
>
> (Psalm 103:8–11, 14)

Heavenly Father, grant that I may live a balanced life before You. Help me to see the tasks You have given me as You see them. May I take pleasure and meaning in being faithful to You. May my life be an encouragement to others to know You. I pray in Jesus' name. Amen.

REVIEW

1. No Little Tasks

With God there are no little *people*, no little *places*, and no little *tasks*.

2. Spiritual Versus Secular

Everything, if it is done for *God*, is *sacred*, regardless of how spiritual it may or may not seem.

3. Keeping the Balance

We cannot spend *equal* amounts of time on our responsibilities, but we can spend *adequate* amounts of time to keep them *balanced*.

As a memory exercise, write in the missing words in the paragraphs below. Notice that they are the same words as the italicized words in the paragraph above.

1. No Little Tasks

With God there are no little _____, no little _____, and no little _____.

2. Spiritual Versus Secular

_____ if it is done for _____ , is _____ regardless of how spiritual it may or may not seem.

3. Keeping the Balance

We cannot spend _____ amounts of time on our responsibilities, but we can spend _____ amounts of time to keep them _____.

RESPONSE

Questions for Group Discussion or Personal Exercises

1. Do some of your weekly activities appear to you to be unimportant to God? Why do you feel this way?

2. Why do you think most of us have been led to believe that life's priorities should be God, family, others, personal life, then work?

3. Where do you feel God is leading you to be more faithful "in the little things?" What activities do you need to evaluate with the perspective of "doing them as unto the Lord?"

TWENTY-SIX

USING YOUR
SPIRITUAL GIFTS

> *Sick or well, blind or seeing, bond or free,*
> *we are here for a purpose, and however we*
> *are situated, we please God better with use-*
> *ful deeds than with many prayers of pious*
> *resignation.*

> Helen Keller

O scar Wilde once wrote, "In this world there are only two
tragedies. One is not getting what one wants, and the other
is getting it."[1] He was trying to warn us that no matter how hard
we work at being successful, success won't satisfy us. By the time we
get there, having sacrificed so much on the altar of success, we will
realize that success was not what we wanted.

Swiss psychiatrist Carl Jung wrote, "About a third of my cases
are suffering from no clinically definable neurosis, but from the
senselessness and emptiness of their lives. This can be described as
the general neurosis of our time."[2]

You don't gain happiness by pursuing happiness. You become
happy by pursing God, who grants to us peace, love, and joy as a
by-product, as it were. Think of the happiest people you know. Are
they the wealthiest people you know? Probably not. Probably the
happiest people you know are those who have found something

299

meaningful to do with their lives, and happiness has stolen into their lives while they were busy doing other things.

I read one time that our business in the world is not to try to make something out of ourselves, but rather to find a job worth doing and lose ourselves in it. There is much truth in that, if understood in a Christian context.

What we long for is the fruit of the Spirit in our lives (Galatians 5:22–23)—not the fruit of self effort, not the fruit of money, not the fruit of achievement, not the fruit of fame, not the fruit of sacrifice or service, but the fruit of the Spirit.

We were all created by God to invest our lives in something greater than ourselves, in something outside ourselves. It is like the insightful bum who said, "I wouldn't stoop to work for nobody that would hire the likes of me." We cannot find meaning in living for anything as small as ourselves.

And as we live for something greater than ourselves (the will of God), God gives us meaning, purpose, and satisfaction. It is easy to understand how non-Christians would get tricked into climbing the ladder of success only to find it is leaning against the wrong wall. But it is remarkable that Christians are also tricked into the same thing. With startling ease, we get deceived into chasing the same mirage—a non-existent pot of gold at the end of a rainbow that isn't there. It is a foundation for life that is as thin as soup which was made by boiling the shadow of a chicken!

God has already answered our struggle for a sense of meaning and purpose in life. He has recruited us to *the* great cause of the ages—advancing the kingdom of Christ to the corners of the globe. And not only that, but He has also gifted us to be successful at everything He asks us to do. If Christ asks us to do something, we can succeed at it. If we cannot succeed at it, then Christ is not asking us to do it. However, success must be defined in God's terms and not man's. Success is simply to be faithful to what God calls us to. The results are up to God. He has given each of us a spiritual gift. As we exercise our spiritual gift according to His leading, we are being faithful to Him, and our actions generate the results which He wants. We cannot fail.

The Body of Christ and Spiritual Gifts

There are many different opinions about spiritual gifts. This is because the Bible has not made the subject crystal clear. However, for all the diversity of opinion around the edges, nearly everyone agrees that at the core, God has gifted us to serve one another in the body of Christ with a spiritual gift or gifts. Our focus in this chapter is not on the areas of disagreement but on the core of agreement.

The primary point to make is this: Each Christian is personally responsible to minister to others. We cannot escape by claiming that we have hired someone else to do the job. God expects each of us to assume personal responsibility for ministry, and the pastors of our church are not to do all the work of the ministry. Rather, they are to help train us to do the work of the ministry (see Ephesians 4:12).

One of the glaring weaknesses of the church today is a passive congregation. It is like the old description of football: There are 50,000 people in the stands desperately in need of exercise, watching twenty people on the field desperately in need of rest.

The church is more like that than we care to admit. The congregation as a whole sits and watches while the pastors and a few committed laymen work their heads off. This is not how God intends it to be. God intends each Christian to be involved in the game, and He has gifted each Christian to be able to play the position He has for him. First Peter 4:10 says, "As each one has received a special gift, employ it in serving one another, as good stewards of the manifold grace of God."

Service and Ministry Gifts

Let us focus, then, on the service and ministry gifts about which there is little disagreement. None of these gifts is defined in Scripture, so as we try to clarify and define them, it is a little subjective. Nevertheless, the following observations may be helpful.

Prophecy: Prophecy (Romans 12:6), in this "service" context, does not mean predicting the future, but rather, proclaiming the truth of the Scripture. Those with this gift have a unique ability to understand and communicate the Bible, and encourage people to respond. They enjoy studying, teaching, and preaching the Bible.

Service: The gift of service (Romans 12:7) is commonly understood to mean the ability to anticipate and meet needs—physical, spiritual, or emotional. People with this gift feel moved to serve others, to respond when there is a demonstrated need or a call to action, tend not to seek leadership positions, and see themselves as being spontaneous.

Teaching: The gift of teaching (Romans 12:7) is marked by a keen interest in personal study of the Bible and good ability to analyze God's truth. When the people with this gift teach, they may not be electrifying speakers, but they are able to communicate clearly the truths and application of Scripture. Those who enjoy research, exacting analysis, and who can spot sloppy teaching or careless research a mile away may have the gift of teaching.

Exhortation: The gift of exhortation (Romans 12:8) is commonly understood as the ability to come along side and encourage, admonish, stir up, and console. Those with this gift often identify closely with others' problems. They get below the surface in conversation with others and urge them to better courses of action. They tend to speak with great urgency.

Giving: The gift of giving (Romans 12:8) is generally understood as being inclined and skilled with the ability to make and distribute money and resources to further the cause of Christ. People with this gift tend to be very cautious about money and very concerned about the judicious use of finances. They enjoy distributing material resources, often without anyone knowing about it, and with no thought of recognition or financial gain.

Leading: The gift of leading (Romans 12:8) is generally understood as having a concern and vision for getting the greatest use of people, money, and time in furthering the cause of Christ. People with this gift gravitate to the front line of leadership, and pave the way in charting a course of action and calling everyone to stay on that course. They tend to be visionary and be able to inspire others to the vision. They enjoy solving problems. They see the "big picture" and enjoy getting all of the "parts" to effectively serve the "whole."

Showing mercy: The gift of showing mercy (Romans 12:8) is commonly understood as giving aid to those who cannot return the mercy—including the aged, children, sick, handicapped, or unlovely. They enjoy helping those whom the majority often ignores. Those with this gift are quick to meet the needs of others in distress and are easily moved by the suffering of others. They often cannot understand why others without this gift are not sensitive to people's needs and hurts.

Each of us has at least one of these gifts and is responsible to be ministering his gift for the benefit of others.

Learning by Doing

The first question that most people have is, "Which gift do I have, and how can I know?" The answer to that can be very involved and difficult to determine for certain. However, there are several guiding principles. First, we are all commanded to be doing the things that others might be gifted in. For example, someone might have the gift of mercy, but all of us are to show mercy. Someone might have the gift of giving, but all of us are to give. Someone might have the gift of service, but all of us are to serve.

Therefore, we should all be busy doing the things that we are commanded to do. Then, as we are busy doing these things, we will find that some of the activities are more enjoyable than others, and some of the activities seem to generate more results and greater affirmation than others. If so, this is very possibly an area of spiritual giftedness. The spiritual gift is something we enjoy doing, and something which others affirm in us. So, by trial and error, by inner and outward affirmation, we come to a gradual conclusion as to what our gift might be.

However, we must not get paralyzed if we still don't know what our gift is. Instead, we need to be busy doing what we see to do. God will use our gift, even if we don't know what it is. It is not necessary to know your spiritual gift(s) to have effective ministry to others, but it can be motivating and reassuring when we do.

Therefore, accept that you are gifted. Believe that you are competent to do anything Christ asks of you. If you cannot do it, He is not asking it of you. If He is asking it of you, you can do it. Be secure. Be confident. Reach out. Do your part. "As each of you has received a special gift, employ it in serving one another" (1 Peter 4:10).

> For just as we have many members in one body and all the members do not have the same function, so we, who are many, are one body in Christ, and individually members of one another. And since we have gifts that differ according to the grace given to us, let each exercise them accordingly. (Romans 12:4–6a)

Father, I offer myself to You for service to Your Body. I accept that You have gifted me, and I gladly serve You and other Christians with my gift. Fill my life with meaning as I serve You in love. In Jesus' name. Amen.

REVIEW

1. The Body of Christ and Spiritual Gifts

We were *created* by God to invest our lives in something *greater* than *ourselves.*

2. Service and Ministry Gifts

Each of us has a *gift* which is to be used in *building* up other *Christians.*

3. Learning By Doing

As we are *faithful* to God doing the things He asks of us, He will *lead* us into a *knowledge* of our spiritual gift(s).

As a memory exercise, write in the missing words in the paragraphs below. Notice that they are the same words as the italicized words in the paragraph above.

1. **The Body of Christ and Spiritual Gifts**

   We were _____ by God to invest our lives in something _____ than _____.

2. **Service and Ministry Gifts**

   Each of us has a _____ which is to be used in _____ up other _____.

3. **Learning By Doing**

   As we are _____ to God doing the things He asks of us, He will _____ us into a _____ of our spiritual gift(s).

RESPONSE

Questions for Group Discussion or Personal Exercises

1. Do you have an inner desire to really be used by God for His glory? Have you participated in a particular kind of service that brought you a sense of fulfillment?

2. On a scale of 1–10, how committed are you to being personally responsible for ministry? On the same scale, how free does your local church make you feel in order to fulfill that responsibility?

3. What are some of the natural consequences of relying on the "professionals" to be the only "ministers"?

4. Which of the gifts mentioned in this chapter have you found most interesting? Most fulfilling? Least fulfilling?

TWENTY-SEVEN

SHARING THE GOOD NEWS

Evangelism is not a professional job for a few trained men, but is instead the unrelenting responsibility of every person who belongs, even in the most modest way, to the company of Jesus.

Elton Trueblood

I love hearing how people become Christians—not just famous people, but regular, ordinary people. Let me tell you several that revolve around my spiritual father, Jake. The stories are told as best I remember them, though some of the names and details are deliberately changed to protect privacy. Jake is the man who led me to the Lord, though I was a ripe plumb who fell into his lap. His son, Joel, wore me down, and in my weakened condition, Jake moved in and got the kill. Joel, who is now a pastor, and I were in high school together and played on the basketball team. Joel was our best player. The first year in college, he went to an engineering school not too far away, where he had an athletic scholarship, and I went to a regional campus of Indiana University.

The next summer Joel and I were talking one evening, sitting on the hood of our cars at the Dairy Queen in our sleepy little hometown, and we began talking about the Lord. I had had a couple of close brushes with death that past year, and I knew I needed to become a Christian sooner or later. I began thinking that I had better make it "sooner," because there might not be any "later." I didn't realize that someone my age could help me become a Christian. I felt a need to talk to someone older, so we went to Joel's house at about 2:00 in the morning and rolled Jake out of bed.

He stumbled out of the bedroom to the kitchen and leaned against the doorway, breathing heavily with his face in his hands. He acted more like he had been shot than merely awakened from a deep sleep. He eventually recovered, and we talked for several hours, and as the birds began singing and the milkman began delivering milk, I was ushered into the kingdom of heaven.

Jake didn't do anything terribly sophisticated. He just cared, and he tried. And Jesus did everything else.

Then I remember Bob Baker. Bob was on my top ten list of those least likely to become a Christian. He had one of the foulest vocabularies I had ever heard. I used to work with him in the kitchen in the high school cafeteria, and he grossed me out daily with his vulgarity. After graduation, Bob married Susan, and they set up house in my hometown in Indiana.

Susan became a Christian and started attending church, but Bob wouldn't darken the door. Jake used to ask him regularly if he would come to church, but Bob was having none of it. In the rural areas of Indiana, they used to have a two-week revival every summer. A guest speaker would come in from out of town, and they would have meetings every night of the week for two weeks. Jake hounded Bob until he finally agreed to come to the revival meetings, but Bob sat toward the back with his arms folded defensively across his chest, his jaw set and lips pointed in a perpetual pout.

Each night after the meeting Jake would work up his courage to go ask Bob if he wanted to talk about the Lord. "No, not tonight Jake." Jake prayed for Bob every day during this time. Night after night passed, and Bob didn't go forward. Jake was afraid the revival would come and go and Bob wouldn't become a Christian.

The last night, Jake went up to Bob after the service and said, "Well, Bob, how about it. Are you ready to become a Christian tonight?" To Jake's astonishment, Bob said, "Well Jake, why don't you and Wilma come out to the house and we'll talk about it." Now the revival didn't get over until late, perhaps 9:30 or 10:00.

But they went out and talked about the Lord until late, but Bob showed no signs of being ready to become a Christian. It was getting very late, perhaps 1:00 or 2:00 in the morning, and Jake was getting a little self-conscious about staying so long. Also, he and Wilma were getting tired. Finally he said, "Well Bob, if you are not ready to become a Christian tonight, Wilma and I will go home, and we'll talk about it another night."

Bob said, "Not so fast. Jake, you hungry?" Jake said, "Well, to tell the truth, I could eat something." Bob said, "Susan, let's fix some bacon and eggs." So Susan fixed four plates of bacon and eggs, and toast and coffee. They chatted some more, and finally finished eating. Then Bob said, "Well, we might as well get this over with. Let's go in around the bed." They all went in the bedroom and knelt around the bed. And there, that night, Bob was ushered into the kingdom of heaven.

Jake didn't do anything special. He didn't do anything terribly sophisticated. He just cared, and he tried. And Jesus did everything else.

Then there was Dave Hill. Dave was a pig farmer—a rough, hard-working, hard-drinking, hard-cussing pig farmer. Jake was a feed salesman, and used to sell pig feed to Dave. He would talk about Jesus to him and his wife, Connie, every chance he got. Connie would listen politely, but Dave used to have a fit. Dave would listen only so long, and then he would jump up and start cussing and walking back and forth, waving his arms in the air. His eyes would dialate and little bubbles of saliva would form at the corners of his mouth. "Get off my blankety blank property before I throw your blankety blank hide out the door," he would scream in a voice that rattled the *neighbor's* windows.

But Dave needed pig feed, and Jake was the one he had to get it from, so Jake would go out again. And if he had the chance, he would talk to him about Jesus again. No one remembers how many times Dave threw Jake off his property, but Jake always came back.

One night, Jake was sitting at their kitchen table, which is the social center of all the homes in rural Indiana, talking to Dave and Connie about the Lord. Finally Connie said, "Dave, I don't care what you do. I'm going to accept Jesus." And there in a barely audible half whisper, Connie prayed, and was ushered into the kingdom of heaven. Dave stared in disbelief. Then he said, "Well Connie, if we are going to do this, I thought we were going to do it together." Connie shot back, "Well, I'm afraid that you're never going to get around to it." Dave said, "Well, I suppose I might as well, too." And that day, Dave was ushered into the kingdom of heaven.

Jake didn't do anything terribly sophisticated. He just cared, and he tried. And Jesus did everything else.

There isn't any magic to it. If Jake were here, he wouldn't say you had to read any books on personal evangelism. He wouldn't say you had to take a seminar to learn how to share your faith. He wouldn't take you through the ten steps on how not to offend anybody, because leading people to Christ isn't found in a program. The secret to leading people to Christ is simply caring enough and trying hard enough. Jesus will do everything else.

Don't you just love to hear stories about how people have become Christians? I know I do. I think everyone does. Don't you wish your life included stories like this of leading people to the Lord? I think all Christians do. It is part of the new birth in Christ, to desire to bring others to Him. And here is the point. You can. All you have to do is care and try. If you need to read a book, take a seminar, or anything else, that is okay. But nothing will replace the heart of it all—caring and trying.

There is a well known sermon illustration which Joe Aldrich uses in his book, *Life-style Evangelism*:

> There is a legend which recounts the return of Jesus to glory after His time on earth. Even in heaven He bore the marks of His earthly pilgrimage with its cruel cross and shameful death. The angel Gabriel approached Him and said, "Master, you must have suffered terribly for men down there."
>
> "I did," He said.
>
> "And," continued Gabriel, "do they know all about how you loved them and what you did for them?"
>
> "Oh, no," said Jesus, "not yet. Right now only a handful of people in Palestine know."
>
> Gabriel was perplexed. "Then what have you done," he asked, "to let everyone know about your love for them?"
>
> Jesus said, "I've asked Peter, James, John, and a few more friends to tell other people about Me. Those who are told will in

turn tell still other people about Me, and My story will be spread to the farthest reaches of the globe. Ultimately, all of mankind will have heard about My life and what I have done."

Gabriel frowned and looked rather skeptical. He knew well what poor stuff men were made of. "Yes," he said, "but what if Peter, James, and John grow weary? What if the people who come after them forget? What if way down in the twentieth century, people just don't tell others about you? Haven't you made any other plans?

Jesus answered, "I haven't made any other plans. I'm counting on them."[1]

If the message of salvation in Christ is true, then it is the most important piece of information in the world. It carries with it the inherent mandate to pass the information on to others. If someone has told us, then we ought to tell someone else.

So how are we doing? If the message of the gospel depended on our involvement, would it flourish or die out? If it depended on us, would Gabriel's apprehension be justified or not? In Mark 16:15, we read, "Go into all the world, and preach the gospel to all creation." Not only is it a self-evident conclusion, but it is a command from Jesus. So the question remains, "how are we doing?"

Personal Level

Evangelism is a lifestyle. Jesus wants our lives to influence others to believe in Him. It is not so much what we do, as what we are. Sharing our faith with others does not come easily for most of us. We are intimidated and threatened by the prospect. We can't get away from the inevitable, however. Unless we are spreading the message, it won't get done.

Many people are turned off by "program" evangelism. It seems canned and forced to them. Usually people must have had repeated exposure to the gospel before they accept it. So when a program of evangelism sweeps through, if a person is not spiritually prepared to accept Christ at that time, the opportunity passes with the program. However, if he has a relationship with someone who is a Christian, then the opportunity is constant. When he is ready, the opportunity is there.

Most of us have been discouraged in our attempts to share our faith with others. Often, the other people want absolutely nothing to do with it. Or, they listen with polite or strained attention and move on the first chance they get. Therefore, we must come to a more complete understanding of "lifestyle" evangelism, so that we can be encouraged to remain faithful to the process. The following four principles are helpful in outlining "lifestyle" evangelism.

Principle #1: Sowing and Reaping

Lifestyle evangelism includes not just "reaping" but also "sowing." A friend of mine tells the following story:

> In my old neighborhood my wife and I prayed, looked for, and took every opportunity to share Christ with our neighbors. After three and a half years, not one person trusted Christ. I was discouraged. But, you see, I was buying the idea that evangelism is just reaping. When Jesus taught his disciples in John 4, He talks about sowing and reaping, and that one will sow and another will reap.
>
> The year after my wife and I moved, one of our former neighbors came to see us. Their marriage was falling apart and they knew my wife and I had something different. We had an opportunity to lead that couple to Christ . . . but still, that was just one couple in a neighborhood that we had poured our lives into.
>
> Now, a year and a half later, five couples have trusted Christ in that neighborhood—all led to Christ by that first couple—and they have a neighborhood Bible study with fifteen non-Christians attending.
>
> Did we do evangelism those three years when no one accepted Christ? Absolutely. We were sowing, we were cultivating and we were watering. But God didn't give us the opportunity to reap. We have to remember that reaping belongs to God.

Principle #2: Being Prepared

We must understand the gospel message ourselves and know how to share it with others. There are many books written to help you know how to do this. Or better yet, find someone who is already doing it and have him show you how. Some churches have training programs. Do what you have to, but get prepared.

Principle #3: Let Your Life Speak

As you do your best to live out your spiritual convictions, people will see a difference in your life. They will notice that you are different, and that difference will give you opportunities to share your faith with others.

Jim Peterson, in his book *Evangelism as a Lifestyle*, tells the story of a time when he was talking with a young woman on an airplane. It became evident that she was looking for companionship when they landed. Jim could have succumbed to the temptation. He could have copped out and switched the subject. Or, he could have said, sternly, "that would be sin." Instead, secure in the wisdom of his convictions, he said to her:

> "I travel a lot and many times I am lonely. I often encounter temptations to be unfaithful to my wife. But I've decided it's not worth it. I know I could deceive her, but the basis of our relationship is our mutual love and confidence. She trusts me and I trust her.
>
> "I've lived long enough to realize that meaning in life is not found in seeing what I can get away with, or in bigger achievements, or in a position, or in how my leisure time is spent. I've learned that meaning is found in relationships. Consequently, I don't intend to destroy the best relationship I have. If I came home having been unfaithful to my wife, even though she might not percieve it, and even though I could keep it from her, I'd know. She would come to me with her blind confidence and I'd have to somehow create a distance between us. We'd be pulled apart and she would never know why. Soon we would be strangers living together under the same roof."
>
> "The ones who would pay most heavily would be my wife and children. That strikes me as the height of selfishness.
>
> She was dumbfounded. Then she added, "I've never heard ideas like yours. Where do they come from?"
>
> "You'd laugh if I told you."
>
> "No, I wouldn't," she said.
>
> "I got them from the Bible," I said. I went on to explain to her what the Christian message is and how it changes a person so he can get his life in order.[2]

Though it didn't happen right away, Jim learned that the woman eventually made the decision to follow Jesus in her life. Certainly, it won't happen like that every time, but the point is,

Jim was confident in his faith and answered in a very natural and engaging way. It made sense. It opened up a door to share the "good news." We need to believe that our faith does make sense, and that if we can learn to be un-defensive, natural, and honest, our lives will open up a constant succession of opportunities to share our faith.

Principle #4: Trust God

In 1 Corinthians 3:6, Paul says, "I planted, Apollos watered, but God was causing the growth. So then, neither the one who plants nor the one who waters is anything, but God who causes the growth." It is God who convinces people to accept the truth of Christ. It is God who opens their minds to understand the truth. It is God who causes people to be born again. We are stewards of a message. As we live a life that supports the gospel message, and as we share with people when we get an opportunity, God is the one who determines the results.

We must relax in His sovereignty. He does not require results from us. He only requires faithfulness to sharing the message. We must trust Him and the power of the Scriptures in people's lives. It is not our clever arguments, our persuasiveness, our compelling logic or our irresistable personalities. It is God, using the Word. We must be faithful to tell people what the Bible says, and share the difference it has made in our lives. Leave everything else to God.

Here are some practical steps to take in becoming more involved in personal evangelism.

- Recognize that there are people out there who want to become a Christian, but no one is reaching out to them. Their lives may be falling apart, and they are longing for someone to help them find the truth. You will not be forcing yourself on anyone. Rather, you will be offering water to a thirsty soul.

- Understand that God is the one who saves people. You don't. All you have to do is be faithful to share when He gives you an opportunity. Rest in His sovereignty.

- Recognize that the message of the gospel is much more powerful if you develop a relationship with a person, rather than just drop the message on them like a water balloon and take off. Make friends with people, and then wait for God to give you the opportunity to share the gospel.

- Your life must support the message you are sharing. If it doesn't, they will consider you a hypocrite. Live a life of integrity.

- Develop accountability and support relationships with other people who are trying to do the same thing you are doing. We all need encouragement. Seek out a few like-minded people. Few people can accomplish this kind of a lifestyle alone.

- Pray for spontaneous opportunities and single out people to pray for. Be ready when the opportunity comes.

- If it seems other people are giving you positive signals, take the initiative with personal contact. We all like to be befriended.

- Have a Bible study in your home. Have Christian friends invite non-Christian friends, so there is a mix.

- Trust God to work, and rely on the Holy Spirit.

- Don't worry if you don't see fruit right away. Paul planted, Apollos watered, but God gave the increase in His time.

Often, coming to the point at which we are willing to share our faith is the last major hurdle a person crosses in his spiritual maturation. We fear that we look foolish in the eyes of others. Properly done, nothing could be further from the truth. More and more, people are understanding that they don't have the answers for life's questions, and even though they might not end up agreeing with your decision, they will respect you for it.

Corporate Level

Not only should we be involved in personal evangelism, but also, we should participate and support evangelism on a corporate level. For example, there are "institutional" opportunities to share your faith, and they are rich and rewarding experiences. Many churches and other Christian organizations have ministries in prisons, in street ministries, in nursing homes, in crisis pregnancy centers, or in orphanages. We can be a tremendous encouragement to others in our support of these structured ministry opportunities.

Support Level

Finally, there are many ministries dedicated to evangelism. The Billy Graham Evangelistic Organization, Campus Crusade for Christ, Navigators, and other such organizations deserve our prayers and our financial support. We can multiply ourselves by sending our financial and prayer support to those who are in full-time evangelistic ministries.

I used to minister with an organization called Walk Thru the Bible Ministries, which holds seminars to give an overview of the Old and New Testaments. I was one of the original team members, and back in the old days when it was a fairly small organization, we did not include a gospel presentation in the seminar.

One day, a fire-breathing, evangelist-type pastor came to our headquarters in Atlanta. "You people ought to be giving a gospel presentation during your seminars!" he charged. He didn't understand, we told him, that this is a teaching seminar for people who are already Christians. "Out of the thousands of people who attend these seminars every year, there are bound to be plenty of people attending who have not yet become Christians. They are sitting under the teaching of the Word of God for eight hours, and the Holy Spirit is working in their hearts. They are sitting there wanting to become Christians, and you are not giving them the chance!" he rejoined.

The possibility seemed inescapable. So we all agreed we would give it a shot. For the next year, we included a brief time at the close of the seminar in which we presented the gospel and invited people to accept Jesus as their personal savior. In the next twelve months, over five thousand people came to Christ! That was, perhaps ten years ago. Who knows how many thousands have come to Christ since then?

We didn't do anything very sophisticated. At the God-directed urging of this concerned brother in Christ, his concern transferred to us. We just cared, and we tried. And Jesus did everything else.

The gospel message is the most important piece of information in the world. Someone shared it with you, and God wants you to share it with someone else. You don't have to do anything very sophisticated. Just care and try.

And Jesus came up to them and spoke to them, saying, "All authority has been given to Me in heaven and on earth. Go therefore and make disciples of all the nations, baptizing them in the name of the Father and the Son and the Holy Spirit, teaching them to observe all that I commanded you; and lo, I am with you always, even to the end of the age." (Matthew 28:18–20)

> *Heavenly Father, I will accept the call to be an evangelist with my lifestyle. Help me to be perceptive and bold, and lead me to those You want me to share with. May I have the privilege of leading others to know You. Amen.*

REVIEW

1. Personal Level

God wants us each to *share* the good news of *salvation* in Christ with others as a part of our *lifestyle*.

2. Corporate Level

Many *opportunities* exist for us to be involved in *organized* efforts to *spread* the good news.

3. Support Level

God is using *many* people to spread the good news beyond what we can do ourselves, and they need our *prayer* and *financial* support.

As a memory exercise, write in the missing words in the paragraphs below. Notice that they are the same words as the italicized words in the paragraph above.

1. **Personal Level**

   God wants us each to _____ the good news of _____ in Christ with others as a part of our _____.

2. **Corporate Level**

   Many _____ exist for us to be involved in _____ efforts to _____ the good news.

3. **Support Level**

   God is using _____ people to spread the good news beyond what we can do ourselves, and they need our _____ and _____ support.

RESPONSE

Questions for Group Discussion or Personal Exercises

1. Think back to your own conversion. What had the greatest impact on your decision? Was it personal relationships with believers, or more of a corporate influence?

2. Do you feel you have to have the gift of evangelism or master some technique before you can begin personal evangelism?

3. List as many activities as you can that fit the category of "sowing."

4. In what area of your life should you be "letting your life speak" a little louder? What would be a "do-able" next step for you in that area?

TWENTY-EIGHT

KNOWING GOD'S WILL

*In our quest for God's guidance we become
our own worst enemies, and our mistakes
attest to our nuttiness in this area.*

J. I. Packer

Perhaps you have heard the story about the young farmer who wanted to know God's will for his life. Each day when he went out to plow corn, he would beg; he would implore God to reveal His will to him. What should he do with his life? What was His will for his life? Then one day as he was plowing corn, the clouds near the horizon seemed to come together in an unmistakable combination of letters . . . uncertain at first, but becoming much clearer momentarily . . . "P"—"C" . . . the clouds seemed to spell.

"P—C . . . P—C . . ." the young farmer pondered over and over. "What could 'P—C' possibly mean?" Then it hit him. PREACH CHRIST! Finally, he knew. He was to become a preacher and preach Christ.

He rushed into his pastor's home and told him the great news and asked if he might have the privilege of preaching his first sermon the next Sunday. The pastor agreed, reluctantly.

After the sermon the following Sunday, the young farmer met the pastor in his study and said, "Well, what do you think?"

The pastor replied, "Son, I'm not sure if the Lord was speaking to you in the clouds the other day or not, but if He was, I think He was telling you to Plow Corn."

We smile, and yet, deep down, we identify with the young farmer. We want to know God's will. We want assurances when we make decisions. We want the security of knowing we are doing exactly what God wants us to do. And we feel sorry for the young farmer. How was he to know? He prayed earnestly and after his prayer saw a "P" and a "C" in the clouds. What is he supposed to think? How was he supposed to know if the "P—C" were from God and what they meant?

How can we know God's will? Especially for newer Christians, this is one of the most commonly asked questions in the Christian life. In exploring the answer, we must distinguish between two things: (1) the moral will of God, and (2) decision making. Let's look at the difference between the two.

The Moral Will of God

When the Bible talks about the "will of God," it is pretty much talking about His moral will. There are only two places in the New Testament where the Bible says, "This is the will of God." The first one is 1 Thessalonians 4:3: "For this is the will of God, your sanctification." Sanctification means having been "set apart for God." Perhaps more directly, it suggests "God's possession, used for God's purposes." We are God's possession, and when we do God's purposes, we are "sanctified." That is the mindset of God's will in the New Testament. It has to do with our moral progress and our growing spiritually, so that we do God's purposes in an ever-increasing way.

The second passage where the phrase "the will of God" is used is 1 Thessalonians 5:18: "Give thanks in all circumstances; for this is the will of God in Christ Jesus for you." It is God's will for us that we give thanks to God in the midst of all circumstances. In order to do that, we must see the circumstances as God sees them; we must trust Him and believe that He is able to work in and through all circumstances to bring good out of them. We must place our hopes and dreams in the world to come, not in this world. Again, the will of God has to do with our character—His moral will.

God lets us know what His moral will for us is, and if we follow His moral will, there is little danger of "missing" His circumstantial will. God has promised repeatedly throughout the Bible to guide His sincere children and to give them wisdom. We do not have to try to "find" His circumstantial will for us, because it is not "lost." It will come to us as we remain in His moral will.

Ray Stedman wrote, in one of his "Discovery Papers":

> This is the will of God, your sanctification, that you may be a body wholly filled and flooded with God Himself. What a challenge, what a glory, what a marvellous thing, that in the midst of this sweeping current of immorality washing everything down the stream to utter destruction, there may be those who are able to stand in wholesome purity, reflecting the love and grace and glory of the life of Jesus Christ. This is the will of God! When you have found that, the matter of guidance takes care of itself. It is easy for God to lead someone who belongs to Him body, soul, and spirit.[1]

So when we ask, "How can I know God's will?" we realize that God's primary concern for us is that we walk in His moral will—laboring continuously to be the kind of person He wants us to be. When we live each moment with this mindset, then, when God wants to redirect us, He can.

Making Decisions

"Easy for you to say," you might add. "It sounds easy when you only talk about it in moral terms. However, I must decide which college to go to. I must decide whom to marry. I must decide which ministry to contribute money to. I must decide whether to put my children in private or public high school. I must make a million decisions, and I don't know how to make them. I don't know what the right thing is to do. How do I make decisions with any confidence that they are the decisions God wants me to make?"

Fair enough! You must make decisions. But if you are walking with the Lord, you do not have to worry about missing God's will. If you are in His moral will and making decisions the best way you know how, you can trust that God can guide you into whatever decisions He thinks are important for you to make in order to carry out His will for you. Again, Stedman wrote:

> If we approach the problem [of assuming that God's will is "circumstances"], we will never come to a satisfying answer. We are starting out on the wrong foot when we come at it in that way. I speak out of years of frustrating experience, during which I attempted to find the will of God by just such a manner. I never came to an answer until I saw that I was approaching the problem wrongly. For the will of God is not a program, it is a relationship. It is not what you do, it is what you are. It is not primarily a question of guidance (that is a part of it, admittedly, but it is a very minor part), it is really a question of acceptance [of his Lordship over every aspect of your life].[2]

Having accepted that, there are some Biblical and common sense principles that will help us in making decisions in life. We can know as much of God's circumstantial will as we need to know.

Principle #1: Scripture

The Bible is God's owner's manual. Just as the car makers put an owner's manual in each vehicle they manufacture, telling the owner how they must operate and maintain their vehicle, so God has given mankind the Bible, telling them how to operate and maintain themselves. We cannot make up our own rules and get away with it. The "machine" was not manufactured with that kind of latitude. The Bible does not speak directly to many of the specific things we face in life (what color of socks to wear in the morning), but it is adequate for the Christian to become all that God wants him to become. And, in principle, it addresses many specific circumstances. It has been said that the Bible does not give us a road map for life, but it does give us a compass.

The Bible is full of many commands and instructions for most of life's decisions. The more we know of God's Word, the more certain we can be of God's will. As examples, the Bible makes it clear that we are to not murder, not commit adultery, not lie, cheat, or steal, not lust, or covet. We are to forgive others, work hard, be honest, love our neighbor, give to the poor, honor our parents, help others in need, not take a fellow Christian to court, and so on. This is but a sliver of an entire giant redwood of truth found in the Bible that will give us the guidance we need for making many of life's decisions. If any decisions violate the principles of Scripture, they are wrong decisions.

We shouldn't use the Bible incorrectly, however. There is an apocryphal story about a man who was seeking guidance from the Lord. He let his Bible fall open at random, and his eyes fell on Matthew 27:5—"Judas went out and hanged himself." He didn't like that, so he let it fall open again, and his eyes fell on Luke 10:37—"Go and do likewise." He didn't like that any better, so he let it fall open again, and his eyes fell on John 13:27—"What you do, do quickly."

We laugh, and yet it is easy to fall into one of two extremes: (1) not looking to the Bible at all for guidance in life, or (2) using it to try to find specific circumstantial guidance for our personal circumstances. Much of the pain that we suffer in life, we bring on ourselves because we violate truth that was already given us in the Bible, but usually in the form of a principle rather than specific circumstantial guidance.

Principle #2: Prayer

A heart attitude of submission and dependence is crucial when looking for guidance from the Lord. Lewis Sperry Chafer, founder of Dallas Theological Seminary, said, "His leading is only for those who are already committed to do as He may lead."[3] Alan Redpath, the great Bible teacher of an earlier generation, said, "Don't expect God to reveal His will for you next week until you practice it today."[4]

These are certainly true statements. God is not a genie in a bottle. Our wish is not His command. He is our God, and we are accountable to Him for our response to His truth. This mindset of submission and dependence is described in Romans 12:1–2:

> So brothers, since God has shown us great mercy, I beg you to
> offer your lives as a living sacrifice to him. Your offering must be

SPIRITUAL DISCIPLINES

only for God and pleasing to him. This is the spiritual way for

you to worship. Do not change yourselves to be like the people

of this world. But be changed within by a new way of thinking.

Then you will be able to decide what God wants for you. And

you will be able to know what is good and pleasing to God and

As the Christian commits himself totally to following Christ, his

mind is changed by God to understand more of His will.

Also, James teaches that we can pray to God for wisdom in

making decisions. "If any of you lacks wisdom, let him ask of God,

who gives to all men generously and without reproach, and it will

Paul prayed for the Colossian believers that they might be

"filled with the knowledge of His will in all wisdom and spiritual

understanding; that [they] may have a walk worthy of the Lord,

fully pleasing Him, being fruitful in every good work and increas-

Principle #3: Counsel

When I am driving in the car with my wife, if there is any possibil-

ity that we might not know exactly at all times where we are, she

will suggest that we stop and ask someone for directions. I don't

know why, but I hate to stop and ask for directions. I suppose it is

an admission of failure. I will take short cuts, only to end up in a

cul-de-sac, or I will cut across a parking lot only to find that there

is no exit to the street on the other side. Because I feel a little

this same problem. I am convinced that there are two kinds of

people, when it comes to being "lost" while driving an automobile.

Those who stop and ask for directions almost immediately, and

those who won't stop and ask unless they have exhausted every

other option first. Some people are that way with spiritual advice

"Where there is no counsel, the people fall, but in the multitude

James Packer once said, "Don't be a spiritual Lone Ranger;

when you think you see God's will, have your perception checked.

Draw on the wisdom of those who are wiser than you are. Take advice."[5]

That is good advice. Even when you think you have not yet seen God's will, ask advice. It's the wise thing to do. Many other people will have insight that you might not have had. Use it!

Principle #4: Wisdom

Proverbs, chapter 2, reads:

> My son, if you will receive my sayings,
> And treasure my commandments within you,
> Make your ear attentive to wisdom,
> Incline your heart to understanding.
> For if you cry for discernment,
> Lift up your voice for understanding;
> If you seek her as silver,
> And search for her as for hidden treasures;
> Then you will discern the fear of the Lord,
> And discover the knowledge of God,
> For the Lord gives wisdom;
> From His mouth come knowledge
>   and understanding. . . .
> Then you will discern righteousness and justice
> And equity and every good course.
> For wisdom will enter your heart,
> And knowledge will be pleasant to your soul;
> Discretion will guard you,
> Understanding will watch over you,
> To deliver you from the way of evil.
>   (Proverbs 2:1–6, 9–12a)

God has given us a capacity for wisdom, and He expects us to develop it and use it. Wisdom will keep us from many bad decisions and will help us walk in God's moral, as well as, His circumstantial will.

With wisdom, we combine what has been learned through Scripture, prayer, counsel from others, and, in the providence and leading of God, make the best decision we can.

Principle #5: Freedom

Not every decision has earthshaking consequences. Whether you wear a blue shirt or white shirt today is not likely to have any consequences. When the decision has no major consequences that you can foresee, you are free to do what you want.

For example, in 1 Corinthians 10:27, Paul writes, "If one of the unbelievers invites you, and you wish to go, eat anything that is set before you, without asking questions for conscience' sake."

The passage did not say, "If one of the unbelievers invites you, search the Scriptures, pray for days, seek the counsel of others, and make a pro and con list." It merely says, "if you want to, go." We should not strain at gnats by trying to relate all decisions to spiritual significance or sovereign importance. Some decisions the Lord gives us to make based on our own inclinations. With major decisions, of course, the matter must be taken more seriously. But with smaller decisions with no foreseeable consequences, we are free to act.

Trusting God

St. Augustine once said, "Love God and do as you please." Of course, this is the kind of statement that could easily be misunderstood or distorted. But what he meant was, if you love God, you are going to obey His commandments. The Apostle John wrote, "If you love me you will keep my commandments" (John 14:15, 15:10). If you disobey His commandments, for the moment, you have stopped loving God. If you love God, you will not do anything that you understand to be wrong. Therefore, if you are only doing that which you think is right, you can love God and do as you please, understanding that God has overseen the process and will accept the decision.

In his booklet entitled *Guidance,* Philip Yancey wrote:

> I have a confession to make. For me, at least, guidance only becomes evident when I look backward, months and years later. Then, the circuitous process falls into place and the hand of God seems clear. But at the moment of decision, I feel mainly confusion and uncertainty. Indeed, almost all the guidance in my life has been subtle and indirect.

This pattern has recurred so often (and clear guidance for the future has occurred so seldom) that I am about to conclude that we have a basic direction wrong. I had always thought of guidance as forward-looking. We keep praying, hoping, counting on God to reveal what we should do next. In my own experience, at least, I have found the direction to be reversed. The focus must be on the moment before me, the present. How is my relationship to God? As circumstances change, for better or worse, will I respond with obedience and trust?[6]

God does have a circumstantial will for us, but there will be times when we will not know what it is. In those times, we do not have to agonize over God's failure to make His way clear to us. We may feel free to use our best judgment, following the principles of Scripture, prayer, counsel, and wisdom.

> Trust in the Lord with all your heart,
> And do not lean on your own understanding.
> In all your ways acknowledge Him,
> And He will make your paths straight.
> (Proverbs 3:5–6)

Father in Heaven, lead me in Your moral will. Make me more like Jesus in my character. Help me to lean on You and to trust You in all of life's directions. And then, dear Lord, do not let me stray from any circumstance in which You may want to use me. Give me peace as I walk with You. Amen.

REVIEW

1. The Moral Will of God

God's *moral* will for us is clearly *presented* in the Scripture and is clearly our *priority* concern.

2. Making Decisions

When making decisions, God will *lead* us as we *apply* the *principles* of Scripture.

3. Trusting God

If we *remain* in God's *moral* will, we have little to fear in missing His *circumstantial* will.

As a memory exercise, write in the missing words in the paragraphs below. Notice that they are the same words as the italicized words in the paragraph above.

1. The Moral Will of God

God's _____ will for us is clearly _____ in the Scripture and is clearly our _____ concern.

2. Making Decisions

When making decisions, God will _____ us as we _____ the _____ of Scripture.

3. Trusting God

If we _____ in God's _____ will, we have little to fear in missing His _____ will.

RESPONSE

Questions for Group Discussion or Personal Exercises

1. Are you confident that you are in God's moral will? Are you in danger of getting into wrong circumstances because of moral drifting?

2. What dangers do we open ourselves up to when we search the Scriptures for direction which God does not intend to provide?

3. For what decisions are you looking for direction from God right now? Who are some other wise people you could call upon for their counsel?

TWENTY-NINE

SPIRITUAL VIGILANCE

The price of liberty is eternal vigilance.

Thomas Jefferson

I will never forget looking at the picture of my brother in the hospital bed. He had been wounded in Vietnam. He normally weighed 180 pounds, and from the looks of the picture, he must have weighed 130. He looked like a skeleton with skin stretched over it.

He was a lieutenant in the Army infantry, which meant that he was point man on reconnaissance missions into hostile territory, and during one of the missions, his radio man right behind him stepped on a land mine. Shrapnel hit him in the back and wounded him so seriously that he was taken to a hospital in Japan. That was where the picture was taken that eventually appeared in our hometown newspaper. He was sitting up in the hospital bed with a "you-don't-think-I'm-going-to-let-a-little-shrapnel-stop-me" look on his face.

I have learned a little more about land mines since then. For example, it was very common for the Army to put mine fields all around the outside of its camps. Then, the men had to memorize the paths to get through the mine field, because they were so cleverly concealed that no one could see them. "Walk straight toward the big tree until you get even with the large rock. Then turn right and walk up to the crest of the knoll. Angle toward the left until you come to the thicket. Walk around the thicket to the right, keeping ten feet between you and the thicket, until you get to the other side. Then, turn left and walk straight toward the opening in the jungle wall."

One slip of the memory, and you were dead. It took total concentration while walking through the mine field, and you walked very carefully.

When you enter the Christian life, you enter, not a playground, but a battlefield. Life isn't a waltz. It's a war. Just as the battlefield is filled with dangers which require total concentration and walking very carefully, so the Christian life is filled with dangers on every side which require total concentration, and walking very carefully.

That's the message of this chapter. In Ephesians 5:1, Paul exhorted us to be imitators of God and walk in love. We saw in the previous chapter that "love gives," and that it was best summed up in the saying of Jesus, "Do unto others as you would have others do unto you."

Exhortations from Ephesians Chapter 5

Paul warned us, in verses 3–14 of chapter 5 of Ephesians, not to fall for any of the satanic counterfeits of love, like immorality, impurity, greed, filthiness, silly talk, or coarse jesting. These things are not even to be mentioned among Christians. It is because of these things that the wrath of God comes on the sons of disobedience. The implicit warning is that if Christians participate in the sins of the sons of disobedience, we will also partake of the judgment on the sons of disobedience.

Paul says, "don't be partakers with them" (v. 7). You used to be darkness, but now you are light in the Lord. *Walk* as children of light. Not only should you not do those things directly, neither should you not participate in them vicariously. "It is disgraceful even to speak of the things which are done by them in secret" (v. 12).

Now if it is disgraceful even to speak of the things which are done by them in secret, how much more of a shame is it to pay five dollars and stand in line to watch it on a 70mm screen in Dolby stereo? If it is a shame even to speak of the things which are done by them in secret, how much more of a shame is it to listen to it all set to music? If it is a shame even to speak of the things which are done by them in secret, how much more of a shame is it to bring it into the home by way of television, watch it in living color, and even babysit the children with it?

When we participate in the sins of the sons of disobedience, either directly or vicariously through the media, we also participate in the judgment of God on those sins. That is why the church is being bludgeoned by the same social problems as the world.

It was the same in the Old Testament. As Israel participated in the sins of the nations living around them, they also participated in the judgments of the nations living around them. If there was going to be no difference with Israel in righteous behavior, then there would be no difference in their tasting the judgment of God.

This warning was rooted, not in hate, but in love; not in retaliation, but in compassion; not because God wants to hold us down, but because He wants to lift us up; not because He wants to limit us, but because He wants to set us free to fly supersonic in our spiritual lives.

It is in this spirit that Paul then urges us: "Therefore . . . because these great dangers exist on the battlefield of our spiritual lives, and because the dangers are so devastating, be careful how you walk."

Then, he goes on to specify three things about this careful walk.

Be Smart

"Don't walk as unwise people, but as wise" (v. 15). In other words, don't be a fool. The theme here could easily be compared to the theme in Proverbs contrasting the fool with the wise man. Some of the major characteristics of the fool in Proverbs are that he:

• engages in immorality, or

• is lazy, or

- is gluttonous, or

- lies, or

- ignores what his parents tell him, or

- resents instruction, or

- is easily influenced by his peers, or

- is dishonest, or

- steals, or

- lives for material possessions, or

- lives for recognition of others, or

- lives for the pursuit of pleasure, or

- uses alcohol and drugs, or

- is any combination of the above.

Solomon says, "don't be a fool."

Do you think you will find happiness by getting a lot of money? Don't be a fool. Do you think you will find happiness by buying that house you want so badly? Don't be a fool. Do you think you will find happiness if you can just date that good-looking guy or girl? Don't be a fool. Do you think you will find happiness if you can just land that job? Don't be a fool. Do you think you will find happiness by drinking or using drugs? Don't be a fool. Do you think you will find happiness by throwing off all authority and doing only what you want? Don't be a fool. Do you think you will find happiness by manipulating others, by being dishonest? Don't be a fool. Do you think you will find happiness if you can just get accepted by a certain group of people? Don't be a fool.

None of this brings happiness. None of it brings lasting meaning. It is all like trying to capture a moonbeam. It is all a lie. There is one thing that satisfies. Solomon says it is loving God and fulfilling His commandments. Everything else is vanity.

Look around. Are the richest people happiest? *No!* There is a higher suicide rate among the wealthy than among those who are not wealthy. The degraded lifestyles of many of the very wealthy, and the extremely high percentage of alcohol and drug abuse among those people, demonstrate that these things do not satisfy. It doesn't mean that you cannot be happy if you have money. But it does mean that if you are happy, it is not because of the money. It is because of other things. It is because you have the rest of your life together. Think, Paul says! Be smart. Don't be a fool.

Be Effective

"Redeem the time" (v. 16). Time is life. If you fiddle around with time, you are fiddling around with life. If you waste time, you waste life. If you misuse time, you misuse life.

If you control time, you control life. If you use time wisely and effectively, you use life wisely and effectively. Time is life. What you do with one, you do with the other.

The effective use of our time is not a small thing. It determines whether or not when we get to the end of our life, we feel that we had a life of meaning. It determines whether or not we have a sense of purpose and significance as we move through each day. If we are going to live wisely, and if we are going to be careful in walking through the battlefield of the spiritual life, we must be effective. We must use our time wisely.

Too many of us float through life like a cork floating down-stream—just going along with the stream of events. Did you know that you don't have to float along with the stream of events? Did you know you can cut across the stream? Did you know you can go upstream? It is harder, but it can be done, and it is infinitely more rewarding. But you must control your time. You must use it wisely. You must make your time flow in the direction of your priorities.

In his book *Growing Strong in the Seasons of Life,* Charles Swindoll writes:

Allow me to introduce a professional thief.

Chances are you'd never pick this slick little guy out of a crowd, but many, over the years, have come to regard him as a formidable giant. Quick as a laser and silent as a moonbeam, he can pick any lock in your office. Once inside, his winsome ways will captivate your attentions. You'll treat him like your closest friend. Ah . . . but watch out. He'll strip you without a blink of remorse.

Master of clever logic that he is, the bandit will rearrange the facts just enough to gain your sympathies. When others call his character into question, you'll find yourself not only believing in him, but actually quoting and defending him. Too late, you'll see through his ruse and give him grudging credit as the shrewdest of all thieves. Some never come to such a realization at all. They stroll to their graves arm-in-arm with the very robber who has stolen away their lives.

His name? Procrastination. His specialty? Stealing time and incentive. Like the proverbial pack rat, he makes off with priceless valuables, leaving cheap substitutes in their place: excuses, rationalizations, empty promises, embarrassment, and guilt.[1]

There are other professional thieves. Another one is "wrong priorities." Another one is "carelessness." Another one is "never saying no." They all have the same result. They steal your time. Therefore, they steal your life. They keep you from pursuing the best things that God has for you. We must redeem the time.

Wisdom is knowledge effectively applied to life's problems. Paul takes us beyond the step of telling us that we need to live life wisely. Now he gets more specific, and says, we must redeem the time, for the days are evil.

To redeem here, means to buy back. We cannot buy back time. Once it is gone, it is gone; but we can structure our lives to capitalize on opportunities, and that is what is meant here.

"Redeem the time, for the days are evil." This is not merely an exhortation to use time effectively. You can use your time effectively in the pursuit of worthless things. The phrase only makes sense if it means redeeming our time in the pursuit of things that counter the evil days in which we live.

While this means that we must use our time wisely in the fulfillment of obligations in the home and at work, it means much more than that. The things that counter evil are the things that advance the kingdom of God. So the redemption of time here means looking for opportunities to use our resources for things that advance the kingdom of Christ.

We must redeem the time, for the days are evil.

Be Discerning

"So then do not be foolish, but understand what the will of the Lord is" (v. 17).

This will come as a shock and disappointment to some of you, but God's will for your life is not to make you rich and famous. God's will for your life is not to give you a life of ease. God's will for your life is not for you to be floating through life on a bed of roses, lying on a cloud. God's will for your life is to make you like Jesus. And He feels perfectly free to use anything at His disposal to accomplish that purpose.

To accomplish that purpose, He uses the Word of God. He requires your personal involvement. He uses other believers. And He uses time and trials. I know of no one who is a deep and insightful person, who has a grip on life, and whose life is a model of peace, love, and joy, and purpose and meaning in Christ, who has not suffered—and gone through that suffering God's way.

When Paul says, "understand what the will of God is," he is not referring to the specific will of the Lord as what college you should go to, or whom you should marry, or what job you should pursue. Rather, it means to understand what the moral will of God is for you. It is clearly revealed to us, and, therefore, we can be instructed to understand it.

The Lord's moral will for us is to walk in love. Anything immoral or impure or greedy, or any filthiness or silly talk or coarse jesting is not even to be named among us. And not only are we not to directly participate in it, we are not to participate in it indirectly or vicariously. It is a shame even to speak of the things that are done by them in secret. We are to walk in the light, because we are light in the Lord. This is the Lord's will. This is what we are not to be foolish to ignore.

Exhortations for Today

This is what the passage says, and now we want to spend some time thinking through what is means to us. If this is what it says to us, so what? How ought our lives to change, specifically? When we ask these questions, I think there are two major things that we can see coming from this passage for our lives today.

Life Goals

The effective use of time is directly related to our life goals. Have you ever asked yourself what it is that you want out of life? There are three stages in which you can ask yourself this question. The first stage is when you are young, enthusiastic, optimistic, with a distinct sense of being invincible and immortal. Then, you ask yourself "What do I want out of life? The sky's the limit!"

The second stage at which you ask yourself this question is at middle age. The vision and enthusiasm of youth has been refined into a realistic sense of the possible. You redefine, reorganize, and tackle realistic objectives, which are usually more limited than before.

The third stage is in the autumn of life in which you say, "I only have a little more time left. What will I do to invest each day with meaning?"

At each point in time, it is legitimate to ask, "What do I want out of life?" Many of us, if we are willing to look realistically at our limitations, can have much of what we want if we are willing to pay the price.

We must be very careful how we define these things, however, or we will climb the ladder of success only to find it is leaning against the wrong wall.

If we are going to redeem the time, and not be foolish, but understand the will of the Lord, we cannot establish goals in life as X amount of money, or this job, or that accomplishment. Those things don't satisfy! If we establish those things as the things we want out of life, we will be foolish, and will fail to understand the will of the Lord. We will not be redeeming the time.

We must establish the same goals for ourselves that God desires for us, and then we can be wise and know happiness. What goals can we have?

- I want a meaningful relationship with God.

- I want a meaningful relationship with my family.

- I want a meaningful relationship with myself.

- I want a meaningful relationship with friends.

- I want a sense of meaning and significance from what I do in my vocation.

- I want a sense of purpose with what I do with my life.

- I want a satisfying ministry.

If you have these things, life will be rich and rewarding for you, regardless of how much money you have. If you do not have these things, you will not have a rich and rewarding life, no matter how much money you have. Money does not produce happiness.

Once you have these goals and are experiencing some degree of satisfaction in meeting them, it is acceptable to have specific, measurable accomplishments, but you must not link your happiness to them. You can work for them, but you must be willing to take them or leave them, as the will of God allows.

Control Your Time

The effective pursuit of life's goals can only be achieved with the effective control of one's time. It is imperative that we have clear goals—that we understand what it is that we want out of life. Because there is not enough time to do what we want, we must allocate our time according to our priorities. If we do not allocate our time according to our priorities, we will find our time flowing to the areas of least importance. If we do not control our time, there are a hundred people who are willing to control it for us. The only problem is that we don't have the same priorities as they do, and our life is not fulfilling.

Here is what I suggest. Write out your life goals. Start with ten, on a three-by-five card, and review those goals every morning when you get up. Put a Scripture passage beside each goal, so that you are sure you can justify the goal scripturally. Then, spend at least fifteen minutes prioritizing the use of your time for that day according to your goals. Make sure that you can justify the use of all of your time.

Then at night, review the goals and evaluate whether or not you used your time wisely, whether or not you redeemed the time, because of the evil days in which we live.

You may want to approach it differently. But what are your priorities? Don't just float through life, letting life happen to you. Seize the initiative. Take control, by the leading of the Lord, so that your time flows in the direction of your priorities.

How are you controlling the events in your life? I have a test that will help you evaluate this.

Quality of Work

- Leaps tall building in a single bound.
- Must take a running start to leap over buildings.
- Can leap over only short buildings.
- Crashes into building when attempting to leap.
- Cannot recognize building or see them beyond one hundred feet.

Timeliness

- Is faster than a speeding bullet.
- Is as fast as a speeding bullet.
- Not quite as fast as a speeding bullet.
- Would you believe a slow bullet?
- Wounds self with bullet when attempting to fire.

Initiative

- Is stronger than a locomotive.
- Is stronger than a bull-elephant.
- Is strong as a bull.
- Looks like a bull.
- Smells like a bull.

Communication

- Talks with God directly.
- Talks with angels.

- Talks to himself.

- Argues with himself.

- Loses those arguments.

You don't have to be able to leap tall buildings with a single bound, be faster than a speeding bullet, stronger than a locomotive, and talk directly with God. You can do less than that and still have a satisfying life with God. But you must have the right goals, and you must control your time.

Here is His will: "Let your light so shine before men that they may see your good works and glorify your Father which is in heaven." That is the exhortation in Ephesians 5:15–17. "Let your light so shine."

Therefore, my beloved brethren, be steadfast, immovable, always abounding in the work of the Lord, knowing that your toil is not in vain in the Lord. (1 Corinthians 15:58)

Our Heavenly Father, help me to see what is important and what is unimportant in life. Help me to use my time for those things that are important. Help me to be spiritually vigilant, that I might not lose my spiritual liberty to carelessness and sin. At the same time, I know that "unless the Lord guards the city, the watchman keeps awake in vain." So, protect me, Lord. In our Savior's name, Amen.

REVIEW

1. Be Smart

Only a *fool* hopes for *happiness* in the things of this *world*.

2. Be Effective

Only as we *control* our *time* do we control our *life*.

3. Be Discerning

Only the proper *goals justify* the effective use of *time*.

As a memory exercise, write in the missing words in the paragraphs below. Notice that they are the same words as the italicized words in the paragraph above.

1. Be Smart

Only a _____ hopes for _____ in the things of this _____.

2. Be Effective

Only as we _____ our _____ do we control our _____.

3. Be Discerning

Only the proper _____ _____ the effective use of _____.

RESPONSE

Questions for Group Discussion or Personal Exercises

1. Engage in a search for wisdom by reading through the book of Proverbs this month. Read one chapter each day. Write down the marks of wisdom and the marks of foolishness as you read.

2. Do you use any kind of system to evaluate your use of time? If so, how is it working for you? Are you satisfied? If not, read *How to Get Control of Your Time and Your Life* by Alan Lakein as a beginning.

3. Have you ever drawn up any life goals? If so, review them and make needed adjustments. If not, why not do so today or after reading Lakein's book.

THIRTY

LIVING A LIFE OF LOVE

What does love look like? It has the hands
to help others. It has the feet to hasten to
the poor and needy. It has eyes to see misery
and want. It has the ears to hear the sighs
and sorrows of men. That is what love
looks like.

St. Augustine

Phillip Keller, in his book *Lessons from a Sheepdog*, writes of a border collie which he bought to herd sheep on his ranch in Canada. The collie was inexpensive because it was a bad dog, ill tempered, and unpredictable. But Keller was short on funds and hoped that the dog might be sufficient to work his sheep until he could afford a better one. The story went something like this.

He said that when he got the dog, it was wild and nearly vicious from an inner core of fear and suspicion. It became quickly clear that the dog had been terribly mistreated—beaten, starved, and neglected—and had no capacity to trust people. When Keller got the bundle of nerves back to his ranch, he spent several days trying to calm the dog and win its trust. He kept it in a cage and came to it repeatedly throughout the day to talk to it and to try to win its confidence. He spoke gently to it, never moved quickly, and tried cautiously to pet it. Nothing worked. The dog remained suspicious and unpredictable, and refused to eat.

SPIRITUAL DISCIPLINES

So after nearly a week of flooding the collie with kindness, there was no change. He realized that the dog would starve itself to death. There was nothing to do but to let it go free and hope that in its freedom, it would eat.

As he released the dog, it disappeared quickly over the hill into the brush-dotted pastureland of his sheep ranch. After several days, he concluded that he would never see the dog again. But he kept food and water out for it and couldn't keep his eyes from roaming the horizon throughout the days in hopes of catching a glimpse. Keller's heart went out to the animal which was so perfect in physical form but so tormented inside because of the inhumanity of man.

Then one day, Keller spotted the dog on a ridge overlooking the pasture where he was. The dog was watching him. Keller spoke to him softly, kindly. The dog disappeared. The next day he appeared again. Again, Keller spoke softly and kindly to him. That evening, some of the food was gone. And so for the next several days, progress seemed to be made. A trust was beginning to form between man and beast, though from a distance. Somehow, Keller writes, the collie sensed his love, his predictability, his trustworthiness.

Eventually, the dog became a common sight around the ranch, and the food and water disappeared regularly. Then one day, the impossible happened. As Phillip Keller sat on a large rock overlooking his grazing sheep, he saw the black and white form float silently to the back of him. Keller sat motionless with his hands behind his back. After an eternity of waiting, his senses were flooded with the touch of a cold, wet nose on his hand. After a moment, Keller turned slightly. The dog stayed. He put his hand on the dog's head, and the hint of a wag stirred at the end of his tail. At that moment, a bond was sealed between man and dog that was never to be broken until the dog's death from old age many years later.

As Philip Keller describes it, the black and white border collie became his constant companion, shadowing him in unwavering devotion, and instant obedience. Keller could not travel for long from the ranch, because when he was gone, the dog refused to eat. It became a veritable extension of Keller himself as it worked the sheep with uncanny instinct and precision. He became the epitome of a sheep dog, with skill, cunning, loyalty, and devotion.[1]

And he became a marvelous illustration of the healing power of love, of the enriching quality of love and the transforming nature of love.

The collie became an example of the progress of love which we see in Ephesians 3:17–19. First, we experience love, then we begin to understand love, and finally, we can truly enter into, and enjoy love. Paul prays that:

> Christ may dwell in your hearts through faith, and that you, being rooted and grounded in love, may be able to comprehend with all the saints what is the breadth and length and height and depth, and to know the love of Christ which surpasses knowledge, that you may be filled up to all the fulness of Christ.

Let us examine Paul's prayer in detail. We can use the imagery of a plant.

The Love of God: Receiving the Seeds

There are two images here that Paul uses—the image of a tree and the image of a building. If we are rooted in love, then in the imagery Paul is using, we are the tree, and God's love is the soil. And we sink our roots deeply into the soil of God's love.

Back in Indiana where I am from, it is common to see weeping willow trees uprooted in wind storms. The reason is that they grow only in moist soil, and the root structure is shallow. When the wind blows, the tree has more resistance to the wind than the roots do in the soil, and as a result, the tree blows over.

In Texas where I live now, however, we have live oak trees. These trees have a root structure below ground that is equal to the limb structure above ground. It would be very uncommon to see a live oak tree blown over in a wind storm. That is the point of being rooted in God's love. Deep in the love of God there is life, there is strength, and there is security. When the winds of adversity blow, the love of God holds us steady and keeps us from being destroyed.

As we experience the love of God, it heals us, like Philip Keller's border collie. As the collie experienced Keller's love, and it was healed, the good side was brought back to life, and it developed the ability to care. By experiencing the love of God, love is born in our hearts.

The Love of God: Cultivating the Vine

Paul prays that they may be able to comprehend with all the saints the magnitude of God's love—the breadth, length, height, and depth of God's love. This has been called the Great Cube of God's love.

We live at a time in history when it is exceedingly difficult to comprehend the love of God, because we have such a distorted view of love. Television and movies have so distorted the true concept of love that the Christian has to work hard to regain a proper view. There are four dimensions of love that have been distorted and need to be corrected, in order to begin to comprehend the love of God.

The first distortion is that love always includes sweeping emotions. The type of love that all significant relationships rely upon is *agape* love. *Agape* is the Greek word for love of this kind. Fundamentally, agape "gives" of its resources for the welfare of another person. Some biblical principles include:

- John 3:16. "God so *loved* the world that He *gave* his only begotten Son . . ." (God didn't get goosepimples over the world.)

- Ephesians 5:25. "Husbands, love your wives just as Christ also *loved* the church and *gave* Himself up for her." (Christ had no goosepimples over the church.)

- 1 Corinthians 13:4–8a. "Love is patient, love is kind and is not jealous. Love does not brag and is not arrogant, does not act unbecomingly; it is not provoked, does not seek its own, does not take into account a wrong suffered, does not rejoice in unrighteousness, but rejoices with the truth; bears all things, believes all things, hopes all things, endures all things. Love never fails.

No high soaring emotions. Only the doing of that which is good for another.

A closely related distortion of love is that you can fall in and out of love. Madison Avenue has caused us to equate emotional bonding with love. There are two different things in this world. There is love, what we just described. Then, there is emotional bonding, which is the emotional attachment that can sometimes happen in life. Emotional bonding is that all-consuming emotional fixation on another person of the opposite sex. It is something that everyone experiences sooner or later. I bonded emotionally to Annette Funicello on the Mickey Mouse Club, and she didn't even know I existed. Love and emotional bonding are not the same, and one of the greatest single points of damage to human relationships is the equating of the two.

Biblically, you do not fall in and out of love. You can fall in and out of emotional bonding. But you cannot fall in and out of love. You "decide" your way into true love, and you must "decide" your way out of it.

In the movie, "My Fair Lady," some poor, lost soul sang about an overpowering feeling he got whenever "she" was near. This is equated with love. And if the next morning, the overpowering feeling is not there, we assume that the love is gone, and we dump that relationship and go on my our searching for another emotional bonding experience which we think is love.

The ideal situation for a marriage is when you are emotionally bonded to the one you have decided to love. And if you are sincere in your decision to love another person, virtually without exception, God gives you the capacity to bond emotionally. But all the *commands* to love in the Bible are *agape*. And that does not require emotional bonding. It cannot, because you cannot command your emotions. You can only command your will.

The third distortion is that love and sex must go together. Today, the value of the world is that if you love someone else of the opposite sex, it is only ultimately demonstrated by engaging in sex. Television is in a feeding frenzy on sexual freedom. I pride myself in having never watched most of the television programs that are on, but even in the ones starring children, they insist on throwing up the issue of sexual relationships outside of marriage as being not only permissible but expected.

Parents, this is poison, and if you give your children the freedom to watch this kind of programming for recreation, you will have to look in the mirror to find someone to blame when your kids start living out the behavior they watch on television.

4. The fourth distortion of Biblical love is that love has the freedom to take. Elvis used to sing, "It's now or never, come hold me tight. Kiss me my darling, be mine tonight. Tomorrow may be too late. It's now or never, my love won't wait." That is utter nonsense. It is the world view of a tom cat. It's the value system of the beasts.

Love can always wait to give. It is lust that cannot wait to get. Love gives, it does not take. Read 1 Corinthians 13:4–8 again. There is nothing in that which says love can be selfish. Love gives of its resources for the welfare of another.

We could go on, but the point is, concerning love, the value system of the world is totally opposed to the value system of God. If it is true that you can only get your deepest longings met in God, then every time you accept and act on the world's definition of love, you are sewing destructive seeds.

Does God hate this concept which the world promotes as love? Without a doubt. But not for legalistic reasons. Not because He has decided to disallow that which is the most fun for us, because He doesn't want us to have fun. His reasons are entirely different.

I am going to keep this next part as brief as I can, because I am going to be plowing very deep, but if you will hang in there with me, you will understand the *true* issues behind sexual relationships and why it is so terribly *important* to keep them pure.

- God is the ultimate being in the universe, and the Trinity (Father, Son, and Holy Spirit) is the ultimate relationship in the universe. The Trinity functions in total love, unity, and harmony, and they take ultimate joy from their relationship with each other. The closer we become like God, the more joy, meaning, and satisfaction we have in life. The farther we depart from being like God, the more pain, emptiness, and dissatisfaction we have in life. And frankly, this is true, regardless of whether or not the people involved are Christians. There are atheists who have happy and meaningful relationships. There are Christians who don't.

- Sexual relationships are a symbolical representation of that loving spiritual unity. God uses sexual relationships between men and women to teach the world what God is like. It is an object lesson.

- When God loves, He creates life in unity and harmony. When man and woman love each other as an expression of their spiritual unity and harmony, they create life. But it is all an object lesson about who God is. God didn't have to choose sex as a means for procreation. He could have had us lie dormant for a week or so once every five years, and divide like an amoeba. So why sex? Because God is using it to show what He is like. That is why Satan has energized our world system to fixate on sex. If he can instill in a culture a desire for permissive sex, he "kills" God.

- When we fulfill God's commands, we present to the world (and to our children, most importantly) a true picture of what God is like. He loves us forever. He loves us unconditionally. He will never leave us or forsake us. He will only ever do that which is best for us. We present that truth to the world by our sexual purity.

When we choose sexual impurity, we present to the world a false picture of God. We say, "Love isn't forever . . . It isn't unconditional. We will leave and forsake other people . . . We won't do what is best for others." We teach the world (and worst, our children) that there is no God who can be trusted, there is no truth to be followed, and there is no safety in relationships.

As a result, a world turns its back on God, sex takes on all the significance of a good burp, and we are left to try to find meaning however we can. However, we can't find it, so we become addicted to whatever activities ease the pain: free sex, booze and drugs, television and movies, music, and recreation. Or if we get tired of trying to find meaning for each twenty-four hour period, we blow our brains out. That is why there are so many teenage suicides today. They see the meaningless of the world which their parents have given them, and they cannot endure the boredom or lack of meaning, so they kill themselves.

Do you see? Sexual purity, because of its link to an accurate picture of God, is at the very center of the only world view that gives any meaning whatsoever to human existence. To abandon the world view that accepts the sanctity of sexual purity is to embrace a world view that has produced drug abuse, runaway crime, homosexuality and AIDS, Satan worship, terrorism, world hunger, totalitarianism, graft, greed and corruption—because all those are expressions of a world view which does not put God at the center. When this world view predominates, people reject God on a wholesale level, and souls go plummeting to hell.

All right, we can come up and take a breath now. I know that that was deep, but I pray to God that it will change your world view. The issue is not only sexual purity. It is much, much greater than that. Ultimately, meaning in life and the eternal destiny of men's souls are at stake.

When we experience God's love, it is often through God's children. Often, it is in the kindnesses of God's children that we first experience the love of God, and a capacity to comprehend the meaning and importance of God's love is awakened in our hearts.

I have most wanted to know God when I have seen people who demonstrated God's love to me. There is great, great power in our loving others as Christ loves us.

The Love of God: Harvesting the Fruit

"To know the love of Christ which surpasses knowledge," says our Ephesians passage. "To know" means to know in a way that goes beyond head knowledge and includes experience—to know by experience the love of Christ. It certainly includes and is based on accurate information, but it goes beyond intellectual assent to "knowing by experience."

When I was young, my mother used to say, "Life can be tough, and you must learn to take the bitter with the sweet." And I would say, "I know." Now, my mother can say, "Life can be tough, and you must learn to take the bitter with the sweet." And I would say, "I know." The words are the same, but the comprehension levels are worlds apart. Then, I knew in my mind. Now, I know by experience. That's the point of knowing the love of Christ—knowing by experience.

"Know the love which surpasses knowledge . . ." How can you do something that is undo-able? The sense of this is the same as drinking from a pure mountain stream. You drink fully of the stream which can never be drunk dry. You drink deeply from that which cannot be drunk. That is, you consume as much as you can from that which cannot be totally consumed. That is the sense in which you deeply know by experience the love of Christ which cannot be fully comprehended and known in its entirety.

Finally, you order your life priorities to reflect the pursuit of loving relationships. That is when life begins to take on the richness and meaning that we long for, and that is when we begin to know by experience the love of Christ which surpasses knowledge. That is when we begin to drink deeply of the fresh water springs of life that can never be depleted.

Helen Keller was blind and deaf, and the emotional toll which this took on her brilliant mind turned her into a volatile, uncontrollable demon. But the character of Anne Sullivan, as she worked carefully with her, is a marvel of patience, wisdom, and hope. Years later in her autobiography, *The Story of My Life*, Helen Keller wrote:

> The most important day in all my life is the one in which my teacher, Anne Mansfield Sullivan, came to me. I am filled with wonder when I consider the immeasurable contrasts between the two lives which it connects. It was the third of March, 1887, three months before I was seven years old.
>
> I guessed vaguely that something unusual was about to happen. I felt approaching footsteps. I stretched out my hand, as I supposed, to my mother. Someone took it, and I was caught up and held close in the arms of her who had come to reveal all things to me, and more than all things else, to love me.
>
> At one point in time, Anne Sullivan gave me a doll, and worked with me to sign the word d-o-l-l over and over again.
>
> I became impatient with her repeated attempts, and seizing the doll, I dashed it to the floor. I was keenly delighted when I felt the fragments of the broken doll at my feet. Neither sorrow nor regret followed my passionate outburst. In the still, dark world in which I lived, there was no strong sentiment or tenderness. I felt my teacher sweep the fragments to one side of the

hearth, and I had the satisfaction that the cause of my discomfort was removed. She brought me my hat, and I knew I was going out into the warm sunshine.

We walked down the path to the well-house, attracted by the fragrance of honeysuckle with which it was covered. Someone was drawing water and my teacher placed my hand under the spout. As the cool stream gushed over one hand, she spelled into the other hand, "w-a-t-e-r", first slowly, then rapidly. I stood still, my whole attention fixed upon the motion of her fingers. Suddenly I felt a mist consciousness of something forgotten—a thrill of returning thought; and somehow the mystery of language was revealed to me. I knew then that w-a-t-e-r meant the wonderful cool something that was flowing over my hand. That living word awakened my soul, gave it light, hope, joy, set it free!

I left the well-house eager to learn. Everything had a name, and each new name gave birth to a new thought. As we returned to the house, every object which I touched seemed to quiver with new life. That was because I saw everything with a strange new sight that had come to me. On entering the door I remembered the doll I had broken. I felt my way to the hearth and picked up the pieces. I tried vainly to put them together. Then my eyes filled with tears; for I realized what I had done, and for the first time I felt repentance and sorrow.

I learned a great many new words that day. I do not remember what all they were; but I do know that mother, father, sister, and teacher were among them . . . words that were to make the world blossom for me, "like Aaron's rod, with flowers." It would have been difficult to find a happier child than I was as I lay in my crib at the close of that eventful day and lived over the joys it had brought me, and for the first time longed for a new day to come.[2]

Anne Sullivan loved her charge, even though she was rejected and spited because of it. But she continued to love—consistently, in big ways and in little ways. And finally, when it seemed like it might be hopeless, the love broke through. Hellen Keller experienced the love, and based on that experience, began to comprehend for the first time what love was. When she did, she was then able to order her life in such a way as to pursue relationships of love—the only thing that gives life meaning.

Love is patient, love is kind and is not jealous; love does not brag and is not arrogant, does not act unbecomingly; it does not seek its own, is not provoked, does not take into account a wrong suffered, does not rejoice in unrighteousness, but rejoices with the truth; bears all things, believes all things, hopes all things, endures all things. Love never fails. (1 Corinthians 13:4–8)

> *Our Father in Heaven, thank You for loving me. Thank You for sending Jesus to show me how much You love me. Help me to love others as You love me. For then, I will be filled with the joy of life, and others will understand better Your love for them. I ask it in the name of the One who loved me clear to the cross. Amen.*

REVIEW

1. The Love of God: Receiving the Seeds

As we *grasp* how much God *loves* us, we will be able to love Him in *return*.

2. The Love of God: Cultivating the Vine

As we operate on God's definition of *love,* our own *capacity* to give and receive love is *increased.*

3. The Love of God: Harvesting the Fruit

After we have *tasted* God's love for us, we will order our lives to *pursue* relationships of *love.*

As a memory exercise, write in the missing words in the paragraphs below. Notice that they are the same words as the italicized words in the paragraph above.

1. The Love of God: Receiving the Seeds

As we _____ how much God _____ us, we will be able to love Him in _____.

2. **The Love of God: Cultivating the Vine**

As we operate on God's definition of _____, our own _____ to give and receive love is _____.

3. **The Love of God: Harvesting the Fruit**

After we have _____ God's love for us, we will order our lives to _____ relationships of _____.

RESPONSE

Questions for Group Discussion or Personal Exercises

1. Is there anyone you can identify today who loves you unconditionally? How do you know? How do they express this kind of love?

2. Which of the four distortions of love do you tend to believe?

3. Read 1 John 3:1. God's love for us is so great! Spend a moment right now thanking God for loving you so much.

4. In your own words, how does sexual purity reflect the nature of God's love to the world?

5. Ask God to help you understand His love more completely and increase your own capacity to give and to receive love.

NOTES

Chapter 1: What Gives Me Meaning in Life?

1. Harold Kushner, *When All You've Ever Wanted Isn't Enough* (New York: Simon and Schuster, Inc., 1986), 165-166.
2. Quoted in John Piper, *Desiring God* (Portland, OR: Multnomah Press, 1986), 15.
3. Ibid., 16.
4. C. S. Lewis, *The Weight of Glory and Other Addresses* (Grand Rapids: Wm. B. Eerdmen's Publishing Co., 1965), 1-2.
5. Juan Carlos Ortiz, *Disciple* (Wheaton, IL: Creation House, 1975), 34-35.

Chapter 2: How Does God See Me?

1. Max Anders, *30 Days to Understanding the Bible* (Dallas, TX: Word Publishing, 1988), 245-246.
2. John MacArthur, Jr., *The MacArthur New Testament Commentary: Ephesians* (Chicago: Moody Press, 1986), 178-179.

Chapter 3: How Do I Fit into God's Plan?

1. Billy Graham, *How to Be Born Again* (Dallas, TX: Word Publishing, 1977), 118-119.

Chapter 4: Love God

1. Soren Kierkegaard as quoted by Anne Ortland, *Up with Worship* (Ventura, CA: Regal Books, 1975), 20.

Chapter 5: Love Others

1. Rudyard Kipling, "*The Thousandth Man*," *Rudyard Kipling's Verse, Definitive Edition* (Garden City, NY: Doubleday and Company, Inc., 1940), 529-530.
2. Charles Colson, *Loving God* (Grand Rapids, MI: Zondervan Publishing House, 1983), 131-132.
3. Anne Ortlund, *Up with Worship* (Ventura, CA: Regal Books, 1975), 102.

Chapter 6: Esteem Yourself

1. Doug Sherman and William Hendricks, *Your Work Matters to God* (Colorado Springs, CO: NavPress, 1988).
2. Arthur Holmes, *Contours of a World View* (Grand Rapids, MI: Wm B. Eerdmen's Publishing Co., 1983), 230–231.
3. Stephen Dunning, Edward Lueders, Hugh Mith, "The Toaster," *Reflections on a Gift of Watermelon Pickle* (Glenview, IL: Scott, Foresman and Company, 1966), 37.

Chapter 7: Be a Steward

1. Colson, *Loving God,* 126.
2. Lloyd Cory, *Quotable Quotations* (Wheaton, IL: Victor Books, 1985), 400–401.

Chapter 8: Be a Servant

1. Edward Arlington Robinson, "Richard Cory" in an anthology entitled *The American Tradition in Literature, Vol. II* (New York: W. W. Norton and Company, 1967), 1042.
2. Harold Kushner, *When Bad Things Happen to Good People* (New York, NY: Pocket Books/Simon and Schuster, 1986), 18.
3. Michael Green, *Illustrations for Biblical Preaching* (Grand Rapids, MI: Baker Book House, 1989), 331–332.

Chapter 9: Work of God

1. C. S. Lewis, *Surprised by Joy* (New York: Harcourt, Brace and Jovanovich, 1955), 228–229.
2. Francis Schaeffer, *True Spirituality* (Wheaton, IL: Tyndale House Publishers, 1971), 42.
3. Ibid.

Chapter 10: Word of God

1. Charles Colson, "What Have We To Do?" *Jubilee,* August 1988, 7.
2. Charles Swindoll, *The Seasons of Life* (Portland, OR: Multnomah Press, 1983), 386–387.

Chapter 11: Personal Commitment

1. Wilbur Rees, "$3.00 Worth of God." as quoted in *When I Relax, I Feel Guilty,* by Tim Hansel (Elgin, IL: David C. Cook Publishing Co., 1979), 49.

Chapter 12: Other Believers

1. Paul Brand, *Fearfully and Wonderfully Made* (Grand Rapids, MI: Zondervan Publishers House, 1980), 27–28.
2. Lawrence J. Crabb, Jr. and Dan B. Allender, *Encouragement* (Grand Rapids, MI: Zondervan Publishing House, 1984), 23–24.

3. John Donne, *Bartlett's Familiar Quotations by John Bartlett* (Boston: Little, Brown and Company, 1980), 254.

Chapter 13: Time and Trials

1. Miles Stanford, *Principles of Spiritual Growth* (Lincoln, NE: Back to the Bible Publications), 12.
2. Anders, *30 Days*, 271-273.
3. C. S. Lewis as quoted by Chuck Colson, *Life Sentence* (Lincoln, VA: Chosen Books, 1979), 31.

Chapter 14: Intellectual Intimidation

1. David Dewitt, *Answering the Tough Ones* (Chicago: Moody Press, 1980), 11-12.
2. Winston Churchill as quoted by Lloyd Cory, *Quotable Quotations* (Wheaton, IL: Victor Books, 1985).
3. Excerpted from the taped "Creation Series," Dr. Ron Chittock, Recorded at Grace Covenant Church.
4. Ibid.
5. Ibid.
6. Ibid.
7. Ibid.
8. Josh McDowell, *Answers* (San Bernadino, CA: Here's Life Publishers, 1980), 16.
9. Francis Schaeffer, *The Church at the End of the Twentieth Century* (Downers Grove, IL: Inter-Varsity Press, 1970), 15.

Chapter 15: Materialism

1. "The Money Society," *Fortune Magazine*, July 6, 1987.
2. Patrick Morley, *The Man in the Mirror* (Nashville, TN: Thomas Nelson Publishers, 1988), 130.
3. Ibid., 130.
4. Kushner, *When All You Ever*, 18.

Chapter 16: Spiritual Discouragement

1. Philip Yancey, *Disappointment with God* (Grand Rapids, MI: Zondervan Publishing House, 1988), 32-33.
2. C. S. Lewis, *A Grief Observed* (New York: Bantam Books, 1976), 4-5.
3. Yancey, *Disappointment*, 165, 170.

Chapter 17: Carelessness

1. Gary Richmond, *A View from the Zoo* (Dallas, TX: Word Publishing, 1987), 115-116.
2. James C. Dobson, *Love Must Be Tough* (Dallas, TX: Word Publishing, 1983), 211-212.

Chapter 18: Toying with Sin

1. Charles Swindoll, *Strengthening Your Grip* (Waco, TX: Word Books, 1982), 62.

Chapter 19: Spiritual Exhaustion

1. Gordon MacDonald, *Ordering Your Private World* (Nashville: Thomas Nelson, Publishers, 1984), 13.
2. Nancy Gibbs, "How America Has Run Out of Time." *Time,* April 24, 1984, 58–59.
3. Ibid.
4. Tim Kimmel, *Little House on the Freeway* (Portland, OR: Multnomah Press, 1987), 17–33.
5. MacDonald, *Ordering,* 138.
6. Morely, *Man in the Mirror,* 22.
7. MacDonald, *Ordering,* 193.

Chapter 20: Spiritual Warfare

1. John White, *The Fight* (Downers Grove, IL: Inter-Varsity Press, 1976), 87.

Chapter 21: Spiritual Armor

1. Ray Stedman, *Spiritual Warfare* (Waco, TX: Word Books, 1978), 17–18.
2. Ibid.

Chapter 22: The Battle for the Mind

1. Clifton Fadiman, *The Little, Brown Book of Anecdotes* (Boston, MA: Little, Brown and Company, 1985), 547.
2. Ibid., 306.

Chapter 23: Prayer

1. Fadiman, 358.
2. Albert M. Wells, Jr., *Inspiring Quotations* (Nashville, TN: Thomas Nelson Publishers, 1988), 121.

Chapter 24: Worship

1. Ortlund, *Up with Worship,* 10.
2. Ibid., 20.
3. Michael Green, *Illustrations for Biblical Preaching* (Grand Rapids, MI: Baker Book House, 1989), 264.

Chapter 25: Balancing Life's Competing Priorities

1. Francis Schaeffer, *No Little People* (Downers Grove, IL: Inter-Varsity Press, 1974), 13, 17–18.
2. Ibid.

Chapter 26: Using Your Spiritual Gifts

1. Oscar Wilde as quoted in Harold Kushner, *When All You Ever Wanted Isn't Enough* (New York, NY: Pocket Books/Simon and Schuster, 1986), 16.
2. Carl Jung as quoted in Kushner, *When All You Ever*, 18.

Chapter 27: Sharing the Good News

1. Joseph C. Aldrich, *Life-Style Evangelism* (Portland, OR: Multnomah Press, 1981), 15–16.
2. Jim Petersen, *Evangelism As a Lifestyle* (Colorado Springs, CO: NavPress, 1980), 80–81.

Chapter 28: Knowing God's Will

1. Ray Stedman, "Finding the Will of God," *Troublesome Issues,* December 13, 1964, 1.
2. Ibid.
3. Philip Yancey, "Vital Issues," *Guidance,* (Multnomah Press, 1983).

Chapter 29: Spiritual Vigilance

1. Charles Swindoll, *Growing Strong in the Seasons of Life* (Portland, OR: Multnomah Press, 1983), 182.

Chapter 30: Living a Life of Love

1. Philip Keller, *Lessons from a Sheep Dog* (Waco, TX: Word Books, 1983), 45–55.
2. Helen Keller, *The Story of My Life* (Garden City, NY: Doubleday and Company, 1954), 34–37.

SUGGESTED READING

Chapter 1: What Gives Me Meaning in Life?

Colson, Charles W. *Loving God.* Grand Rapids, MI: Zondervan Publishing House, 1987.

Packer, J. I. *Knowing God.* Downers Grove, IL: InterVarsity Press, 1973.

Piper, John. *Desiring God.* Portland, OR: Multnomah Press, 1986.

Yancey, Philip. *Disappointment with God.* Grand Rapids, MI: Zondervan Publishing House, 1988.

Chapter 2: How Does God See Me?

Crabb, Larry. *Inside Out.* Colorado Springs CO: NavPress, 1988.

Gillham, Bill. *Lifetime Guarantee.* Eugene, OR: Harvest House, 1988.

Stanford, Miles J. *Principles of Spiritual Growth.* Lincoln, Nebraska: Back to the Bible, 1969.

Chapter 3: How Do I Fit into God's Plan?

Anders, Max. *30 Days to Understanding the Bible.* Dallas, TX: Word Publishing, 1988, 1994.

Mears, Henrietta C. *What the Bible is All About.* Minneapolis: World Wide Publications, 1966.

Boa, Ken and Bruce Wilkinson. *Talk Thru the Old Testament.* Nashville: Thomas Nelson Publishers, 1983.

Chapter 4: Love God

Ortlund, Anne. *Up with Worship.* Glendale, CA: Regal Books, a division of G/L Publications, 1975.

Allen, Ron and Borror, Gordon. *Worship, the Missing Jewel.* Portland, OR: Multnomah Press, 1982.

MacArthur, John. *The Ultimate Priority.* Chicago: Moody Press, 1983.

Chapter 5: Love Others

Smalley, Gary and Trent, John. *The Blessing.* Nashville, TN: Thomas Nelson Publishers, 1986.

Smalley, Gary and Trent, John. *The Gift of Honor.* Nashville, TN: Thomas Nelson Publishers, 1987.

Swindoll, Charles R. *Dropping Your Guard.* Waco, TX: Word Books, 1983.

Crabb, Larry and Allender, Dan. *Encouragement.* Grand Rapids, MI: Zondervan Publishing House, 1984.

Schaeffer, Francis. *The Mark of the Christian.* Downers Grove, IL: InterVarsity Press, 1970.

Chapter 6: Esteem Yourself

Brand, Paul and Yancey, Philip. *In His Image.* Grand Rapids, MI: Zondervan Publishing House, 1984.

Wagner, Maurice. *The Sensation of Being Somebody.* Grand Rapids, MI: Zondervan Publishing House, 1975.

Minirth, Frank and Meier, Paul. *Happiness is a Choice.* Grand Rapids, MI: Baker Book House, 1978.

Brand, Paul and Yancey, Philip. *Fearfully and Wonderfully Made.* Grand Rapids, MI: Zondervan Publishing House, 1980.

Chapter 7: Be a Steward

Swindoll, Charles R. *Improving Your Serve.* Waco, TX: Word Books, 1981.

Swindoll, Charles R. *The Quest for Character.* Portland, OR: Multnomath Press, 1987.

Foster, Richard, *The Celebration of Discipline.* New York: Harper and Row, Publishers, 1978.

Chapter 8: Be a Servant

Getz, Gene. *Building Up One Another.* Wheaton, IL: Victor Books, 1987.

Swindoll, Charles R. *Dropping Your Guard.* Waco, TX: Word Books, 1983.

Chapter 9: The Work of God

Stedman, Ray. *Authenic Christianity.* Portland, OR: Multnomah Press, 1975.

Sproul, R. C., *The Holiness of God*. Wheaton, IL: Tyndale House Publishers, 1988.

Chapter 10: The Word of God

Lindsell, Harold. *The Battle for the Bible*. Grand Rapids, MI: Zondervan Publishing House, 1976.

Packer, J. I. *God Has Spoken*. Downers Grove, IL: InterVarsity Press, 1979.

Chapter 11: Personal Commitment

McDonald, Gordon. *Ordering Your Private World*. Nashville, TN: Thomas Nelson Publishers, 1984.

Foster, Richard. *The Celebration of Discipline*. New York: Harper and Row Publishers, 1978.

Chapter 12: Other Believers

Getz, Gene. *Building Up One Another*. Wheaton, IL: Victor Books, 1987.

Stedman, Ray. *Body Life*. Glendale, CA: G/L Publications, 1979.

McGinnis, Alan Loy. *The Friendship Factor*. Minneapolis: Augsburg Publishing House, 1979.

Chapter 13: Time and Trials

Yancey, Philip. *Disappointment with God*. Grand Rapids, MI: Zondervan Publishing House, 1988.

Swindoll, Charles R. *Three Steps Forward, Two Steps Back*. Nashville, TN: Thomas Nelson Publishers, 1980.

Lewis, C. S. *The Problem of Pain*. New York: The MacMillian Company, 1971.

Chapter 14: Intellectual Intimidation

Boa, Ken and Moody, Larry. *I'm Glad You Asked*. Wheaton, IL: Victor Books, 1977.

McDowell, Josh. *Evidence that Demands a Verdict*. San Bernadino, CA: Campus Crusade for Christ International, 1972.

Little, Paul. *Know Why You Believe*. Downers Grove, IL: InterVarsity Press, 1968.

Chapter 15: Materialism

Morley, Patrick. *Man in the Mirror*. Nashville, TN: Thomas Nelson Publishers, 1989.

White, John. *The Golden Cow.* Dowers Grove, IL: InterVarsity Press, 1979.

Kushner, Harold. *When All You've Ever Wanted Isn't Enough.* New York: Pocket Books, 1986.

Chapter 16: Spiritual Discouragement

Yancey, Philip. *Disappointment with God.* Grand Rapids, MI: Zondervan Publishing House, 1988.

Kreeft, Peter. *Making Sense Out of Suffering.* Ann Arbor, MI: Servant Books, 1986.

Chapter 17: Carelessness

MacDonald, Gordon. *Restoring Your Spiritual Passions.* Nashville, TN: Oliver-Nelson, 1986.

Swindoll, Charles R. *Living Above the Level of Mediocrity.* Waco,TX: Word Books, 1987.

Chapter 18: Toying with Sin

Hybels, Bill. *Who You Are When Nobody's Looking.* Downers Grove, IL: InterVarsity, 1987.

Engstrom, Ted. Integrity. Waco, TX: Word Books, 1987.

Chapter 19: Spiritual Exhaustion

McDonald, Gordon. *Ordering Your Private World.* Nashville, TN: Oliver-Nelson, 1984.

McDonald, Gordon. *Rebuilding Your Broken World.* Nashville,TN: Thomas Nelson Publishers, 1986.

Swindoll, Charles R. *Strengthening Your Grip.* Waco, TX: Word Books, 1982.

Chapter 20: Spiritual Warfare

Stedman, Ray. *Spiritual Warfare.* Portland, OR: Multnomah Press, 1975.

Eims, LeRoy. *No Magic Formula.* Colorado Springs: Navpress, 1977.

Chapter 21: Spiritual Armor

Stedman, Ray. *Spiritual Warfare.* Portland, OR: Multnomah, 1975.

Eims, LeRoy. *No Magic Formula.* Colorado Springs: Navpress, 1977.

Chapter 22: The Battle for the Mind

Schaeffer, Francis. *How Should We Then Live.* Old Tappan, New Jersey: Fleming H. Revell Company, 1976.

Thurman, Chris. *The Lies We Believe.* Nashville, TN: Thomas Nelson Publishers, 1989.

Chapter 23: Prayer

Hunter, Bingham. *The God Who Hears.* Downers Grove, IL: InterVarsity Press, 1986.

Hybels, Bill. *Too Busy Not to Pray.* Downers Grove, IL: InterVarsity Press, 1988.

Eastman, Dick. *The Hour that Changes the World.* Direction Books, Baker Books.

Chapter 24: Worship

Hybels, Bill. *Too Busy Not to Pray.* Downers Grove, IL: InterVarsity Press, 1988.

Colson, Charles. *Loving God.* Grand Rapids, MI: Zondervan Publishing House, 1983.

Henrichsen, Walter and Jackson, Gayle. *A Layman's Guide to Applying the Bible.* Grand Rapids, MI: Zondervan Publshing House, 1985.

Chapter 25: Balancing Life's Competing Priorities

Sherman, Doug. *How to Balance Competing Time Demands.* Colorado Springs: NavPress, 1989.

Howard, J. Grant. *Balancing Life's Demands.* Portland, OR: Multnomah Press, 1983.

Chapter 26: Using Your Spiritual Gifts

Stedman, Ray. *Body Life.* Glendale, CA: Regal Books, 1979.

Gangel, Kenneth O. *Unwrap Your Spiritual Gifts.* Wheaton, IL: Victor Books, 1983.

Chapter 27: Sharing the Good News

Hendricks, Howard. *Say It With Love.* Wheaton, IL: Victor Books, 1972.

Peterson, Jim. *Evangelism as a Lifestyle.* Colorado Springs: Navpress, 1981.

Aldrich, Joseph C. *Life-Style Evangelism.* Portland, OR: Multnomah Press, 1982.

McCloskey, Mark. *Tell It Often—Tell It Well.* San Bernardino, CA: Here's Life Publishers, 1985.

Bright, Bill. *Witnessing Without Fear.* San Bernardino, CA: Here's Life Publishers, 1987.

Chapter 28: Knowing God's Will

Packer, J. I. *Knowing God.* Downers Grove, IL: InterVarsity Press, 1973.

Willard, Dallas. *The Spirit of the Disciplines: Understanding How God Changes Lives.* New York: Harper & Row, 1988.

Sproul, R. C. *Knowing God's Will.*

Chapter 29: Spiritual Vigilance

Engstrom, Ted. *The Pursuit of Excellence.* Grand Rapids, MI: Zondervan Publishing House, 1982.

Lakein, Alan. *How to Get Control of Your Time and Your Life.* New York: A Signet Book, 1973.

Chapter 30: Living a Life of Love

Smalley, Gary and Trent, John. *The Blessing.* Nasshville, TN: Thomas Nelson Publishers, 1986.

Smalley, Gary and Trent, John. *The Gift of Honor.* Nashville, TN: Thomas Nelson Publishers, 1987.

Smalley, Gary and Trent, John. *Love is a Decision.* Waco, TX: Word Books, 1988.

Dobson, James. *Dare to Discipline.* Wheaton, IL: Tyndale House Publishers, 1981.

Dobson, James. *What Wives Wish Their Husbands Knew About Women.* Wheaton, IL: Tyndale House Publishers, 1983.

Dobson, James. *Love Must Be Tough.* Waco, TX: Word Books, 1983.

Dobson, James. *Straight Talk To Men and Their Wives.* Waco, TX: Word Books, 1980.